Real-Resumes for Computer Jobs

Anne McKinney, Editor

PREP PUBLISHING

FAYETTEVILLE, NC

PREP Publishing
1110½ Hay Street
Fayetteville, NC 28305
(910) 483-6611

Library of Congress Cataloging-in-Publication Data

Real-resumes for computer jobs / Anne McKinney, editor.
        p.   cm. -- (Real-resumes series)
      ISBN 1-885288-08-5
      1. Résumés (Employment) 2. Computer industry. I. McKinney, Anne, 1948- II. Series.

      HF5383 .R3958 2001
      808'.06665--dc21   2001021000
                                                                        CIP

Printed in the United States of America

Table of Contents

Introduction: The Art of Finding a Job 1

PART ONE: SOME ADVICE ABOUT YOUR JOB HUNT 4
Step One: Planning Your Job Hunt and Assembling the Right Tools 4
Step Two: Using Your Resume and Cover Letter 6
Step Three: Preparing for Interviews 9
Step Four: Handling the Interview and Negotiating Salary 11
Researching Companies and Locating Employers 13

PART TWO: COVER LETTERS FOR COMPUTER JOBS 17
The Anatomy of a Cover Letter 20
Sample Cover Letters for Job Hunting 22
Changing careers from teaching 23
Changing careers from the aviation industry 24
Changing careers from military service 25
Changing careers with a cover letter that emphasizes hardware knowledge 26
Changing careers from the government sector 27
Launching a career in the computer industry 28
Changing careers from a slow-growth industry to a high-tech environment 29
Changing careers into the computer sales field 30
Changing careers with the goal of becoming more involved in fiber optics 31
Changing careers from federal service to the private sector 32
Sixteen Questions Career Changers Ask About Cover Letters 33
Question 1: What is the "direct approach?" 34
Question 2: How do I address a letter to an ad that provides names and addresses?. 35
Question 3: What's the best way to answer a "blind ad?" 36
Question 4: How do I respond to a recruiter or headhunter who has approached me? 37
Question 5: How do I apply for internal openings? 38
Question 6: How do I ask for consideration for multiple job openings? 39
Question 7: How do I e-mail or fax my resume and cover letter? 40
Question 8: If I want to "drop a name" in a cover letter, what's the best way? 41
Question 9: If I'm relocating soon, how do I say that? 42
Question 10: If I've recently relocated, what do I say in the cover letter? 43
Question 11: What if I want to reopen a door that I closed previously? 44
Question 12: What if they ask for salary requirements? 45
Question 13: What if they ask for salary history? 46
Question 14: How do I make it clear that I want my approach to be confidential? 47
Question 15: How do I write a follow-up letter after an interview? 48
Question 16: How do I resign—gracefully? 49
Another Letter of Leave Taking 50

PART THREE: REAL-RESUMES FOR COMPUTER JOBS 51
Automated Systems Team Chief (Robert Hederman) 54
Chief of Communication Systems Construction (Arthur Tipton) 56
Cisco Certified Network Associate (Jeanne Wu) 58
Communications Advisor (Cassandra Wills) 60
Communications Supervisor (Henry Sprague) 62

Computer Center Supervisor (David Ensor) 64

Computer Center Supervisor (Marty Fish) 66

Computer Products Sales (Edward Grimes III) 68

Computer Programmer (Mason Jenkins) 70

Computer Programmer (Timothy Mays) 72

Computer Information Systems Products (Casey Holtz) 74

Computer Operator (Susan West) 76

Computer Programming Student (Charles Harding) 78

Computer Sales Representative (John Jarcho) 80

Computer Sales Specialist (Samantha Love) 82

Computer Science Graduate (Adam Henke) 84

Computer Science Student (David Curtins) 86

Computer Science Student (Kyle Sweeney) 88

Computer Science Student (Stephen Klink) 90

Computer Specialist (Kyle Myslinsky) 92

Computer Specialist (Wayne Luke) 94

Computer Technician (Rachel Clinton) 96

Electrical Engineeer (Willie Horton) 98

Electronics Engineering Student (Richard White) 100

Electronics Maintenance Supervisor (Charles Stout) 102

Electronics Management Graduate (William Duff) 104

Electronics Repair Technician (Mark Goodman) 106

Electronics Technology Student (Pete Dawkins) 108

Fiber Optics Instructor (Steven Hutt) 110

Forced Entry Switch Section Supervisor (Doug Kenna) 112

Hardware Repair Specialist (Michael Irvin) 114

Microsoft Certified Professional (John Tessler) 116

Microsoft Certified Professional (Kenny Stevens) 118

Microsoft Certified Systems Engineer (Anthony Hopkins) 120

MIS Vice President (Robert Schniepp) 122

Mobile Subscriber Equipment Team Chief (Dawn Hollander) 124

Multichannel Transmission Systems Supervisor (Grace Mayweather) 126

Multimode System Operator (Johnathon Little) 128

Network Analyst (Charles Folkart) 130

Network Engineer (John Lasak) 132

Network Engineering Student (Daniel Lewis) 134

Network Manager (Lucia Villar) 136

Network Manager (Edward Marow) 138

Network Surveillance Engineer (Kaye Green) 140

Network Switching Chief (Denise Ching) 142

Network Switching Manager (Sean Keller) 144

Network Switching Systems Supervisor (Mike Novogratz) 146

Network Switching Systems Supervisor (Robert Porter) 148

Programmer and Analyst (Evan Dreyer) 150

Senior Systems Analyst (Robert Larson) 152

Signal Communications Analyst (Adam Howard) 154

Systems Administrator (Benjamin Long) 156

Systems Analyst (Philip Dees) 158

Systems Analyst (Jon Du Pre) 160

Telecommunications Maintenance Technician (Elmer Oliphant) 162

Telecommunications Operator (Robin Olds) 164

Telecommunications Supervisor (Betty Merritt) 166
Telecommunications Supervisor (Syd Moran) 168
Telecommunications Support Systems Supervisor (Josiah Dubber) 170
Telecommunications Team Supervisor (Frederick Lark) 172
Test Plans Analyst (Spartan Agnew) 174
Website Designer/Systems Technician (Jason Fincher) 176

A WORD FROM THE EDITOR:
ABOUT THE REAL-RESUMES SERIES

Welcome to the Real-Resumes Series. The Real-Resumes Series is a series of books which have been developed based on the experiences of real job hunters and which target specialized fields or types of resumes. As the editor of the series, I have carefully selected resumes and cover letters (with names and other key data disguised, of course) which have been used successfully in real job hunts. That's what we mean by "Real-Resumes." What you see in this book are *real* resumes and cover letters which helped real people get ahead in their careers.

The Real-Resumes Series is based on the work of the country's oldest resume-preparation company known as PREP Resumes. If you would like a free information packet describing the company's resume preparation services, call 910-483-6611 or write to PREP at 1110½ Hay Street, Fayetteville, NC 28305. If you have a job hunting experience you would like to share with our staff at the Real-Resumes Series, please contact us at preppub@aol.com or visit our website at http://www.prep-pub.com.

The resumes and cover letters in this book are designed to be of most value to people already in a career change or contemplating a career change. If we could give you one word of advice about your career, here's what we would say: Manage your career and don't stumble from job to job in an incoherent pattern. Try to find work that interests you, and then identify prosperous industries which need work performed of the type you want to do. Learn early in your working life that a great resume and cover letter can blow doors open for you and help you maximize your salary.

This book is dedicated to those seeking jobs in the computer field. We hope the superior samples will help you manage your current job campaign and your career so that you will find work aligned to your career interests.

As the editor of this book, I would like to give you some tips on how to make the best use of the information you will find here. Because you are considering a career change, you already understand the concept of managing your career for maximum enjoyment and self-fulfillment. The purpose of this book is to provide expert tools and advice so that you *can* manage your career. Inside these pages you will find resumes and cover letters that will help you find not just a job but the type of work you want to do.

Overview of the Book

Every resume and cover letter in this book actually worked. And most of the resumes and cover letters have common features: all are one-page, all are in the chronological format, and all resumes are accompanied by a companion cover letter. The book is divided into three parts. **Part One** provides some advice about job hunting. Step One begins with a discussion of why employers prefer the one-page, chronological resume. In Step Two you are introduced to the direct approach and to the proper format for a cover letter. In Step Three you learn the 14 main reasons why job hunters are not offered the jobs they want, and you learn the six key areas employers focus on when they interview you. Step Four gives nuts-and-bolts advice on how to handle the interview, send a follow-up letter after an interview, and negotiate your salary. At the end of Part One, you'll find advice about how to research and locate the companies and organizations to which you want to send your resume.

Since the cover letter plays such a critical role in a career change, **Part Two** of the book is entitled Cover Letters for Computer Jobs. You will learn from the experts how to format your cover letters and you will see suggested language to use in marketing your computer training, knowledge, or experience. It has been said that "A picture is worth a thousand words" and, for that reason, you will see numerous examples of effective cover letters used by *real* individuals to find their first job in the computer field, change industries, or assume new kinds of responsibilities within the field. Part Two ends with answers to the 16 most commonly asked questions about cover letters and job hunting, and the answers are provided in the form of actual cover letters.

Parts One and Two lead up to the most important part of the book, which is Real-Resumes for Computer Jobs—**Part Three.** In this section you will see people in varying stages of change. Some of the individuals whose resumes and cover letters you see wanted to change the product, company, or service they were selling, managing, or representing. As Part Three evolves, you discover resumes and cover letters used by people who wanted to find a completely different type of work to do. Then there are resumes and cover letters of people who wanted a change but who probably wanted to remain in their industry. Many of you will be especially interested by the resumes and cover letters of individuals who knew they definitely wanted a career change but had no idea what they wanted to do next. Other resumes and cover letters show individuals who knew they wanted to change fields and had a pretty good idea of what they wanted to do next. Part Three ends with resumes and cover letters of folks who moved from self-employment, usually in small companies, to something totally different.

Whatever your background or training, you'll find resumes and cover letters that will "show you the ropes" in job hunting. Bear in mind that you can learn a lot from any of the resumes in this book. For example, if you are already a part of the computer industry, you will find many resumes used by individuals to advance in the industry. If you are seeking your first job in the computer field, you will find numerous examples of resumes and cover letters used to launch careers.

Before you proceed further, think about why you picked up this book.

- Are you nearing completion of a degree but have little or no hands-on experience?
- Are you dissatisfied with the type of work you are now doing?
- Would you like to change careers, change companies, or change industries?
- Are you satisfied with your industry but not with your niche or function within it?
- Do you want to transfer your skills to a new product or service?
- Even if you have excelled in your field, have you "had enough?" Would you like the stimulation of a new challenge?
- Are you aware of the importance of a great cover letter but unsure of how to write one?
- Are you preparing to launch a second career after retirement?
- Have you been downsized, or do you anticipate becoming a victim of downsizing?
- Do you need expert advice on how to plan and implement a job campaign that will open the maximum number of doors?
- Do you want to make sure you handle an interview to your maximum advantage?
- Would you like to master the techniques of negotiating salary and benefits?
- Do you want to learn the secrets and shortcuts of professional resume writers?

> The "direct approach" is the style of job hunting most likely to yield the maximum number of job interviews.

Using the Direct Approach

As you consider the possibility of a job hunt or career change, you need to be aware that most people end up having at least three distinctly different careers in their working lifetimes, and often those careers are different from each other. Yet people usually stumble through each job campaign, unsure of what they should be doing. Whether you find yourself voluntarily or unexpectedly in a job hunt, the direct approach is the job hunting strategy most likely to yield a full-time permanent job. The direct approach is an active, take-the-initiative style of job hunting in which you choose your next employer rather than relying on responding to ads, using employment agencies, or depending on other methods of finding jobs. You will learn how to use the direct approach in this book, and you will see that an effective cover letter is a critical ingredient in using the direct approach.

> Using references in a skillful fashion in your job hunt will inspire confidence in prospective employers and help you "close the sale" after interviews.

Lack of Industry Experience Not a Major Barrier to Entering New Field

"Lack of experience" is often the last reason people are not offered jobs, according to the companies who do the hiring. If you are changing jobs, you will be glad to learn that experienced professionals often are selling "potential" rather than experience in a job hunt. Companies look for personal qualities that they know tend to be present in their most effective professionals, such as communication skills, initiative, persistence, organizational and time management skills, and creativity. Frequently companies are trying to discover "personality type," "talent," "ability," "aptitude," and "potential" rather than seeking actual hands-on experience, so your resume should be designed to aggressively present your accomplishments. Attitude, enthusiasm, personality, and a track record of achievements in any type of work are the primary "indicators of success" which employers are seeking, and you will see numerous examples in this book of resumes written in an all-purpose fashion so that the professional can approach various industries and companies.

The Art of Using References in a Job Hunt

You probably already know that you need to provide references during a job hunt, but you may not be sure of how and when to use references for maximum advantage. You can use references very creatively during a job hunt to call attention to your strengths and make yourself "stand out." Your references will rarely get you a job, no matter how impressive the names, but the way you use references can boost the employer's confidence in you and lead to a job offer in the least time. You should ask from three to five people, including people who have supervised you, if you can use them as a reference during your job hunt. You may not be able to ask your current boss since your job hunt is probably confidential. A common question in resume preparation is: "Do I need to put my references on my resume?" No, you don't. And even if you create a page of references at the same time that you prepare your resume, you don't need to mail your references page with the resume and cover letter. The potential employer is not interested in your references until he meets and gets interested in you, so the earliest you need to have references ready is at the first interview. An excellent attention-getting technique is to take to the first interview not just a page of references (giving names, addresses, and telephone numbers) but an actual letter of reference written by someone who knows you well and who preferably has supervised or employed you. A professional way to close the first interview is to thank the interviewer, shake his or her hand, and then say you'd like to give him or her a copy of a letter of reference from a previous employer. Hopefully you already made a good impression during the interview, but you'll "close the sale" in a dynamic fashion if you leave a letter praising you and your accomplishments. For that reason, it's a good idea to ask employers during your final weeks in a job if they will provide you with a written letter of recommendation which you can use in future job hunts. Most employers will oblige, and you will have a letter that has a useful "shelf life" of many years. Such a letter often gives the prospective employer enough confidence in his opinion of you that he may forego checking out other references and decide to offer you the job in the next few days. Whom should you ask to serve as references? References should be people who have known or supervised you in a professional, academic, or work situation. References with big titles, like school superintendent or congressman, are fine, but remind busy people when you get to the interview stage that they may be contacted soon. Make sure the busy official recognizes your name and has instant positive recall of you! If you're asked to provide references on a formal company application, you can simply transcribe names from your references list. In summary, follow this rule in using references: If you've got them, flaunt them! If you've obtained well-written letters of reference, make sure you find a polite way to push those references under the nose of the interviewer so he or she can hear someone other than you describing your strengths. Your references probably won't ever get you a job, but glowing letters of reference can give you credibility and visibility that can make you stand out among candidates with similar credentials and potential!

With regard to references, it's best to provide the names and addresses of people who have supervised you or observed you in a work situation.

The approach taken by this book is to (1) help you master the proven best techniques of conducting a job hunt and (2) show you how to stand out in a job hunt through your resume, cover letter, interviewing skills, as well as the way in which you present your references and follow up on interviews. Now, the best way to "get in the mood" for writing your own resume and cover letter is to select samples from the Table of Contents that interest you and then read them. A great resume is a "photograph," usually on one page, of an individual. If you wish to seek professional advice in preparing your resume, you may contact one of the professional writers at Professional Resume & Employment Publishing (PREP) for a brief free consultation by calling 1-910-483-6611.

PART ONE: SOME ADVICE ABOUT YOUR JOB HUNT

What if you don't know what you want to do?

Your job hunt will be more comfortable if you can figure out what type of work you want to do. But you are not alone if you have no idea what you want to do next! You may have knowledge and skills in certain areas but want to get into another type of work. What *The Wall Street Journal* has discovered in its research on careers is that most of us end up having at least three distinctly different careers in our working lives; it seems that, even if we really like a particular kind of activity, twenty years of doing it is enough for most of us, and we want to move on to something else!

Figure out what interests you and you will hold the key to a successful job hunt and working career. (And be prepared for your interests to change over time!)

That's why we strongly believe that you need to spend some time figuring out **what interests you** rather than taking an inventory of the skills you have. You may have skills that you simply don't want to use, but if you can build your career on the things that interest you, you will be more likely to be happy and satisfied in your job. Realize, too, that interests can change over time; the activities that interest you now may not be the ones that interested you years ago. For example, some professionals may decide that they've had enough of retail sales and want a job selling another product or service, even though they have earned a reputation for being an excellent retail manager. We strongly believe that interests rather than skills should be the determining factor in deciding what types of jobs you want to apply for and what directions you explore in your job hunt. Obviously one cannot be a lawyer without a law degree or a secretary without secretarial skills; but a professional can embark on a next career as a financial consultant, property manager, plant manager, production supervisor, retail manager, or other occupation if he/she has a strong interest in that type of work and can provide a resume that clearly demonstrates past excellent performance in *any* field and *potential* to excel in another field. As you will see later in this book, "lack of exact experience" is the last reason why people are turned down for the jobs they apply for.

"Lack of exact experience" is the last reason people are turned down for the jobs for which they apply.

How can you have a resume prepared if you don't know what you want to do?

You may be wondering how you can have a resume prepared if you don't know what you want to do next. The approach to resume writing which PREP, the country's oldest resume-preparation company, has used successfully for many years is to develop an "all-purpose" resume that translates your skills, experience, and accomplishments into language employers can understand. What most people need in a job hunt is a versatile resume that will allow them to apply for numerous types of jobs. For example, you may want to apply for a job in pharmaceutical sales, but you may also want to have a resume that will be versatile enough for you to apply for jobs in the construction, financial services, or automotive industries.

Based on 20 years of serving job hunters, we at PREP have found that **an all-purpose resume** and **specific cover letters tailored to specific fields** is often your best approach to job hunting rather than trying to create different resumes for different occupational areas. Usually, you will not even need more than one "all-purpose" cover letter, although the cover letter rather than the resume is the place to communicate your interest in a narrow or specific field. An all-purpose resume and cover letter that translate your experience and accomplishments into plain English are the tools that will maximize the number of doors which open for you while permitting you to "fish" in the widest range of job areas.

Your resume will provide the script for your job interview.

When you get down to it, your resume has a simple job to do: Its purpose is to blow as many doors open as possible and to make as many people as possible want to meet you. So a well-written resume that really "sells" you is a key that will create opportunities for you in a job hunt.

This statistic explains why: The typical newspaper advertisement for a job opening receives more than 245 replies. And normally only 10 or 12 will be invited to an interview.

But here's another purpose of the resume: it provides the "script" the employer uses when he interviews you. If your resume has been written in such a way that your strengths and achievements are revealed, that's what you'll end up talking about at the job interview. Since the resume will govern what you get asked about at your interviews, you can't overestimate the importance of making sure your resume makes you look and sound as good as you are.

Your resume is the "script" for your job interviews. Make sure you put on your resume what you want to talk about or be asked about at the job interview.

So what is a "good" resume?

Very literally, your resume should motivate the person reading it to dial the phone number you have put on the resume. (If you are relocating, that's one reason you should think about putting a local phone contact number on your resume, if possible, when your contact address is several states away; employers are much more likely to dial a local telephone number than a long-distance number when they're looking for potential employees.)

If you have a resume already, look at it objectively. Is it a limp, colorless "laundry list" of your job titles and duties? Or does it "paint a picture" of your skills, abilities, and accomplishments in a way that would make someone want to meet you? Can people understand what you're saying?

The one-page resume in chronological format is the format preferred by most employers.

How long should your resume be?

One page, maybe two. Usually only people in the academic community have a resume (which they usually call a *curriculum vitae*) longer than one or two pages. Remember that your resume is almost always accompanied by a cover letter, and a potential employer does not want to read more than two or three pages about a total stranger in order to decide if he wants to meet that person! Besides, don't forget that the more you tell someone about yourself, the more opportunity you are providing for the employer to screen you out at the "first-cut" stage. A resume should be concise and exciting and designed to make the reader want to meet you in person!

Should resumes be functional or chronological?

Employers almost always prefer a chronological resume; in other words, an employer will find a resume easier to read if it is immediately apparent what your current or most recent job is, what you did before that, and so forth, in reverse chronological order. A resume that goes back in detail for the last ten years of employment will generally satisfy the employer's curiosity about your background. Employment more than ten years old can be shown even more briefly in an "Other Experience" section at the end of your "Experience" section. Remember that your intention is not to tell everything you've done but to "hit the high points" and especially impress the employer with what you learned, contributed, or accomplished in each job you describe.

Once you get your resume, what do you do with it?
You will be using your resume to answer ads, as a tool to use in talking with friends and relatives about your job search, and, most importantly, in using the "direct approach" described in this book.

When you mail your resume, always send a "cover letter."
A "cover letter," sometimes called a "resume letter" or "letter of interest," is a letter that accompanies and introduces your resume. Your cover letter is a way of personalizing the resume by sending it to the specific person you think you might want to work for at each company. Your cover letter should contain a few highlights from your resume—just enough to make someone want to meet you. Cover letters should always be typed or word processed on a computer—never handwritten.

Never mail or fax your resume without a cover letter.

1. Learn the art of answering ads.
There is an "art," part of which can be learned, in using your "bestselling" resume to reply to advertisements.

Sometimes an exciting job lurks behind a boring ad that someone dictated in a hurry, so reply to any ad that interests you. Don't worry that you aren't "25 years old with an MBA" like the ad asks for. Employers will always make compromises in their requirements if they think you're the "best fit" overall.

What about ads that ask for "salary requirements?"
What if the ad you're answering asks for "salary requirements?" The first rule is to avoid committing yourself in writing at that point to a specific salary. You don't want to "lock yourself in."

What if the ad asks for your "salary requirements?"

There are two ways to handle the ad that asks for "salary requirements."
First, you can ignore that part of the ad and accompany your resume with a cover letter that focuses on "selling" you, your abilities, and even some of your philosophy about work or your field. You may include a sentence in your cover letter like this: "I can provide excellent personal and professional references at your request, and I would be delighted to share the private details of my salary history with you in person."

Second, if you feel you must give some kind of number, just state a range in your cover letter that includes your medical, dental, other benefits, and expected bonuses. You might state, for example, "My current compensation, including benefits and bonuses, is in the range of $30,000-$40,000."

Analyze the ad and "tailor" yourself to it.
When you're replying to ads, a finely-tailored cover letter is an important tool in getting your resume noticed and read. On the next page is a cover letter which has been "tailored to fit" a specific ad. Notice the "art" used by PREP writers of analyzing the ad's main requirements and then writing the letter so that the person's background, work habits, and interests seem "tailor-made" to the company's needs. Use this cover letter as a model when you prepare your own reply to ads.

Date

Mr. Arthur Wise
Chamber of Commerce of the U.S.
9439 Goshen Lane
Dallas, TX 22105

Dear Mr. Wise:

I would appreciate an opportunity to show you in person, soon, that I am the resourceful and technically astute individual you are looking for as your Network Manager for the Chamber of Commerce in Texas.

Here are just three reasons why I believe I am the effective young professional you seek:

- *I myself am "sold" on the Chamber of Commerce* and have long been an admirer of its goal of forming a cohesive business organization to promote the well-being of communities and promote business vigor. As someone better known than I put it long ago, "the business of America is business." I wholeheartedly believe that the Chamber's efforts to unite, solidify, and mobilize American business can be an important key in unlocking the international competitiveness and domestic vitality of our economy. I am eager to contribute to that effort.

- *I am a proven computer professional* with a demonstrated ability to integrate new technology into an organization's existing infrastructure. In my current job as a project manager, I have established LANs and WANs which have greatly increased efficiency.

- *Single and available for frequent travel, I realize from your advertisement that the position requires frequent travel.* I am fortunate to have the natural energy, industry, and enthusiasm required to put in the long hours necessary.

You will find me, I am certain, a friendly, good-natured person whom you would be proud to call part of the Chamber's "team." Although I have worked primarily in profit-making environments, I am confident that I could enthusiastically and gracefully transition my skills into a trade association environment. I would enjoy the opportunity to contribute my strong networking knowledge to the Chamber.

I hope you will call or write me soon to suggest a convenient time when we might meet to discuss your needs further and how I might serve them.

Yours sincerely,

Your Name

Employers are trying to identify the individual who wants the job they are filling. Don't be afraid to express your enthusiasm in the cover letter!

2. Talk to friends and relatives.

Don't be shy about telling your friends and relatives the kind of job you're looking for. Looking for the job you want involves using your network of contacts, so tell people what you're looking for. They may be able to make introductions and help set up interviews.

About 25% of all interviews are set up through "who you know," so don't ignore this approach.

3. Finally, and most importantly, use the "direct approach."

More than 50% of all job interviews are set up by the "direct approach." That means you actually send a resume and a cover letter to a company you think might be interesting to work for.

The "direct approach" is a strategy in which you choose your next employer.

To whom do you write?

In general, you should write directly to the *exact name* of the person who would be hiring you: say, the vice-president of marketing or data processing. If you're in doubt about to whom to address the letter, address it to the president by name, and he or she will make sure it gets forwarded to the right person within the company who has hiring authority in your area.

How do you find the names of potential employers?

You're not alone if you feel that the biggest problem in your job search is finding the right names at the companies you want to contact. But you can usually figure out the names of companies you want to approach by deciding first if your job hunt is primarily geography-driven or industry-driven.

In a **geography-driven job hunt,** you could select a list of, say, 50 companies you want to contact **by location** from the lists that the U.S. Chambers of Commerce publish yearly of their "major area employers." There are hundreds of local Chambers of Commerce across America, and most of them will have an 800 number which you can find through 1-800-555-1212. If you and your family think Atlanta, Dallas, Ft. Lauderdale, and Virginia Beach might be nice places to live, for example, you could contact the Chamber of Commerce in those cities and ask how you can obtain a copy of their list of major employers. Your nearest library will have the book which lists the addresses of all chambers.

In an **industry-driven job hunt,** and if you are willing to relocate, you will be identifying the companies which you find most attractive in the industry in which you want to work. When you select a list of companies to contact **by industry,** you can find the right person to write and the address of firms by industrial category in *Standard and Poor's, Moody's,* and other excellent books in public libraries. Many Web sites also provide contact information.

Many people feel it's a good investment to actually call the company to either find out or double-check the name of the person to whom they want to send a resume and cover letter. It's important to do as much as you feasibly can to assure that the letter gets to the right person in the company.

At the end of Part One, you will find some advice about how to conduct library research and how to locate organizations to which you could send your resume.

What's the correct way to follow up on a resume you send?

There is a polite way to be aggressively interested in a company during your job hunt. It is ideal to end the cover letter accompanying your resume by saying, "I hope you'll welcome my call next week when I try to arrange a brief meeting at your convenience to discuss your current and future needs and how I might serve them." Keep it low key, and just ask for a "brief meeting," not an interview. Employers want people who show a determined interest in working with them, so don't be shy about following up on the resume and cover letter you've mailed.

STEP THREE: Preparing for Interviews

But a resume and cover letter by themselves can't get you the job you want. You need to "prep" yourself before the interview. Step Three in your job campaign is "Preparing for Interviews." First, let's look at interviewing from the company's point of view.

What are the biggest "turnoffs" for companies?

One of the ways to help yourself perform well at an interview is to look at the main reasons why companies *don't* hire the people they interview, according to companies that do the interviewing.

Notice that "lack of appropriate background" (or lack of experience) is the *last* reason for not being offered the job.

The 14 Most Common Reasons Job Hunters Are Not Offered Jobs (according to the companies who do the interviewing and hiring):

1. Low level of accomplishment
2. Poor attitude, lack of self-confidence
3. Lack of goals/objectives
4. Lack of enthusiasm
5. Lack of interest in the company's business
6. Inability to sell or express yourself
7. Unrealistic salary demands
8. Poor appearance
9. Lack of maturity, no leadership potential
10. Lack of extracurricular activities
11. Lack of preparation for the interview, no knowledge about company
12. Objecting to travel
13. Excessive interest in security and benefits
14. Inappropriate background

Department of Labor studies have proven that smart, "prepared" job hunters can increase their beginning salary while getting a job in *half* the time it normally takes. (4½ months is the average national length of a job search.) Here, from PREP, are some questions that can prepare you to find a job faster.

Are you in the "right" frame of mind?

It seems unfair that we have to look for a job just when we're lowest in morale. Don't worry *too* much if you're nervous before interviews. You're supposed to be a little nervous, especially if the job means a lot to you. But the best way to kill unnecessary

It pays to be aware of the 14 most common pitfalls for job hunters.

fears about job hunting is through 1) making sure you have a great resume and 2) preparing yourself for the interview. Here are three main areas you need to think about before each interview.

Do you know what the company does?

Don't walk into an interview giving the impression that, "If this is Tuesday, this must be General Motors."

Research the company before you go to interviews.

Find out before the interview what the company's main product or service is. Where is the company heading? Is it in a "growth" or declining industry? (Answers to these questions may influence whether or not you want to work there!)

Information about what the company does is in annual reports as well as newspaper and magazine articles. Just visit your nearest library and ask the reference librarian to guide you to materials on the company. Internet searches will yield valuable information. At the end of Part One, you will find many suggestions about how to research companies.

Do you know what you want to do for the company?

Before the interview, try to decide how you see yourself fitting into the company. Remember, "lack of exact background" the company wants is usually the last reason people are not offered jobs.

Understand before you go to each interview that the burden will be on you to "sell" the interviewer on why you're the best person for the job and the company.

How will you answer the critical interview questions?

Anticipate the questions you will be asked at the interview, and prepare your responses in advance.

Put yourself in the interviewer's position and think about the questions you're most likely to be asked. Here are some of the most commonly asked interview questions:

Q: *"What are your greatest strengths?"*
A: Don't say you've never thought about it! Go into an interview knowing the three main impressions you want to leave about yourself, such as "I'm hard-working, loyal, and an imaginative cost-cutter."

Q: *"What are your greatest weaknesses?"*
A: Don't confess that you're lazy or have trouble meeting deadlines! Confessing that you tend to be a "workaholic" or "tend to be a perfectionist and sometimes get frustrated when others don't share my high standards" will make your prospective employer see a "weakness" that he likes. Name a weakness that your interviewer will perceive as a strength.

Q: *"What are your long-range goals?"*
A: If you're interviewing with Microsoft, don't say you want to work for IBM in five years! Say your long-range goal is to be *with* the company, contributing to its goals and success.

Q: "What motivates you to do your best work?"
A: Don't get dollar signs in your eyes here! "A challenge" is not a bad answer, but it's a little cliched. Saying something like "troubleshooting" or "solving a tough problem" is more interesting and specific. Give an example if you can.

Q: "What do you know about this company?"

A: Don't say you never heard of it until they asked you to the interview! Name an interesting, positive thing you learned about the company recently from your research. Remember, company executives can sometimes feel rather "maternal" about the company they serve. Don't get onto a negative area of the company if you can think of positive facts you can bring up. Of course, if you learned in your research that the company's sales seem to be taking a nose-dive, or that the company president is being prosecuted for taking bribes, you might politely ask your interviewer to tell you something that could help you better understand what you've been reading. Those are the kinds of company facts that can help you determine whether you want to work there or not.

Q: "Why should I hire you?"

A: "I'm unemployed and available" is the wrong answer here! Get back to your strengths and say that you believe the organization could benefit by a loyal, hard-working cost-cutter like yourself.

In conclusion, you should decide in advance, before you go to the interview, how you will answer each of these commonly asked questions. Have some practice interviews with a friend to role-play and build your confidence.

STEP FOUR: Handling the Interview and Negotiating Salary

Now you're ready for Step Four: actually handling the interview successfully and effectively. Remember, the purpose of an interview is to get a job offer.

Eight "do's" for the interview

According to leading U.S. companies, there are eight key areas in interviewing success. You can fail at an interview if you mishandle just one area.

1. Do wear appropriate clothes.
You can never go wrong by wearing a suit to an interview.

2. Do be well groomed.
Don't overlook the obvious things like having clean hair, clothes, and fingernails for the interview.

3. Do give a firm handshake.
You'll have to shake hands twice in most interviews: first, before you sit down, and second, when you leave the interview. Limp handshakes turn most people off.

4. Do smile and show a sense of humor.
Interviewers are looking for people who would be nice to work with, so don't be so somber that you don't smile. In fact, research shows that people who smile at interviews are perceived as more intelligent. So, smile!

5. Do be enthusiastic.
Employers say they are "turned off" by lifeless, unenthusiastic job hunters who show no special interest in that company. The best way to show some enthusiasm for the employer's operation is to find out about the business beforehand.

Go to an interview prepared to tell the company why it should hire you.

A smile at an interview makes the employer perceive of you as intelligent!

6. Do show you are flexible and adaptable.
   An employer is looking for someone who can contribute to his organization in a flexible, adaptable way. No matter what skills and training you have, employers know every new employee must go through initiation and training on the company's turf. Certainly show pride in your past accomplishments in a specific, factual way ("I saved my last employer $50.00 a week by a new cost-cutting measure I developed"). But don't come across as though there's nothing about the job you couldn't easily handle.

7. Do ask intelligent questions about the employer's business.
   An employer is hiring someone because of certain business needs. Show interest in those needs. Asking questions to get a better idea of the employer's needs will help you "stand out" from other candidates interviewing for the job.

8. Do "take charge" when the interviewer "falls down" on the job.
   Go into every interview knowing the three or four points about yourself you want the interviewer to remember. And be prepared to take an active part in leading the discussion if the interviewer's "canned approach" does not permit you to display your "strong suit." You can't always depend on the interviewer's asking you the "right" questions so you can stress your strengths and accomplishments.

Employers are seeking people with good attitudes whom they can train and coach to do things their way.

An important "don't": Don't ask questions about salary or benefits at the first interview.
Employers don't take warmly to people who look at their organization as just a place to satisfy salary and benefit needs. Don't risk making a negative impression by appearing greedy or self-serving. The place to discuss salary and benefits is normally at the second interview, and the employer will bring it up. Then you can ask questions without appearing excessively interested in what the organization can do for you.

"Sell yourself" before talking salary
Make sure you've "sold" yourself before talking salary. First show you're the "best fit" for the employer, and then you'll be in a stronger position from which to negotiate salary.

Interviewers sometimes throw out a salary figure at the first interview to see if you'll accept it. Don't commit yourself. You may be able to negotiate a better deal later on. Get back to finding out more about the job. This lets the interviewer know you're interested primarily in the job and not the salary.

Now...negotiating your salary
You must avoid stating a "salary requirement" in your initial cover letter, and you must avoid even appearing **interested** in salary before you are offered the job.

Don't appear excessively interested in salary and benefits at the interview.

Never bring up the subject of salary yourself. Employers say there's no way you can avoid looking greedy if you bring up the issue of salary and benefits before the company has identified you as its "best fit."

When the company brings up salary, it may say something like this: "Well, Mary, we think you'd make a good candidate for this job. What kind of salary are we talking about?"

Never name a number here, either. Give the ball back to the interviewer. Act as though you hadn't given the subject of salary much thought and respond something like this: "Ah, Mr. Jones, salary. . .well, I wonder if you'd be kind enough to tell me what salary you had in mind when you advertised the job?" Or ... "What is the range you have in mind?"

Don't worry, if the interviewer names a figure that you think is too low, you can say so without turning down the job or locking yourself into a rigid position. The point here is to negotiate for yourself as well as you can. You might reply to a number named by the interviewer that you think is low by saying something like this: "Well, Mr. Lee, the job interests me very much, and I think I'd certainly enjoy working with you. But, frankly, I was thinking of something a little higher than that." That leaves the ball in your interviewer's court again, and you haven't turned down the job either, in case it turns out that the interviewer can't increase the offer and you still want the job.

Salary negotiation can be tricky.

Last, send a follow-up letter.
Finally, send a letter right after the interview telling your interviewer you enjoyed the meeting and are certain (if you are) you are the "best fit" for the job. The people interviewing you will probably have an attitude described as either "professionally loyal" to their companies or "maternal and proprietary" if the interviewer also owns the company. In either case, they are looking for people who want to work for *that* company in particular. The follow-up letter you send might be just the deciding factor in your favor if the employer is trying to choose between you and someone else.

Sample follow-up letters are shown in the next section. Be sure to modify the model letter according to your particular skills and interview situation.

A follow-up letter can help the employer choose between you and another qualified candidate.

Researching companies and locating employers

Figuring out the names of the organizations to which you want to mail your resume is part of any highly successful job campaign. Don't depend on only answering the ads you read in printed or electronic form, waiting for the ideal job to appear in **newspapers or magazines,** many of which are published online. If you are geographically oriented and need to find work in a particular city or town, check out the Sunday advertisements in the classified sections which suit you best, such as "administrative" or "professional" or "technical." Also aggressively research possible employers. Here is some information which you can use in researching the names of organizations for which you might be interested in working.

In electronic and printed form, most libraries have a variety of information available on various organizations throughout the U.S. and worldwide. If your local library has computers, you will probably have access to a vast network of information. Many printed materials might be available only for use in the reference room of the library, but some items may be checked out. Listed below are some of the major sources to look for, but be sure and check at the reference desk to see if there are any resources available in a printed or online form related to the specific types of companies you wish to investigate.

The Worldwide Chamber of Commerce Directory
Most chambers of commerce annually produce a "list of major employers" for their market area (or city). Usually the list includes the name, address, and telephone number of the employer along with information about the number of people employed, kinds of products and services produced, and a person to contact about employment. You can obtain the "list of major employers" in the city where you want to work by writing to that chamber. There is usually a small charge.

The *Worldwide Chamber of Commerce Directory* is an alphabetical listing of American and foreign chambers of commerce. It includes:

> All U.S. Chambers of Commerce (with addresses and phone numbers)
> American Chambers of Commerce abroad
> Canadian Chambers of Commerce
> Foreign Chambers of Commerce in principal cities worldwide
> Foreign Embassies and Consulates in the U.S.
> U.S. Consulates and Embassies throughout the world

Standard and Poor's Register of Corporations, Directors, and Executives

Standard and Poor's produce three volumes annually with information concerning over 77,000 American corporations. They are:

Volume 1—**Corporations.** Here is an alphabetical listing of a variety of information for each of over 77,000 companies, including:

- name of company, address, telephone number
- names, titles, and functions of several key officers
- name of accounting firm, primary bank, and law firm
- stock exchange, description of products or services
- annual sales, number of employees
- division names and functions, subsidiary listings

Volume 2—**Directors and Executives.** This volume lists alphabetically over 70,000 officers, directors, partners, etc. by name. Information on each executive includes:

- principal business affiliation
- business address, residence address, year of birth
- college and year of graduation, fraternal affiliation

Volume 3—**Index.**

Moody's Manuals

Moody's Manuals provide information about companies traded on the New York and American Stock Exchanges and over the counter. They include:

Moody's Industrial Manual

Here, Moody's discusses detailed information on companies traded on the New York, American, and regional stock exchanges. The companies are listed alphabetically. Basic information about company addresses, phone numbers, and the names of key officers is available for each company listed. In addition, detailed information about the financial and operating data for each company is available. There are three levels of detail provided:

Complete Coverage. Companies in this section have the following information:

- *financial information* for the past 7 years (income accounts, balance sheets, financial and operating data).
- *detailed description of the company's business* including a complete list of subsidiaries and office and property sites.
- *capital structure information,* which includes details on capital stock and long-term debt, with bond and preferred stock ratings and 2 years of stock and bond price ranges.
- *extensive presentation of the company's last annual report.*

Full Measure Coverage. Information on companies in this section includes:
- *financial information for the past 7 years* (income accounts, balance sheets, financial and operating data).
- *detailed description of company's business,* with a complete list of subsidiaries and plant and property locations.
- *capital structure information,* with details on capital stock and long-term debt, with bond and preferred stock ratings and 2 years of stock and bond price changes.

Comprehensive Coverage. Information on companies in this section includes:
- *5 years of financial information* on income accounts, balance sheets, and financial and operating ratios.
- *detailed description of company's business,* including subsidiaries.
- *concise capital structure information,* including capital stock and long-term debts, bond and preferred stock ratings.

Moody's OTC Manual

Here is information on U.S. firms which are unlisted on national and regional stock exchanges. There are three levels of coverage: complete, full measure, and comprehensive (same as described above). Other Moody's manuals include: *Moody's Public Utility Manual, Moody's Municipal and Government Manual,* and *Moody's Bank and Finance Manual.*

Dun's Million Dollar Directory

Three separate listings (alphabetical, geographic, and by products) of over 120,000 U.S. firms. There are three volumes:
Volume 1—The 45,000 largest companies, net worth over $500,000.
Volume 2—The 37,000 next largest companies.
Volume 3—The 37,000 next largest companies.

U.S. industrial directories

Ask your librarian to guide you to your library's collection of industrial directories. Almost every state produces a manufacturing directory, for example, and many libraries maintain complete collections of these directories. You may find information on products and the addresses and telephone numbers of industrial companies.

Thomas' Register of Manufacturers

16 volumes of information about manufacturing companies.
Volumes 1-8—Alphabetical listing by product.
Volumes 9-10—Alphabetical listing of manufacturing company names, addresses, telephone numbers, and local offices.
Volumes 11-16—Alphabetical company catalog information.

Information About Foreign Companies

If you'd like your next job to be overseas or with an international company, you can find much helpful information in the library. You approach these companies in the same way as you would approach U.S.-based companies.

Directory of Foreign Manufacturers in the U.S.

Alphabetical listing of U.S. manufacturing companies which are owned and operated by parent foreign firms. The information provided includes the name and address of the U.S. firm, the name and address of the foreign parent firm, and the products produced.

Directory of American Firms Operating in Foreign Countries
Alphabetical listing of the names, addresses, chief officers, products, and country operated in of U.S. firms abroad.

International Firms Directory
This lists foreign corporations.

Hoover's Handbook of World Business
This lists corporations in Asia and Europe.

Principal International Businesses
This is a comprehensive directory of international businesses.

Information Available From The Internet

Information about companies is also available through the Internet. You can use all the search engines to help you in your search for company information and company website addresses. It is not the purpose of this book to recommend websites by name, but you can type in "jobs" or "employment" or "careers" as a key word using any search engine and you will be introduced to organizations that will allow you to post your resume online. You can also usually find an organization's website by typing in the following website addresses, just substituting the name of the company you want to find, such as "Dell," for "organizationname":

       http://www.organizationname.com
       http:/www.organizationname.org
       http://www.organizationname.net

However, sometimes finding what you are looking for takes trial and error. For example, if you wanted to find Hewlett Packard's website, you would find it either by typing in "Hewlett Packard" as a key word or by typing in http://www.HP.com. Not all website addresses are perfectly obvious, straightforward, or intuitive, but the search engines usually perform in an excellent fashion when you type in key words in a trial-and-error "surfing" or fact-finding mode.

Many people are aware of the importance of having a great resume, but most people in a job hunt don't realize just how important a cover letter can be. The purpose of the cover letter, sometimes called a **"letter of interest,"** is to introduce your resume to prospective employers.

"A Picture Is Worth a Thousand Words."

As a way of illustrating how important the cover letter can be, we have chosen to show you on the next two pages the cover letter and resume of an individual in career change who is seeking his first job in the computer field. If the employer received only his resume without a cover letter, this individual would appear to offer merely 14 years of experience in the farm industry. What the cover letter allows him to do is to explain that he worked extensively with computers in the agricultural industry prior to going back to college at middle age to finish his Computer Science degree.

The cover letter is the critical ingredient in a job hunt such as David Curtin's because the cover letter allows him to say a lot of things that just don't "fit" on the resume. For example, he can emphasize his ability to relate well to customers.

Finally, the cover letter gives him a chance to stress his maturity and work experience. This will set him apart from other newly minted college grads who will be lacking in experience.

You will see on the next two pages that the cover letter gives you a chance to "get personal" with the person to whom you are writing whereas the resume is a more formal document. Even if the employer doesn't request a cover letter, we believe that it is *always* in your best interest to send a cover letter with your resume. The aim of this book is to show you examples of cover letters designed to blow doors open so that you can develop your own cover letters and increase the number of interviews you have.

A cover letter is an essential part of a job hunt.

Please do not attempt to implement a job hunt without a cover letter such as the ones you see in Part Two and in Part Three of this book. A cover letter is the first impression of you, and you can influence the way an employer views you by the language and style of your letter.

Your cover letter and resume are "companion" documents.

Date

Exact Name of Person
Exact Title
Exact Name of Company
Address
City, State, Zip

A cover letter and resume are "companion" documents.

When you look at this resume, you see how important a cover letter can be in a job hunt. Without the cover letter, this person might seem lacking in the raw ingredients which lead to success in the computer field.

Dear Exact Name of Person (or Dear Sir or Madam if answering a blind ad):

With the enclosed resume, I would like to express my interest in exploring employment opportunities with your organization.

As you will see from my resume, I hold a degree in Computer Science and previously completed extensive coursework at the University of Georgia in Electrical Engineering. After the University of Georgia, I became employed by the Case Company and worked for that corporation for 14 years as a Product Support Manager. I resigned from my position with the Case Company and became a full-time Computer Science student in 2000 when the company asked me to accept a promotion which required relocation to their home office in Wisconsin. At that point, I decided to complete the college degree which I had begun many years earlier, and I have worked part-time as a business consultant while completing my B.S. I have completed courses related to HTML, Java, Visual Basic, C and C++, UNIX, and Interfacing, and I am making plans to pursue Oracle in my spare time.

While providing all types of wholesale support and sales to 20 retail dealers in my job as a Product Support Manager with the Case Company, I was extensively involved in training the dealers' employees in computer operations. The Case Company decided in 1994 that it would require its dealer-customers to communicate with the company through online methods, so it became a major part of my job to work with dealers' platforms which included UNIX, AS 400, and Windows NT. I trained the dealers' employees in computer operations, and I also trained technicians to perform troubleshooting using high-tech computer equipment.

A key part of my job was helping dealers maximize the profitability of their retail businesses, so I became very skilled at interpreting financial documents including proformas, balance sheets, and other paperwork. I take pride in the fact that I helped all my dealer customers improve their bottom line through my recommendations related to market share, product line conversions and product mix, warranty policies and procedures, and stock ordering. I was consistently in the top 5% of the company's managers in a variety of areas including customer satisfaction.

If you can use a versatile professional who offers a versatile background which includes extensive customer service experience as well as computer knowledge, I hope you will contact me soon to suggest a time we might meet. Thank you for your time.

Sincerely,

David Curtins

DAVID CURTINS

1110½ Hay Street, Fayetteville, NC 28305 • preppub@aol.com • (910) 483-6611

OBJECTIVE

I want to contribute to an organization that can use a resourceful professional with an extensive technical background in electrical engineering and computer science along with vast experience in business consulting, operations management, and sales.

EDUCATION

B.S. degree in Computer Science, Phillips College, Weston, GA, 2001.
- Completed course work related to Java, Visual Basic, C and C++, UNIX, Interfacing, and other subjects. Will pursue Oracle studies in my spare time.
- **Previous course work in Electrical Engineering:** Began college with a major of pre-med and changed to Electrical Engineering, University of Georgia.

Technical computer training: Extensive training related to UNIX, AS 400, Windows NT, and other platforms sponsored by the Case Corporation.
- Skilled at interpreting schematics, diagrams, and blueprints; highly proficient in working with electrical circuitry. Highly skilled with Word, PowerPoint, Excel.

Financial training: Am skilled at reading profit-and-loss statements, pro formas, balance sheets, and other financial documents.

Graduated from Jeff Davis High School, Hazlehurst, GA, 1983.
- Was a school leader: was voted "Mr. Junior" and "Mr. Senior."

EXPERIENCE

BUSINESS CONSULTANT & FULL-TIME COMPUTER SCIENCE STUDENT. (2000-present). After working for the Case Company for 14 years, I resigned from the corporation when the company wanted me to accept a promotion and relocation to its home office in Racine, WI; I decided to resign and complete my college degree.

PRODUCT SUPPORT MANAGER. Borders Company, Racine, WI (1988-2000). Was responsible for 20 retail dealers and served as their wholesale source of supply for agricultural items such as plow tools.
- Became skilled in all aspects of business consulting as I worked with retailers to improve their profitability and merchandising mix; developed plans to foster better relationships between dealers and their customers.
- Developed innovative plans to help dealers increase the service part of their business. Utilized PowerPoint to make presentations and conduct training.
- Functioned as a business consultant; was trained to read financial statements and profit-and-loss statements.
- In 1994, after the company made the decision to require dealers to communicate their orders and other matters online, was extensively trained in computer operations related to UNIX, AS 400, Windows NT, and other platforms. Became skilled in assisting customers in their networking needs, and trained the dealers' employees in computer use and troubleshooting.
- Trained technicians to perform troubleshooting using high-tech computer troubleshooting equipment.

Highlights of achievements:
- Increased parts sales from $3.9 million in 1991 to $6.8 million in 1999.
- Boosted customer satisfaction rating from 62% in 1997 to 84% in 1999.
- Developed effective business plans which established goals for numerous product lines and which established objectives for operating income, market share, product line conversions, warranty policies and procedures, customer complaints, service reports, stock order goals, and claim audits.

PERSONAL

Outstanding references on request. Extremely resourceful and effective problem solver.

Date

**Addressing the Cover
Letter:** Get the exact
name of the person to
whom you are writing. This
makes your approach
personal.

Raytheon
P.O. Box 6056
Greenville, TX 75403
Attn: Mr. Smith

Dear Mr. Smith:

With the enclosed resume, I would like to make you aware of my knowledge of and education in communications and fiber optic technology, and to express my strong interest in offering my skills to your company. I recently spoke with a former Raytheon employee, Mr. Lonzo G. Bustos, and he recommended that I forward my resume to your attention.

Second Paragraph: You
have a chance to talk
about whatever you feel is
your most distinguishing
feature.

As you will see, I have just completed my Associate's Degree in Electronics Technology. My major area of concentration was Communications and Fiber Optics. I have worked with fiber optics previously while employed by Quanta Systems on a contract job in which we installed optical module boxes and fiber optic cable along a 5-mile perimeter.

Third Paragraph: You
bring up your next most
distinguishing qualities and
try to
sell yourself.

Though my previous work experience is not as highly technical in nature, I think you will see that I have proven myself to be a hard-working and reliable employee, as well as a capable supervisor. Most of the jobs shown on my resume were jobs I held while simultaneously completing courses toward my A.S. degree. Now that I have finished my degree, I am anxious to utilize my knowledge of communications and fiber optics technology. My strong work ethic, education, and technical know-how would be an asset to your organization.

Final Paragraph: He asks
the employer to contact
him. (Make sure *your*
reader knows what the
"next step" is.)

If you can use a highly motivated, intelligent young communications and fiber optics professional, I hope you will contact me to suggest a convenient time when we might meet to discuss your present and future needs, and how I might meet them.

Sincerely,

Pete Dawkins

Date

Exact Name of Person
Exact Title
Exact Name of Company
Address
City, State, Zip

Dear Exact Name of Person: (or Dear Sir or Madam if answering a blind ad):

    With the enclosed resume, I would like to make you aware of my exceptional technical skills as well as my strong background as a talented manager, articulate trainer, and highly skilled information systems and telecommunications professional.

    As you will see from my resume, I have earned a Master of Science in Computer Systems Engineering, graduating summa cum laude with a cumulative GPA of 3.9. I have further augmented my education with numerous technical courses, including Lifespan 2000/2012 fiber optics systems, Novell NetWare Systems Administrator 4.0 (LAN), and Microsoft courses in Network Essentials, NT Server & Workstation, Exchange, SQL, SMS, and TCP/IP. In addition, I have extensive military training in the telecommunications field including courses in Mobile Subscriber Equipment and Tactical Satellite/Microwave Systems.

    Recently I have excelled as a Fiber Optics Instructor, traveling worldwide to provide corporate training and technical support in installation, troubleshooting, maintenance, and configuration of ACCESS family fiber optic systems to customers worldwide which include Sprint, MCI, AT&T, and others. In previous positions, I have designed and implemented corporate Wide Area Networks and managed an ISDN technical support center for GTE, providing technical assistance with modem and terminal adapter configurations including Frame Relay, T1, and T-3 systems.

    You will also see from my resume that I was Project Manager for the implementation of a $500 million Novell LAN and provided training, supervision, and oversight for GTE-Mobile Subscriber Equipment training as well as authoring a number of training materials for Army leadership development and management courses.

    If you can use a highly skilled information telecommunications and information systems professional, I hope you will welcome my call soon when I try to arrange a brief meeting to discuss your goals and how my background might serve your needs. I can provide outstanding references at the appropriate time.

                       Sincerely,

                       Steven Hutt

Sample Cover Letters for Job Hunting

The cover letters in this section are written for people who need a very creative and resourceful cover letter. These cover letters are designed to accompany resumes of individuals trying to embark on a course of employment which is different from what they have been doing most recently.

Career-change cover letters are designed to help you find employment in a new field or industry. In this type of cover letter, you must "make sense" of yourself to the prospective employer. Otherwise, the prospective employer may look at your resume and ask himself, "Why is an air traffic controller writing to me about this programming job?" The career-change cover letter is the employer's first impression of you and can explain why you are approaching him or her.

If you don't know what you want to do next, it's best to make your cover letter "all purpose."

In a job hunt, the all-purpose cover letter can be a time saver because it can serve as a "standard" or "model" or "template" which you can use each time you send out your resume. You may wish to modify it from time to time, but the all-purpose cover letter is there, already written, often in your computer, when you see an ad you want to answer or when you identify an employer whom you wish to contact in order to explore suitable opportunities for someone of your skills and abilities. The all-purpose cover letter can be used for employers in your current field or for employers in other industries.

When you are seeking your first job in a new field, use language that makes you "look" and "sound" as though you would be a credit to the profession you are trying to enter.

Most people know the frustration of not having any experience in the field in which they are seeking employment. There are particular techniques that should be used when writing a cover letter to try to obtain the first job in one's field. This type of cover letter "builds a bridge" to a new field. Sometimes you just get tired of doing something you've done effectively for many years and feel that a change is needed in order to retain your enthusiasm and interest. But whether the job hunter is young or mature, the career-change cover letter must reach out personally to prospective employers and explain why the prospective employer's business is of interest. That's what *anyone* in a job hunt must do: reach out personally to the potential employer and make the employer believe that you are serious about your desire to make a career change, not just "having a bad day."

Date

Exact Name of Person
Title or Position
Name of Company
Address (number and street)
Address (city, state, and zip)

Dear Exact Name of Person: (or Sir or Madam if answering a blind ad)

With the enclosed resume, I would like to express my interest in exploring employment opportunities with your organization and make you aware of my versatile abilities which could complement your goals. Although I have been very successful as a Mathematics Teacher and have enjoyed the challenge of educating young minds, I have decided that I would like to apply my mathematical skills to benefit a company in the computer industry.

As you will see from my enclosed resume, I earned my B.S. in Mathematics with a Computer Science Concentration from Michigan State University where I maintained a 3.5 GPA. During my senior year I worked as many as 40 hours a week as a Research Assistant and Tutor.

In my most recent job as a middle school math teacher, I refined my communication, organizational, and time management skills while organizing and directing numerous projects. On my own initiative, I planned the school's first science fair. Earlier while serving in the U.S. Army for four years, I was handpicked for supervisory positions ahead of my peers and commended for my effective leadership style.

Both my management experience in the military and my teaching experience have helped me refine my verbal and written communication skills. I am highly regarded for my ability to persuade, motivate, and lead, and I am certain I could utilize those skills and talents in order to positively impact a company's bottom line.

If you can use a proven performer with an ability to work well with others, I hope you will contact me to suggest a time when we might talk to discuss your needs. Single and available for worldwide relocation, I would cheerfully travel as frequently as your needs require. I can provide excellent references at the appropriate time.

Sincerely,

Julie M. Vogel

Changing careers from teaching
This career-change letter emphasizes the communication skills and versatility of a young professional with teaching experience as well as a distinguished military record. Lack of experience in a particular field is not a main reason why employers choose not to interview applicants. Employers are looking for a track record of accomplishment in whatever you have done so far.

Date

Exact Name of Person
Exact Title
Exact Name of Company
Address
City, State, Zip

**Changing careers from
the aviation industry**

Dear Exact Name of Person: (or Dear Sir or Madam if answering a blind ad):

In this letter, an electronics technician is attempting to make a career change from the aviation industry. He hopes to get closer to the "forefront of technology" but he knows it is not wise to state all his specific desires in a cover letter which introduces him and his background. Notice that he emphasizes his background in quality assurance, which should be an attractive feature to any industry.

With the enclosed resume, I would like to introduce you to my considerable technical skills which are related to your needs.

As you will see from my resume, I am working for McDonnell Douglas Aircraft Corporation and have earned the respect of superiors and peers for my ability to quickly learn and master new computer software and hardware. Currently assigned as an Aircraft Instrumentation and Telemetry System Technician, I was nominated for early promotion based on my job knowledge and leadership. I have been credited with playing a major role in the success of a unit which has won numerous honors including the governor's award for "Quality in the Workplace," a high-level maintenance effectiveness award, and an "Outstanding Unit Award."

Selected for special projects and teams, I have participated in the development of aircraft modifications and earned recognition from the Undersecretary of Defense and the McDonnell Douglas Aircraft Corporation for my efforts. One of my special projects was applying technical expertise to complete modifications on cockpit cameras.

If you can use a self starter with excellent electronics and mechanical skills along with the ability to work independently or as a contributor to team efforts, I hope you will welcome my call soon when I try to arrange a brief meeting to discuss your goals and how my background might serve your needs. I can provide outstanding references at the appropriate time.

Sincerely,

Michael Irvin

Alternate Last Paragraph:
I hope you will write or call me soon to suggest a time when we might meet to discuss your needs and goals and how my background might serve them. I can provide outstanding references at the appropriate time.

Date

Exact Name of Person
Exact Title
Exact Name of Company
Address
City, State, Zip

Dear Exact Name of Person (or Dear Sir or Madam if answering a blind ad):

With the enclosed resume, I would like to make you aware of my background as a versatile and experienced professional with a history of success in areas which include computer operations, logistics and supply, production control, and employee training and supervision.

As you will see, I am completing requirements for my Bachelor's degree in Computer Science from Methodist College which I expect to receive this winter. I am proud of my accomplishment in completing this course of study while simultaneously meeting the demands of a career in the U.S. Army. In my current military assignment as a Technical Inspector, I ensure the airworthiness of aircraft which is required to relocate anywhere in the world on extremely short notice in response to crisis situations.

Throughout my years of military service, I have been singled out for jobs which have required the ability to quickly make sound decisions and have continually maximized resources while exceeding expected standards and performance guidelines. I have been responsible for certifying multimillion-dollar aircraft for flight service, training and supervising employees who have been highly productive and successful in their own careers, and applying technical computer knowledge in innovative ways which have further increased efficiency and productivity.

I offer a combination of technical, managerial, and supervisory skills and a level of knowledge which will allow me to quickly achieve outstanding results in anything I attempt. Known for my energy and enthusiasm, I am a creative professional with a strong desire to make a difference in whatever environment I find myself.

I hope you will contact me to suggest a time when we might meet to discuss your needs. I can assure you in advance that I could rapidly become an asset to your organization.

Sincerely,

Kyle Sweeney

Changing careers from military service
In this letter, a military professional is seeking to change fields. Notice how he tries to make the employer understand what he learned in military service which could be transferable knowledge. In a career change, experienced professionals often must sell their personality and potential more than their actual work experience in order to "blow the door open."

Exact Name of Person
Exact Title
Exact Name of Company
Address
City, State, Zip

Changing careers with a cover letter that emphasizes hardware knowledge
In this letter, a young person completing his bachelor's degree reaches out to employers in various fields. He emphasizes his track record of initiative in seeking out opportunities for training in his spare time.

Dear Exact Name of Person: (or Dear Sir or Madam if answering a blind ad):

With the enclosed resume, I would like to make you aware of my background as an experienced network manager with extensive training and exceptional technical skills related to local and wide area network maintenance. I am skilled in areas including but not limited to hardware upgrading, maintenance, and repair as well as software installation and configuration.

As you will see from my resume, I have excelled in technical training programs which included courses on Introduction to LAN "Network Essentials," Microsoft TCP/IP, and Windows NT Server 4.0.

I have supplemented this formal training with extensive hands-on experience in set-up, maintenance, and administration of Local and Wide Area Networks using Windows, Windows NT2000 Server, and TCP/IP. Other training was related to Exchange Server, Enterprise, and numerous other network and workstation applications. In addition, my comprehensive knowledge of hardware upgrading, maintenance, configuration, and repair has been tested in challenging situations both in office and field environments.

Pursuing completion of a Bachelor of Science in Management Information Systems (MIS), I am currently preparing to take the six-test battery of examinations leading to certification as a Microsoft Certified Systems Engineer.

If you can use a highly skilled information systems professional with exceptional technical skills in hardware, software, and network administration, I hope you will welcome my call soon when I try to arrange a brief meeting to discuss your goals and how my background might serve your needs. I can provide outstanding references at the appropriate time.

Sincerely,

John Tessler

Date

Exact Name of Person
Exact Title
Exact Name of Company
Address
City, State, Zip

Dear Exact Name of Person (or Dear Sir or Madam if answering a blind ad):

With the enclosed resume, I would like to make you aware of my interest in exploring employment opportunities with your organization. After completing nearly 10 years of distinguished federal service—and although I was strongly encouraged to remain in the Department of Defense—I recently resigned and am in the process of permanently relocating to your area. I am seeking employment in the private sector.

In spite of a hectic schedule which involved frequent travel for training projects and worldwide missions, I completed nearly two years of college course work while excelling in my full-time positions. Most recently, I have completed courses at a Microsoft Certified Education Center, and I am in the process of obtaining my Microsoft Certified System Engineer (MCSE). On my own initiative, I recently structured a local area computer network which enabled my company to economize on scarce resources by efficiently sharing data and peripherals. I offer knowledge of computer operations and computer network systems.

After beginning federal service, I was quickly identified as a leader and promoted ahead of my peers. I excelled in supervisory roles in engineering and other organizations, and the numerous awards I received praised my ability to mentor junior employees and inspire them to excel. I flawlessly maintained accountability of up to $500,000 in assets and was noted for my "aggressive emphasis on maintenance and safety."

My troubleshooting and problem-solving skills are strong, and I have applied them in reducing maintenance backlogs as well as in organizing and managing special projects designed to improve the technical skills of employees. I am highly proactive in seeking out opportunities for self-improvement and for advancement of my skills and knowledge.

If you can use a highly motivated self-starter with unlimited personal initiative, I hope you will contact me to suggest a time when we might discuss your needs. I can provide excellent references.

Yours sincerely,

Kenny Stevens

Date

Launching a career in the computer industry

This letter holds the key to this individual's intense desire to become employed in the computer field. He understands that he is essentially "raw material" in a prospective employer'e eyes, so he is accentuating that fact. He tries to make an asset of his youth and inexperience.

Dear Sir or Madam:

With the enclosed resume, I would like to make you aware of my interest in exploring employment opportunities with your organization and introduce you to my background and credentials related to your business.

As you will see from my resume, I have recently earned my Microsoft Certified Systems Engineer (MCSP) and Microsoft Certified Professional (MCP) through coursework from Internet Technologies (I.T.). I am seeking my first full-time job in the internet technology field. I plan to continue my technical education in my spare time at night and on weekends so that I can acquire other certifications which will be beneficial to my employer.

I feel that I have much to offer a company, even though I am only 19 years old. I have worked since I was 13, and I have demonstrated my ability to rapidly master any new technical task. While working in part-time and then in full-time positions with Premier Builders since 2000, I have mastered many complex technical trades activities. I have become a skilled carpenter and framer, and I have worked in nearly all areas of the construction industry on projects related to residential construction. I have earned a reputation as a highly reliable hard worker who knows how to produce high-quality results under tight deadlines. I have earned respect for my natural mechanical abilities and problem-solving skills, and since childhood I have been operating, maintaining, and repairing farm equipment such as tractors, bush hogs, and bailers.

A highly artistic individual with natural talents related to drawing, I am certain I could apply that flair for creativity within a technical company aiming for maximum customer appeal.

I hope you will contact me to suggest a time when we could meet in person to discuss suitable employment opportunities with your firm. I can provide excellent references. Thank you.

Yours sincerely,

Anthony Hopkins

Date

Exact Name of Person
Title or Position
Name of Company
Address (number and street)
Address (city, state, and zip)

Dear Exact Name of Person: (or Dear Sir or Madam if answering a blind ad.)

With the enclosed resume, I would like to make you aware of my considerable background in the management of information systems and in the development of state-of-the-art software and business applications.

As you will see from my resume, I was recruited in 1994 by a fast-growing corporation experiencing rapid expansion to oversee the design and implementation of its MIS activities at 80 store locations. I was promoted to Vice President of Management Information Systems in the process of making major contributions to efficiency, productivity, and profitability. We have replaced store computers with a Windows-based system that reduced manual record keeping and since then I have been designing the implementation of the second phase of this re-engineering project. We are also developing an intranet for stores, supervisors, and other office personnel, and I have personally designed and conducted training and support for all job levels, from top executives, to store management, to entry-level employees.

In my prior position, I was promoted in a track record of advancement with a company which developed software products for the telecommunications industry. During that time I transformed a failing operation which was losing money into an efficient and profitable business while reengineering a product which became the industry's #1 seller.

My software knowledge is vast, as you will also see from my resume, and I offer recent experience with C++ as well as Intranet and HTML.

I can provide outstanding personal and professional references at the appropriate time, and I can assure you in advance that I have a reputation for building and maintaining effective working relationships with people at all organizational levels. If my skills, experience, and talents interest you, please contact me. Thank you in advance for your professional courtesies.

Sincerely,

Robert Schniepp

Changing careers from a slow-growth industry to a high-tech environment
In this letter, an individual with impressive credentials is seeking to attract an employer on the forefront of technology. He feels that he wants to return to a more creative environment in which he would be involved in thinking up new technologies, rather than installing the same technology in store after store.

Date

Exact Name of Person
Title or Position
Name of Company
Address (number and street)
Address (city, state, and zip)

Changing careers into the computer sales field
In this letter, a store manager is seeking to transfer her strong bottom-line orientation and impressive accomplishments in boosting sales and profit into the computer industry.

Dear Exact Name of Person: (or Dear Sir or Madam if answering a blind ad)

I would appreciate an opportunity to talk with you soon about how I could contribute to your organization through my excellent sales, communication, and customer service skills. I am responding to your advertisement for a Computer Sales Representative. I am very knowledgeable of the Dallas, TX, area and offer an outstanding personal and professional reputation in the community.

As you will see from my enclosed resume, I have been highly successful in sales and operations management with a major corporation. Beginning as a Customer Service Manager, I was promoted to manage stores with increasing sales volumes of $7 million, $8.5 million, and $11.5 million annually. In my current position, I have raised total sales by 20% and profit levels by 25% through my aggressive sales orientation.

Although I am held in high regard by my employer and can provide outstanding references at the appropriate time, I have decided that I would like to apply my sales, customer service, and communication skills within the pharmaceutical sales field. I am certain that my sales ability and strong bottom-line orientation would be ideally suited to pharmaceutical sales. As a store manager, I have provided oversight of store merchandising, vendor relations, and product mix.

With a B.S.B.A. degree, I possess an educational background which complements my sales and management experience. My highly developed communication skills, assertive personality, and time-management ability have allowed me to effectively manage as many as 100 employees. I offer a reputation as a forceful yet tactful salesperson who is able to present ideas as well as products in a powerful and convincing fashion.

I can assure you that this is a very deliberate attempt on my part to transition into the pharmaceutical sales field, and I hope you will call or write me soon to arrange a brief meeting to discuss your current and future needs and how I might serve them. Thank you in advance for your time.

Sincerely,

Gloria Pena

Date

Exact Name of Person
Exact Title
Exact Name of Company
Address
City, State, Zip

Dear Exact Name of Person (or Dear Sir or Madam if answering a blind ad):

Changing careers with the goal of becoming more involved in fiber optics
In this case, a talented person with experience in numerous functional areas is presenting herself to employers in numerous industries in an "all-purpose" cover letter.

With the enclosed resume, I would like to make you aware of my experience, training, and skills related to the areas of telecommunications, fiber optics, and cellular communications.

As you will see from my resume, I have received licenses or certifications in areas of technical expertise with Fiber Optics: OSP, Digital Group Modems and Mast, and GTE Multichannel Transmissions. Trained in splicing and installing fiber optics cable, I offer abilities related to the operation, maintenance, and troubleshooting of multichannel radios, digital group modems, UHF and SHF radios, and antennas.

During my four years of employment with GTE Dynamics, I have worked at locations worldwide and I quickly advanced to a supervisory job overseeing up to eight people. While earning a reputation as a technically skilled and knowledgeable young professional, I made contributions which impacted on the effectiveness of maintenance activities. I excelled in responsibilities which included making regular preventive maintenance checks, supervising telecommunications specialists, and personally operating and maintaining equipment.

If you can use a fast learner with strong technical skills and a reputation as one who can be counted on to get the job done right and on time, I hope you will contact me soon to suggest a time when we might meet to discuss your needs. I can assure you in advance that I can provide outstanding references and could quickly become an asset to your organization.

Sincerely,

Grace Mayweather

Alternate last paragraph:
If you can use a fast learner with strong technical skills and a reputation as one who can be counted on to get the job done right and on time, I hope you will welcome my call soon to briefly discuss my qualifications and how I might contribute to your organization's continued growth and success. I can assure you in advance that I can provide outstanding references and could quickly become an asset to your organization.

Date

Exact Name of Person
Exact Title
Exact Name of Company
Address
City, State, Zip

Dear Exact Name of Person (or Dear Sir or Madam if answering a blind ad):

With the enclosed resume, I would like to make you aware of my interest in exploring employment opportunities with your organization.

As you will see from my resume, I have served my country with distinction in the Central Intelligence Agency. In my current position as a Computer Operator with the CIA, I have been rated as "absolutely superior in all areas" and commended for "unparalleled work ethic and dedication to goals" while operating a computerized console in a highly classified environment. I have volunteered my time extensively to community projects, and I was proud to play a role in winning the "best team" rating in the Pacific. In an earlier job as a Satellite Systems Technician at the Air Intelligence Agency's largest field site in Misawa, Japan, I was commended in writing as "superb operator" and was praised for exhibiting "great initiative, attention to detail, and leadership."

I hold one of the nation's highest security clearances: Top Secret/Sensitive Compartmented Information (TS/SCI). I offer a proven ability to excel in training, and I was named Honor Graduate from the six-month Communications Signals Collection/ Processing Course.

I am highly proactive in seeking out opportunities for self-improvement and for advancement of my skills and knowledge. I am currently completing courses in sequence at the World Technology Education Center which will lead to the Microsoft Certified System Engineer (MSCE) certification as well as the Cisco Certified Network Associate (CCNA) certification. Currently I am receiving training with UNIX through the National Security Agency.

Although I have been strongly encouraged to remain in military service and assured of continuous rapid promotion, I have decided to leave the military and seek opportunities in the civilian workplace. If you can use my versatile talents and skills, as well as my reputation for strong personal initiative, I hope you will contact me to suggest a time when we might discuss your needs. I can provide excellent references.

Yours sincerely,

Johnathon Little

In this section you will find answers to common questions about cover letters. Lots of "oddball" situations come up in job hunting, and you will find the answers to many of those questions in this section. In this section you will find out how to phrase the answers to delicate questions such as questions about salary.

Question 1: What is the "direct approach?"
Question 2: How do I address a letter to an ad that provides names and addresses?
Question 3: What's the best way to answer a "blind ad?"
Question 4: How do I respond to a recruiter or headhunter who has approached me?
Question 5: How do I apply for internal openings?
Question 6: How do I ask for consideration for multiple job openings?
Question 7: How do I e-mail or fax my resume and cover letter?
Question 8: If I want to "drop a name" in a cover letter, what's the best way?
Question 9: If I'm relocating soon, how do I say that in the cover letter?
Question 10: If I've recently relocated, what do I say in the cover letter?
Question 11: What if I want to reopen a door that I closed previously?
Question 12: What if they ask for salary requirements?
Question 13: What if they ask for salary history?
Question 14: How do I make it clear that I want my approach to be confidential?
Question 15: How do I write a follow-up letter after an interview?
Question 16: How do I resign—gracefully?

Date

Exact Name of Person
Title or Position
Name of Company
Address (number and street)
Address (city, state, and zip)

THE
DIRECT APPROACH

Question 1: What is the
"direct approach?"
You need to master the
technique of using the
"direct approach" in
your job hunt. By
using the direct
approach, you create
an all-purpose letter,
such as the one on this
page, which you can
send to numerous
employers introducing
yourself and your
resume. The direct
approach is a
proactive, aggressive
approach to a job
campaign, and it sure
beats waiting around
until the "ideal job"
appears in the
newspaper (and 200
other people see it,
too). Figure out the
employers you wish to
approach either (1) by
geographical area or
(2) by industry and
directly approach them
expressing your
interest in their
company. Believe it or
not, most people get
their jobs through the
direct approach!

Dear Exact Name of Person: (or Dear Sir or Madam if answering a blind ad)

I would appreciate an opportunity to talk with you soon about how I could contribute to your organization through my extensive background in sales including my recent experience as a Financial Consultant. I am confident I could be highly successful in the computer sales field with an industry giant such as Dell Computer.

As you will see from my resume, I hold the Series 7, Series 63, Series 24, and Series 65 licenses and am a Registered Member of numerous exchanges and associations of securities dealers. In 2000 I left a Wall Street firm to relocate to the South, where my wife and her family live. Since 2000 I have been working for Merrill Lynch, and after my training and licensing, I established 364 accounts and produced $5 million in managed money in my first six-month period of production. Although I am excelling in my job, I have decided that I wish to establish a career in sales in the computer industry.

Much of my rapid success as a Financial Consultant stems from my exceptional sales abilities in addition to my entrepreneurial background. I offer an extensive background in working with business owners and entrepreneurs.

I can provide outstanding personal and professional references, and I would be delighted to make myself available at your convenience for a personal interview. Thank you in advance for your professional courtesies and consideration.

Yours sincerely,

Elias Johnson III

Date

Exact Name of Person
Title or Position
Name of Company
Address (number and street)
Address (city, state, and zip)

Dear Exact Name of Person: (or Sir or Madam if answering a blind ad.)

With the enclosed resume, I would like to express my interest in the position of Network Administrator which you advertised in the Sunday "Gazette."

As you will see, I offer expertise as a network and telecommunications analyst, manager, and administrator as well as in management information systems and Wide and Local Area Networks (WANs and LANs). Presently the Network and Telecommunications Analyst for a medical center, I ensure connectivity, compatibility, and performance of a network of 60 servers which provide computer access to more than 3,000 hospital employees. Among my contributions while providing this vital support has been a project to upgrade and troubleshoot the time and attendance system. In another project, I implemented an ATM backbone within the medical center.

Earlier as a Network Manager and LAN Administrator for a major medical center, I assisted in the design and implementation of a project to convert an unmanaged ethernet to a managed switched ethernet network running on a fiber optics backbone. My contributions to the success of this project included installing and setting up the first remote connections, performing system backups, providing disk and printer management as well as e-mail administration, and monitoring system security and performance.

Previously I gained experience as a Hardware Specialist, Minicomputer System Operator, Network Technician, and Systems Analyst. For one organization in Germany, I expertly handled the details of disposing of and replacing 75% of outdated and obsolete equipment in a position usually reserved for a more experienced professional.

If you can use a creative, innovative professional who offers special skills in managing and troubleshooting automated systems, I hope you will contact me to suggest a time when we might meet to discuss your needs. I can provide outstanding references at the appropriate time.

Sincerely,

Charles Folkart

ANSWERING ADS

Question 2: How do I respond to an ad that provides the name and address?
It's easy enough to reply to an ad when you have the name and address of the person you're writing to, but there's more to this question than meets the eye. Read the ad carefully and tailor your letter as precisely to the ad as possible.

Date

P.O. Box 66
Dallas, TX 90345

ANSWERING ADS

Question 3: What's the best way to answer a "blind ad?"
"To whom it may concern" or "Dear Sir or Madam" is the proper salutation for a letter responding to a "blind ad" or an ad which does not reveal the company name or the name of the person to whom you are writing. Sometimes companies don't put their name in the ad because they don't want their competitors to know they are hiring. Sometimes companies don't give their name because they think it might encourage telephone calls about the job.

To whom it may concern:

With the enclosed resume, I would like to respond to your advertisement in the *Dallas Chronicle* for a Computer Operator and make you aware of the considerable computer skills I could put to work for you.

As you will see from my resume, I am skilled in all aspects of office activities and am proficient with WordPerfect and the Windows programs including Word, Excel, and Access. I am a very cheerful and adaptable person, as has been demonstrated by my ability to adapt rapidly and become quickly productive while working in long-term and short-term temporary assignments for major corporations, small businesses, and utility companies. I am skilled at operating a multiline switchboard system, and I offer a proven ability to rapidly master new software applications.

A resourceful and enthusiastic individual, I have always found ways to contribute to increased efficiency in all of my jobs. For example, in one job with an electrical supply company, I implemented a new computer program which resulted in increased efficiency in supply parts ordering.

If you can use an experienced young professional known for an excellent attitude as well as superior work habits including reliability, dependability, and honesty, I hope you will contact me to suggest a time when we might meet to discuss your needs. I can assure you in advance that I could rapidly become an asset to your organization.

Sincerely,

Simone Guardado

Date

Mr. John Smith
XYZ Management Recruiters
Address (number and street)
Address (city, state, and zip)

Dear Mr. Smith:

After reviewing the materials you sent me regarding the Des Moines Public Schools Network Manager, I believe that my professional and personal attributes are complementary to the needs of the school system.

In my current position as Network Manager of Fort Leavenworth Schools, I am entrusted with serving 5,700 students and supervising a staff of 660. The challenges in this district serving military dependents have been many and varied. With the cooperation of the staff and the greater school community, we have been successful in securing outstanding financial support for new technology initiatives from both the Department of Defense and Congress.

As Network Manager in Huntsville, AL, and at Fort Leavenworth, I provided the management expertise for expansion of technology in the instructional program. During this past year, one of Fort Leavenworth's elementary schools was chosen as a testbed site for President Clinton's Technology Initiative (PTI). This pilot project will afford our students and staff an opportunity to share innovative programs and instructional strategies.

Thank you for your interest in my qualifications, and I look forward to talking with you soon about the next step you suggest in my formally applying for the position as Network Manager of the Des Moines School System.

Yours sincerely,

Andrew J. Foster

RESPONDING TO RECRUITERS

Question 4: How do I respond to a recruiter or "headhunter" who has approached me?
Don't take any shortcuts when responding to a recruiter who has approached you to see if you might be interested in a new situation. In Mr. Foster's case, he has been approached by a management recruiting firm handling the search for a network administrator of a major school district. As always, make sure your cover letter "sells" you!

Date

Exact Name of Person
Title or Position
Name of Company
Address (number and street)
Address (city, state, and zip)

**APPLYING FOR
INTERNAL OPENINGS**

**Question 5: How do I
apply for internal
openings?**
We recommend
sacrificing no formality
when applying for
internal promotions. As
you see from this
cover letter, you still
need to "sell" your
interest and
qualifications, even
when the insiders
know you.

Dear Exact Name of Person: (or Dear Sir or Madam if answering a blind ad)

With the enclosed resume, I would like to make you aware of my interest in the position of **Computer Analyst II with the Vermont Department of Revenue.** As you will see from my enclosed resume, I offer a background as a seasoned accounting professional with exceptional analytical, communication, and organizational skills. In my current job, I perform essentially as a Financial Management Analyst in my role as a Field Auditor and Revenue Officer with the Vermont Department of Revenue.

With the Department of Revenue, I have advanced in a track record of increasing responsibilities. In my current position as a Field Auditor, I analyze financial reports of businesses and individuals, reconciling various general ledgers as well as investment and checking accounts in order to accurately determine tax liability. Earlier as a Revenue Officer, I consulted with taxpayers to assist them in determining the validity of deductions and calculating the amount of individual income tax owed. In both of these positions, I trained my coworkers, sharing my extensive knowledge of Internal Revenue Service and Vermont Department of Revenue codes and laws while educating department personnel on correct procedures related to professional auditing and collections.

I hold an Associate of Applied Science degree in Accounting from Central Berkshire Community College and a Bachelor of Science in Computer Science from the University of Oregon at Portland.

Please favorably consider my application for this internal opening, and please also consider my history of dedicated service to the Vermont Department of Revenue. I feel certain that I could excel in this job and could be a valuable asset to the department.

Sincerely,

Kevin Strafford

Date

Exact Name of Person
Title or Position
Name of Company
Address (number and street)
Address (city, state, and zip)

Dear Exact Name of Person: (or Sir or Madam if answering a blind ad)

With the enclosed resume, I would like to make you aware of the considerable skills I could put to work for the Baltimore Family Health System. Although I would like you to consider me for any situation where my versatile skills could be of value to you, I am particularly interested in the following positions:
Programmer
Systems Coordinator
Network Analyst II (Information Systems)

You will see that I offer skills compatible with those and other business office positions. I hold a B.S. in Computer Science and have acquired experience in internal business auditing activities, payroll calculation and administration, computer operations, and office management. I have worked for only two companies and have been promoted to increasing responsibilities in both organizations because of my initiative, productivity, and office skills. I am proficient in utilizing numerous software programs including Excel, Lotus, and many others.

With a reputation as a congenial individual with outstanding customer service and public relations skills, I can provide outstanding personal and professional references at the appropriate time. Although I am excelling in my current position and am highly regarded by my employer, it is my desire to work in a medical environment.

If you can use an energetic and highly motivated hard worker who offers versatile skills and abilities, I hope you will contact me to suggest a time when we might meet to discuss your needs and how I might serve them. Thank you in advance for your time.

Yours sincerely,

Holly M. Vargo

Date

BY FAX TO: Human Resources Department
910-483-2439
Reference Job Code XYZ 9034

E-MAILING OR FAXING YOUR RESUME AND COVER LETTER

Question 7: How do I e-mail or fax my resume? The answer is: always with a cover letter. When you fax your resume and the cover letter introducing your resume, we recommend that you put the fax number on the top of the letter. In this way you identify to the receiver how you contacted them (remember, they may be receiving dozens of other resumes and cover letters), and you also have a record of the fax number on the top of your copy of the letter. Never send any type of correspondence in business without dating it.

Dear Sir or Madam:

With the enclosed resume, I would like to make you aware of my interest in employment as a Computer Sales Representative with Dell Computer. I believe you are aware that Walter Freeman, one of your Representatives, has recommended that I talk with you because he feels that I could excel in the position as a Computer Sales Representative.

As you will see from my enclosed resume, I offer proven marketing and sales skills along with a reputation as a highly motivated individual with exceptional problem-solving abilities. Shortly after joining my current firm as a Mortgage Loan Specialist, I was named Outstanding Loan Officer of the month through my achievement in generating more than $20,000 in fees.

I believe much of my professional success so far has been due to my highly motivated nature and creative approach to my job. For example, when I began working for my current employer, I developed and implemented the concept of a postcard that communicated a message which the consumer found intriguing. The concept has been so successful that it has been one of the main sources of advertisements in our office and the concept has been imitated by other offices in the company.

In addition to my track record of excelling in the highly competitive financial services field, I gained valuable sales experience in earlier jobs selling copying equipment and sleep systems. I have also applied my strong leadership and sales ability in the human services field, when I worked in adult probation services. I am very proud of the fact that many troubled individuals with whom I worked told me that my ability to inspire and motivate them was the key to their becoming productive citizens.

If you can use a creative and motivated self-starter who could enhance your goals for market share and profitability, I hope you will contact me to suggest a time when we could meet in person to discuss your needs and goals and how I could meet them. I can provide strong personal and professional references at the appropriate time.

Yours sincerely,

Cheri Garcia

Date

Exact Name of Person
Title or Position
Name of Company
Address (number and street)
Address (city, state, and zip)

Dear Exact Name of Person: (or Sir or Madam if answering a blind ad)

With the enclosed resume, I would like to make you aware of my interest in joining your organization in some capacity which could utilize my extensive experience related to systems analysis. I am responding to your recent advertisement for a Systems Analyst, and I am confident that my extensive knowledge of banking could be valuable to you.

I am somewhat familiar with your organization because I had the pleasure of working by telephone last year with several of your employees on matters related to skip tracing, and I was impressed with the professionalism of your personnel. Ms. Lenette Wilson, in particular, was especially helpful to me and gave me an outstanding impression of your organization.

My family and I have recently relocated to Little Rock from El Paso, TX, where I excelled in a track record of achievement as an Assistant Systems Analyst. I began working for the Ft. Bliss Credit Union in an entry-level position and then was promoted to handle complex responsibilities related to network management. I received numerous Customer Service Awards and achieved an extremely low data reject rate while overseeing the processing of large volumes of data.

In addition to excelling as a Collections Officer, I became knowledgeable of consumer lending and banking while handling money orders, bank checks, IRA withdrawals, travelers checks, savings bonds, coin exchanges, night deposit posting, handling the closing of members' accounts, filing members' open-account cards, processing returned checks, as well as processing and filming checks to National Credit Union Headquarters.

If you can use a hard-working young professional who offers a reputation as a thorough, persistent, and highly motivated individual, I hope you will contact me to suggest a time when we might meet to discuss your needs and goals and how I could help you achieve them. I would be delighted to discuss the private details of my salary history with you in person, and I can provide outstanding personal and professional references.

Sincerely,

Athena Zibart

NAME DROPPING

Question 8: If I want to "drop a name" in a letter, what's the best way?
It's nice to play the "who you know" game socially and in business, and it can help you get in the door for interviews, too. If a current employee has recommended that you write to the organization, or if you have worked with members of the organization on some project, you can "drop a name" gracefully. In so doing, you will add warmth to a cover letter that will exude a very personalized tone.

Date

Exact Name of Person
Title or Position
Name of Company
Address (number and street)
Address (city, state, and zip)

Dear Exact Name of Person: (or Sir or Madam if answering a blind ad)

With the enclosed resume, I would like to initiate the process of being considered for employment within your organization. Because of family ties, I am in the process of relocating to the Houston area by a target date of December 5. Although I already have a Houston address which is shown on my resume, it is my brother's home and I would prefer your contacting me at the e-mail address shown on my resume or at my current telephone number if you wish to talk with me prior to December 5th.

Since graduating from the University of North Carolina at Chapel Hill with a degree in Mathematics with a Computer Science concentration, I have a track record of rapid promotion with a corporation headquartered in Miami Beach. I began as an Assistant Branch Manager and Head Buyer, was cross-trained as a Sales Representative, and have been promoted to my current position in which I manage the selling process related to 3,500 different products. In that capacity, I am entrusted with the responsibility for nearly $15 million in annual expenditures, and I maintain excellent working relationships with more than 150 vendors of name-brand consumer products sold through chain and convenience stores.

In my job, rapid change is a daily reality, and I have become accustomed to working in an environment in which I must make rapid decisions while weighing factors including forecasted consumer demand, distribution patterns, inventory turnover patterns, and vendor capacity and character. I have earned a reputation as a persuasive communicator and savvy negotiator with an aggressive bottom-line orientation.

If you can use my versatile experience in sales, purchasing, distribution, and operations management, I hope you will contact me to suggest a time when we might meet to discuss your needs and how I might serve them. I can provide excellent personal and professional references, and I assure you in advance that I am a hard worker who is accustomed to being measured according to ambitious goals for profitability in a highly competitive marketplace.

Yours sincerely,

Dale P. Jensen

Date

Exact Name of Person
Title or Position
Name of Company
Address (number and street)
Address (city, state, and zip)

Dear Exact Name of Person: (or Sir or Madam if answering a blind ad)

With the enclosed resume, I would like to make you aware of my background in accounts management, personnel supervision, and customer service as well as my strong organizational, interpersonal, and communication skills. My husband and I have relocated back to Rochester, where our respective families are from.

While recently completing my Bachelor of Science degree in Computer Science, I excelled academically and was named to the Dean's List seven times. Prior to earning my degree, I excelled in both military and civilian environments.

In one job in North Carolina, I began as a Receptionist answering a 30-line phone system for a 1100-employee company which provided on-line computer services. I rapidly advanced to Accounts Manager and Shift Supervisor, which placed me in charge of eight people. In that job I made hundreds of decisions daily which involved committing the company's technical resources. In addition to dispatching technicians and managing liaison with companies such as The Bank of Chicago, United Carolina Bank, and Stein Mart, I was authorized to commit company resources valued at up to $500,000.

With my husband's retirement, we are eager to replant our roots in New York, and I am seeking employment with a company that can use a highly motivated hard worker who is known for excellent decision-making, problem-solving, and organizational skills. If you can use a resourceful and versatile individual with administrative and computer skills, I hope you will contact me to suggest a time when we can discuss your present and future needs and how I might meet them. I can provide outstanding personal and professional references, and I thank you in advance for your time and consideration.

Sincerely,

Antoinette Pardue

RECENTLY RELOCATED

Question 10: If I've recently relocated, what do I say in the cover letter?
Employers like the sound of the fact that you have relocated permanently back to the place where you're from. That fact tends to communicate that you might be a permanent and stable employee in the work force of a local employer.

Date

Exact Name of Person
Title or Position
Name of Company
Address (number and street)
Address (city, state, and zip)

REOPENING A DOOR

Dear Exact Name of Person: (or Sir or Madam if answering a blind ad)

Question 11: What if I want to reopen a door I closed previously?

Employers can get their feelings hurt if you turn down a job they offer you. This lady had pulled out of the last round of interviews for a job with a newspaper, and months later she realized she'd made a mistake. This letter accompanying her resume reopened the door for her and led to an offer (and acceptance) of a job.

As I hope you will recall, several months ago I interviewed with you for a position involving responsibility for computer sales with the Microsoft Corporation. I very much appreciated your many kindnesses to me during the interviewing process.

During the time when I was interviewing with you for a position, my current employer approached me and asked if I would take on a special project which involved performing outside sales for the business. Since I had worked at Cross Roads Chrysler-Buick for five years and was very familiar with the customer base and with the company's style of doing business, he wanted me in particular to take on the project and I felt, because of his business circumstances at the time, that I had a personal and moral obligation to serve the company in that role.

For that reason I was unable to follow through with the final stage of becoming an employee of the Microsoft Corporation.

That project has now been completed and I feel I have loyally completed my obligation to the company in that regard. I would like to ask that you reconsider me for an advertising sales position with the Microsoft Corporation. I can provide outstanding personal and professional references, including from my current employer, and I can assure you that I would offer the Microsoft Corporation the same loyalty as I have consistently shown to my current employer.

My resume is enclosed to refresh your memory about my skills and professional qualifications. You may also recall that we first became acquainted years ago when I was attending St. Joseph's Episcopal Church.

I have a high opinion of you and of the Microsoft Corporation, and I hope you will consider me for any position which requires a positive, highly motivated individual with a proven track record of excellent performance in sales and customer service. Thank you again for your past courtesies, and I hope you will welcome my call soon when I try to contact you to see if you have needs I could fill. Best wishes for the holiday season and the New Year.

Yours sincerely,

Samantha Griggers

Date

Exact Name of Person
Title or Position
Name of Company
Address (number and street)
Address (city, state, and zip)

Dear Exact Name of Person: (or Sir or Madam if answering a blind ad)

I would like to make you aware of my strong interest in the position of Computer Training and Development Manager advertised in the *Houston Chronicle*. As you will see, I have a track record of success as an experienced instructor and training program developer as well as proven skills in employee supervision, staff development, and production management.

As you will see, I have excelled as an instructor, course developer, and technical writer. Training and counseling junior personnel have always been key responsibilities.

With a versatile background which includes experience in the telecommunications field, I have been involved in areas including logistics, planning and scheduling, and safety. I offer a reputation as a skilled communicator who has been especially effective in providing instruction in individual and group situations. I am especially proud of the Associate's degree I earned while excelling in my full-time job.

With regard to my salary requirements, I would be delighted to discuss the private details of my salary history with you in person. I can assure you that I can provide excellent references at the appropriate time.

If you can use an experienced professional who is dedicated to setting and achieving high standards in all areas of performance, I hope you will contact me to suggest a time when we might meet to discuss your needs. I am confident that I could become an asset to Dickinson Associates.

Sincerely,

Chico Flores, Jr.

Date

Exact Name of Person
Title or Position
Name of Company
Address (number and street)
Address (city, state, and zip)

WHEN THEY ASK FOR SALARY HISTORY

Question 13: What if they ask for salary history?
You may be asked to provide your salary history in writing, but be sure to add in everything so that the prospective employer receives a fair picture of your total compensation. Please note that we recommend that you handle a request for salary history as it is handled in the letter on the previous page rather than by providing the intimate details of your salary history in a letter.

Dear Exact Name of Person: (or Sir or Madam if answering a blind ad)

I would like to take this opportunity to thank you for considering me for the job on June 4 as a Sales Representative for ABS Computer Systems.

I enjoyed meeting with you and being able to learn more about the company. I believe that ABS has a quality product line and I would be honored to represent these products.

I would also like to thank you for considering my busy schedule as a State Probation and Parole Officer and allowing me to come back for the second interview in the same afternoon. I am an extremely reliable and dependable professional, and I appreciated your professional courtesies in helping me be away from my current job as little as possible.

In response to your question about my salary history, I am currently making in the neighborhood of $45,000 with a raise anticipated within two months that could take me to close to $50,000. I enjoy a full benefits package with my current employer.

I am very interested in the position we discussed, and I can provide exceptionally strong personal and professional references at the appropriate time. Thank you for talking with me and helping me learn more about your fine company, and I hope to hear from you soon.

Sincerely,

Kim Chiang

Date

Exact Name of Person
Title or Position
Name of Company
Address (number and street)
Address (city, state, and zip)

Dear Exact Name of Person: (or Sir or Madam if answering a blind ad)

WHEN CONFIDENTIALITY
MATTERS

With the enclosed resume, I would like to make you aware of my interest in the possibility of putting my strong management, production operations, and sales background to work for your company. Please treat my inquiry as highly confidential at this point. Although I can provide outstanding personal and professional references at the appropriate time, I do not wish my current employer to be aware of my interest in your company.

Question 14: How do I make it clear that I want my approach to be confidential?
Here's another example of the wording to use when you want to stress that you wish your approach to be confidential.

As you will see from my enclosed resume, I have been in the multipurpose concrete applications business my entire working life. I began in entry-level positions with Fabrico Concrete in New Orleans and was promoted to Plant Manager and Sales Manager. Then I joined Alfred Wright and Son, Inc. in Lafayette, LA, where I tripled production and transformed that company into an attractive acquisition candidate which caught the attention of Handy Concrete. When Handy Concrete Company bought Alfred Wright in 1996, I became a Division Manager and in 1998 was promoted to Regional Manager.

In my current position I manage computer operations at 10 divisions while supervising three Division Managers and overseeing activities of technicians at 10 locations. I also supervise four sales and customer service professionals in addition to preparing budgets for each of the 10 divisions. I have played a key role in the extensive automation of the company's records and accounting system, and I would like to continue my work in the automated management area.

If you can use a professional with computer knowledge and versatile management skills transferable to any industry, I hope you will contact me to suggest a time when we might meet. Should you have ambitious goals in either the production management or sales area, I feel certain that my experience could be useful.

Sincerely,

Eugene H. Dubois, Jr.

Exact Name of Person
Title or Position
Name of Company
Address (number and street)
Address (city, state, and zip)

FOLLOW-UP LETTER

Question 15: How do I write a follow-up letter after an interview?
Notice the last paragraph. A follow-up letter is an excellent opportunity to send your requests for reimbursement for any out-of-pocket expenses you incurred in connection with the interview.

Dear Exact Name of Person: (or Sir or Madam if answering a blind ad)

I want you to know how much I enjoyed talking with you in Sioux Falls on Friday, January 12th.

I am intensely interested in working with you to develop retail applications in the convenience store industry. I believe you are aware that I performed essentially that job for the construction industry in a previous position. With Newcombe Computer Systems, I rose from System Programmer to Director of Development as I transformed a failing operation into an efficient and profitable business.

In my current job as Vice President of Management Information Systems (MIS), I played a key role in making many changes within FashionPlus, a major retail chain, which made the company an acquisition target. Now that we are a part of a larger retail company, I am directing network systems development for this vastly larger organization. I understand your company's growth goals, as you explained them to me, and I feel I could become a valuable part of your strategic planning and implementation process.

One of my strengths is that I have a vast knowledge of many different areas, ranging from accounting systems and accounting development, to user interface, to putting together specifications, to the continual troubleshooting of problems and refinement of systems. It has been my responsibility to sit with technical experts in all functional areas and be able to assure the attainment of specific goals in their area of operation. I am confident that I could apply my expertise related to UNIX, NT, and programming within your industry, and I am skilled at establishing effective working relationships at all levels.

Thank you for giving me so much of your time and for letting me become better acquainted with your needs. I am enclosing a copy of my mileage statement (423 miles) and a copy of the hotel statement. I believe I could become a valuable member of your management team.

Sincerely,

James W. White

Date

Exact Name of Person
Title or Position
Name of Company
Address (number and street)
Address (city, state, and zip)

Dear Exact Name of Person:

It is with genuine sadness and many mixed feelings that I must inform you that I will be resigning from my position at Cranford, Sweeney & Co., CPAs, effective July 26.

The firm of Hill, Gilbert & Wilkins in Spokane, also a public accounting firm, has offered me a position as a Network Analyst at a salary of nearly $50,000 annually, and I feel it is a time in my life when I must move on.

Leaving the firm of Cranford, Sweeney & Co., CPAs, is very difficult for me professionally and emotionally. After I received my Microsoft certifications, you gave me my first job in the computer field, and I have thoroughly enjoyed the family atmosphere coupled with the professional style of both you and Mr. Cranford. You have taught me so much about how to solve problems, how to work more efficiently, and how to handle difficult clients. I am deeply grateful for your encouragement, professional mentoring, and strong personal example.

Although the decision to leave Cranford, Sweeney & Co., CPAs, is difficult, I really feel that I have no choice. As a single parent who provides full financial support of my daughter, I am driven by the desire to provide a gracious standard of living for my small family. I will be placing her in a Christian school in Spokane so that she can continue learning in the same Christian environment as she has had in Tacoma.

I hope you know that I have always given 110% to your firm in terms of my financial knowledge, intelligence, and problem-solving ability, and I hope you feel that I have made contributions to its reputation. I feel I am separating more from a family than from an employer, and I felt I wanted to put this information in writing to you as a first step because getting the words out verbally would be a difficult emotional experience for me.

Thank you from the bottom of my heart for all you have done for me professionally and personally.

Yours sincerely,

Elizabeth J. Ritchie

LETTERS OF RESIGNATION

Question 16: How do I resign—gracefully?
Here's an example of a letter that will be an emotional experience for the people receiving it as it was for the person who signed It. Employers are often not happy when you leave them, so a great letter of resignation can ease the hurt.

TO: John Smith
    Elaine Bryant
    Meredith Kleinfield

**ANOTHER LETTER OF
LEAVE TAKING**

Dear Friends and Valued Colleagues:

**Question 16: How do I
resign — gracefully?**
A letter of resignation
can be a highly
emotional experience,
both for the person
sending it and for the
individuals receiving it.
It gives you a formal
opportunity to declare
your last day on the
job and to thank
appropriate people.

It is with much sadness as well as with great personal affection for all of you that I wish to inform you that I will be leaving the Ford Motor Company. My final departure date can be worked out according to your wishes, but I would suggest Wednesday, December 20, 2000.

A sales position has become available at The Dell Company, and I believe the hours of employment will be better suited to my needs as a single parent.

Because I have been employed with Ford Motor Company for the past ten years, I feel as though I am "leaving home," and in that nostalgic frame of mind, it is my desire to tell you how much I have appreciated your training me, helping me, and giving me opportunities to try new things and gain new skills. I am very truly grateful to you, and I hope you know that I always gave my best effort.

I can assure you that I will continue to be a highly productive source of referrals for you even when I am gone, because I believe wholeheartedly in the products and the product line we all have represented. If I can ever help any of you individually in any way, too, please let me know.

In the meantime, please accept my sincere thanks for all the kindnesses and professional courtesies you have shown me.

Yours sincerely,

Mary Anne Murphy

Real-Resumes

for

Computer Jobs

In this section, you will find resumes and cover letters of computer professionals—and of people who want to work in the computer field. How do computer professionals differ from other job hunters? Why should there be a book dedicated to people seeking jobs in the computer field? Based on more than 20 years of experience in working with job hunters, this editor is convinced that resumes and cover letters which "speak the lingo" of the field you wish to enter will communicate more effectively than language which is not industry specific. This book is designed to help people (1) who are seeking to prepare their own resumes and (2) who wish to use as models "real" resumes of individuals who have successfully launched careers in the computer field or advanced in the field. You will see a wide range of experience levels reflected in the resumes in this book. Some of the resumes and cover letters were used by individuals seeking to enter the field; others were used successfully by senior professionals to advance in the field.

Newcomers to an industry sometimes have advantages over more experienced professionals. In a job hunt, junior professionals can have an advantage over their more experienced counterparts. Prospective employers often view the less experienced workers as "more trainable" and "more coachable" than their seniors. This means that the mature professional who has already excelled in a first career can, with credibility, "change careers" and transfer skills to other industries.

Computer professionals might be said to "talk funny." They talk in language like UNIX, WANS, LANs, and other industry-specific terms.

Newcomers to the field may have disadvantages compared to their seniors. Almost by definition, the inexperienced computer professional—the young person who has recently earned a college degree, or the individual who has recently received certifications respected by the industry—is less tested and less experienced than senior managers, so the resume and cover letter of the inexperienced professional may often have to "sell" his or her potential to do something he or she has never done before. Lack of experience in the field she wants to enter can be a stumbling block to the junior manager, but remember that many employers believe that someone who has excelled in anything—academics, for example—can excel in many other fields.

Some advice to inexperienced professionals...

If senior professionals could give junior professionals a piece of advice about careers, here's what they would say: Manage your career and don't stumble from job to job in an incoherent pattern. Try to find work that interests you, and then identify prosperous industries which need work performed of the type you want to do. Learn early in your working life that a great resume and cover letter can blow doors open for you and help you maximize your salary.

Exact Name of Person
Exact Title
Exact Name of Company
Address
City, State, Zip

**AUTOMATED SYSTEMS
TEAM CHIEF**

Dear Exact Name of Person: (or Dear Sir or Madam if answering a blind ad):

With the enclosed resume, I would like to introduce you to my background as a natural leader with a talent for training and supervising others along with strong technical computer skills which I could put to work for your organization.

As you will see from my resume, I proudly served in the Department of Defense for four years where I earned a reputation as a detail-oriented quick learner known for high levels of creativity and initiative. I have become recognized as a young professional who can be counted on to give my time freely to advise and guide others. With excellent skills in many areas, I have been effective in training others to achieve superior results in physical fitness, professional skills, and technical areas. I have mentored personnel who exceeded expectations in all measurable areas of performance.

Skilled in the installation and operation of computer software, I offer special knowledge of automated systems and telecommunications combined with a natural talent for providing assistance and passing my knowledge on to others. The recipient of Commendation Medals for "sustained superior performance" and specific professional accomplishments, I earned advancement to the ranks of supervisory personnel as a noncommissioned officer selected ahead of my peers in the minimum time possible.

If you can use a talented young professional who meets challenges head-on and thrives on them, please feel free to call me soon to arrange a brief meeting to discuss your goals and how my background might serve your needs. I can provide outstanding references at the appropriate time.

Sincerely,

Robert Hederman

Alternate Last Paragraph:
I hope you will welcome my call soon to arrange a brief meeting when we might meet to discuss your needs and goals and how my background might serve them. I can provide outstanding references at the appropriate time.

ROBERT HEDERMAN

1110½ Hay Street, Fayetteville, NC 28305   •   preppub@aol.com   •   (910) 483-6611

OBJECTIVE

To offer a reputation as an adaptable quick learner known to an organization that can benefit from my technical aptitude, ability to effectively train and work well with others, creativity, and experience in working with computers and telecommunications.

EDUCATION & TRAINING

Completed extensive military training which included technical programs on weapons systems and the operation of radio and wire communications equipment as well as courses on hazardous material handling and combat lifesaving.

COMPUTERS AND OTHER TECHNICAL KNOWLEDGE

Skilled in the installation and operation of computer software, am highly knowledgeable of Microsoft PowerPoint, Word, Excel, and Access, as well as Internet Explorer, Outlook, Windows NT2000, and WordPerfect. Offer special knowledge of DoD logistics software.

In addition to my skill with computers, am familiar with telecommunications equipment such as:

radios: AN/GRA-39, TA-312, AN/PRC-127, AN/PRC-119, TA-1, MSRT, OE-254 antenna array, PLGR, AN/PSN-11, and AN/CYX-10

other: HTU - Handheld Terminal Unit, wheeled vehicles, Avenger and Stinger weapons systems, and IFF (Identify Friend or Foe) and related programming equipment

EXPERIENCE

Became known as a "model of professionalism" with a tremendous amount of technical skill and an authoritative and fair manner, Department of Defense (1999-present):
AUTOMATED SYSTEMS TEAM CHIEF. Washington, DC (2000-present). Excelled in producing well-trained and knowledgeable personnel as a team leader; was responsible for communications equipment worth $200,000.

- Was recognized with a Commendation Medal in recognition of sustained superior performance with an emphasis on my technical and tactical expertise.
- Earned advancement to a supervisory position in the minimum possible time, ahead of my peers, while scoring 197 of 200 promotion points.
- Completed approximately 100 hours of correspondence school course work.
- Recognized for my ability to remain calm and in control under pressure and deadlines.
- Contributed my own time to train subordinates who went on to earn promotions, including one "marginal" performer who earned a passing grade during job skill testing, and others who received first-round "pass" scores in knowledge testing.
- Mentored one subordinate who went on to compete in and win "Employee of the Month."
- Chosen as Quality Assurance Manager, received a 100% score in a major inspection and "no faults noted" ratings in a major inspection of organizational maintenance.
- Developed internal programs which allowed substandard performers to bring scores to an average of 290 and my small-unit personnel to average 299 points—the highest in the organization.

SYSTEMS TEAM CHIEF. Washington, DC (1999-00). Trained, mentored, and supervised the performance of one subordinate while ensuring the maintenance, security, and operation of a $1.5 million automated system and associated equipment.

- Gained technical experience while using an advanced state-of-the-art computerized system used to enter precise measurements used in live-fire training projects.
- Received an award in recognition of leading my section to recognition as the best in the parent organization.

PERSONAL

Entrusted with a Secret security clearance. Meet challenges with enthusiasm.

Exact Name of Person
Exact Title
Exact Name of Company
Address
City, State, Zip

**CHIEF OF COMMUNICATIONS
SYSTEMS CONSTRUCTION**

Dear Exact Name of Person: (or Dear Sir or Madam if answering a blind ad):

With the enclosed resume, I would like to make you aware of my distinguished background of effectiveness in managing communications systems installation projects as well as my strong knowledge of such diverse areas as technical school operations, procurement, and inventory control.

As you will see from my resume, I built a reputation as an adaptable professional while excelling in managing multiple simultaneous projects in demanding technical environments for the U.S. Air Force. Accustomed to working under harsh weather conditions and within tight deadlines, I have overseen projects in Alaska and Greenland; The Philippines, Japan, and Korea; and throughout Europe.

Presently pursuing an associate's degree after earlier studying Electronics Systems Technology, I also received extensive military training which emphasized management and leadership as well as techniques for effective instructors. In my final military assignment prior to retirement, I served as Chief of Communications Systems Construction with the responsibility for planning, coordinating, and managing projects throughout the world. As operations director of a 55-person work center, I oversaw antenna and communications systems installation, enhances, and reconstruction projects which ensured continuous communications support for activities vital to national security.

Earlier jobs in quality assurance inspection, training program instruction and management, and engineering installation operations supervision allowed me to refine my reputation as a creative, energetic professional who could be counted on to complete projects on time and within budget. Cited on numerous occasions for solving difficult problems in ways which reduced expenditures and still allowed the project to be completed ahead of schedule, I was often sought out to provide technical guidance as well as counseling for subordinates.

If you can use an experienced communications technician with excellent time and resource management skills, I hope you will welcome my call soon when I try to arrange a brief meeting to discuss your goals and how my background might serve your needs. I can provide outstanding references at the appropriate time.

Sincerely,

Arthur Tipton

ARTHUR TIPTON

1110½ Hay Street, Fayetteville, NC 28305 • preppub@aol.com • (910) 483-6611

OBJECTIVE
To offer a strong background in the management of communications systems installation and operations to an organization that can benefit from my leadership and expertise.

EDUCATION & TRAINING
Currently attending Mississippi Gulf Coast Community College, Gulfport, MS.
Studied Electronics Systems Technology at the Community College of the Air Force.
Received extensive U.S. Air Force training in management techniques and leadership skills.

TECHNICAL SKILLS & KNOWLEDGE
Communications: use all cable locators and troubleshooting test equipment.
Computers: am proficient in Windows 95 & 98; MS Word, Excel, Access, and PowerPoint.
Construction equipment: operate trenchers, backhoes, line trucks, and tractor-trailers.

EXPERIENCE
Advanced to manage worldwide communications systems, U.S. Air Force:
CHIEF OF COMMUNICATIONS SYSTEMS CONSTRUCTION. Keesler AFB, MS (1999-present). Provided oversight to a team of 55 communications systems construction professionals, including 11 junior managers and 44 technicians; directed installation, enhancement, and reconstruction of antenna and communications systems in locations throughout the world.
- Planned, coordinated, and oversaw multiple simultaneous projects, including installation of a $9 million air traffic control system for ten FAA communications sites and an antenna installation project which saved $35,000 by using salvaged materials.
- Controlled a $3 million annual operating budget, handling inventory control, purchasing, and procurement; developed a preventive maintenance program for antenna systems.
- "Expertly planned" the removal of a major antenna system and its relocation without damage to structural steel, avoiding $50,000 in expenses.
- Located and corrected a design error in eight National Weather Service Next Generation Radar systems, reducing their vulnerability to lightning strikes.

DIRECTOR OF PLANS AND OPERATIONS. Keesler AFB, MS (1995-99). Managed a technical school program, supervising a staff of three personnel providing instruction to over 300 students; developed lesson plans and coordinated training sites and materials; was handpicked to assist in rewriting skills tests for senior installation and maintenance managers.

ENGINEERING INSTALLATION SUPERVISOR. Keesler AFB, MS (1993). Provided on-site supervision and safety guidance during antenna, steel tower, rigid radome, and associated systems installation, removal, and maintenance activities; earned promotion to QA Inspector based on results obtained in this position.
- Completed projects that included disassembly of a long-range radar facility in Alaska and a radar facility in Oklahoma ahead of schedule in spite of severe weather delays.

CENTRALIZED ANTENNA SYSTEMS SUPERVISOR. Germany (1989-93). Managed 20 technicians maintaining more than $19.5 million worth of antenna systems at 85 NATO sites throughout Europe; oversaw scheduling of installation, repair, and maintenance.
- Supervised an eight-person team in a special project to install a three-antenna system at am airport in Germany which involved surveying, engineering, and correcting a potential hazard for flight training missions by resolving air-to-ground communications problems.

Highlights of earlier experience: Advanced in supervisory and leadership roles.

PERSONAL
Secret/NATO Secret security clearance. Reputation for creativity and a high level of energy.

Exact Name of Person
Title or Position
Name of Company
Address (number and street)
Address (city, state, and zip)

CISCO CERTIFIED NETWORK ASSOCIATE

Dear Exact Name of Person: (or Sir or Madam if answering a blind ad.)

With the enclosed resume, I would like to express my interest in exploring employment opportunities with your organization.

As you will see, I served my country in the U.S. Army where I earned rapid advancement to supervisory roles while becoming known for my technical expertise related to telecommunications wiring and networking. Although I was strongly encouraged to remain in military service and become an officer, I made the decision to explore private sector opportunities.

Having recently completed the first semester of the CCNA (Cisco Certified Network Associate) course, I am planning to complete my bachelor's degree in my spare time. My educational background also includes two years of coursework in Management Information Systems and military training including the GTE Network Switching Systems Operator/Maintainer Course. This combination of education and military training has given me the opportunity to become familiar with equipment from major manufactures including IBM, GTE, Cisco, and Lucent Technologies.

In my job as a Telecommunications Supervisor, I controlled a $1 million inventory while gaining recognition for my ability to maximize human and material resources and maintain the highest levels of productivity from five-person teams of telecommunications specialists. My company provided 3,000 people with secure voice and data communications services. Entrusted with a Secret security clearance, I am proficient in installing, operating, and maintaining a wide range of cable, switching, and secure communications covering wide geographic areas as well as in overseeing others providing these services.

If you can use a mature and dedicated hard worker who would be committed to producing quality results while applying expertise in telecommunications operations and supervision, I hope you will contact me to suggest a time when we might meet to discuss your needs. I can provide outstanding references at the appropriate time.

Sincerely,

Jeanne Wu

JEANNE WU

1110½ Hay Street, Fayetteville, NC 28305　　•　　preppub@aol.com　　•　　(910) 483-6611

OBJECTIVE	To offer expert technical knowledge and experience emphasizing telecommunications wiring and networking to an organization that can benefit from my skills in resource and personnel management along with my ability to excel under deadline pressure.
EDUCATION & TRAINING	Completed semester one, **CCNA (Cisco Certified Network Associate)** course, Central Texas Community College, Dallas, TX, certification expected February 2002.

- Am planning to complete my bachelor's degree in my spare time; after high school graduation, entered military service so I could take advantage of GI Bill opportunities.

Received military training including the GTE Network Switching Systems Operator & Maintainer Course and leadership development programs.

Completed nearly two years of coursework in Management Information Systems, 1997.

TECHNICAL EXPERTISE

Through training and experience, am familiar with equipment from IBM, GTE, Cisco (routers), Lucent Technologies, and other major manufacturers.

- Installed and supervised others in the installation of RF towers; skilled in planning and installing RF sites. Experienced in working with switched and routed networks.
- Proficient in working with running, splicing, and termination of network and telecommunications cabling including all copper, coaxial and UTP; have installed and monitored digital packet switched networks. Became skilled in working over wide geographic areas.
- Offer hands-on experience in training and supervising others in team environments to install, operate, and maintain network equipment to include RF towers, patch panels, voice and data switching equipment, half and full duplex RF and wire communication components, Ethernet bus segments, junction boxes, and subscriber voice lines.
- Knowledge of and experience with network protocols. Monitored networks on a UNIX-based system which utilized X.25 protocols and Ethernet standards.
- Controlled COMSEC (communications security) equipment and materials.
- Installed, operated, and troubleshot the AN/TTC-48 Super secure system.

EXPERIENCE

Earned a reputation as a positive, results-oriented leader with strong technical skills and the ability to train, motivate, and guide others to exceed standards, U.S. Army:
TELECOMMUNICATIONS SUPERVISOR. Ft. Bragg, NC (1998-2001). Excelled in finding ways to get the work done with fewer personnel and no loss in quality or productivity while supervising five-person teams of telecommunications specialists; controlled $1 million worth of high-tech equipment and systems.

- Strongly encouraged to remain in military service and become an officer, made the decision to explore private sector opportunities.
- Supported 3,000 people in multiple organizations with secure voice and data telecommunications services; was a key player during fielding of a first-of-its-kind combined switching RF unit.
- Was honored for "hard work and innovation" and received a medal for my "knowledge of the Network Encryption System (NES)" which resulted in "flawless support."

SUPERVISOR, NETWORK SWITCHING SYSTEMS. Korea (1997-98). After becoming known as a productive and effective technician and earning promotion to this supervisory role within eight months, trained and supervised three people; ensured that individuals were proficient in telecommunication equipment installation and maintenance.

- Installed, monitored, and troubleshot networks using network diagrams and operating procedures; trained teams of specialists in field environments.

PERSONAL

Entrusted with a Secret security clearance. Am an effective instructor and public speaker.

Exact Name of Person
Exact Title
Exact Name of Company
Address
City, State, Zip

**COMMUNICATIONS
ADVISOR**

Dear Exact Name of Person (or Dear Sir or Madam if answering a blind ad):

With the enclosed resume, I would like to make you aware of my experience in the information technology industry and of the technical expertise I have gained and refined while serving in the National Security Agency.

As you will see from my enclosed resume, I offer a reputation as a technically skilled professional who is able to quickly master the latest technology. As a top-level Consultant, I am currently assigned as a Communications Advisor, and I travel extensively worldwide in order to advise the Special Operations community. In this job, I have been in a position to direct others in installing, operating, and maintaining voice and data networks. In an organization with a fast operations tempo and the responsibility for responding to short-notice crisis situations throughout the world, I have advanced ahead of my peers while earning a reputation as an astute problem solver.

An honors graduate from both middle and senior management courses, I have been awarded several medals and honors in recognition of my professionalism, drive, initiative, and high standards. I have also been entrusted with a Top Secret/SCI security clearance.

In my present assignment, I have been involved in fielding and in the research and development stages of new computer, data, and radio systems. Known for my initiative and wide-ranging technical knowledge, I have been credited with saving the government thousands of dollars by using off-the-shelf systems and creatively using available technology to ensure reliable communications in support of critical real-world missions.

I am confident that I possess the desire to excel in information technology as well as the aptitude, flexibility, and potential which would allow me to become a valuable candidate for employment with an organization seeking qualified technical professionals. If you can use a top-notch technical expert with the ability to think strategically and solve tough technical problems, I hope you will accept my call soon to suggest a time when we might talk about your needs. I can provide outstanding references at the appropriate time.

Sincerely,

Cassandra Wills

CASSANDRA WILLS

1110½ Hay Street, Fayetteville, NC 28305 • preppub@aol.com • (910) 483-6611

OBJECTIVE	To offer excellent hands-on technical skills and experience in information technology and computer networking to an organization that can use a physically and mentally tough professional known as a quick learner with excellent resource management abilities.

TECHNICAL KNOWLEDGE

Entrusted with a Top Secret/SCI security clearance, offer familiarity with a wide range of equipment and systems which include:

Microsoft 95 and 98 networks	INMARSAT telephones	Cisco routers
digital video capture/transmission	wide variety of antennas	E-commerce
COMSEC (communications security) devices		Windows NT 4.0
Saturn B Terminal voice-over IP data systems		Microsoft Office Suite
Harris and Motorola radios (including Spectra and Quantar)		surveillance equipment
hand-held and vehicle-mounted Racal radio systems		power generation systems

EDUCATION & TRAINING

Am pursuing a bachelor's degree, University of Kentucky, campus at Ft. Campbell, KY.
Earned recognition as a Distinguished Honor Graduate of two advanced management training programs and excelled in more than 14 months of training including the Special Operations Course, FBI firearms training, high-risk survival, and antiterrorist driving training.
Working on **A+ certification**, have completed training and am preparing to take the test.

EXPERIENCE

Am building a reputation for sound judgment, quick thinking, and strong electronics skills as a member of the National Security Agency:
COMMUNICATIONS ADVISOR AND SPECIALIST. Ft. Campbell, KY (1995-present). Install, operate, and maintain a $2 million inventory of equipment and am heavily involved in the fielding, research, and development of computer, data, and radio systems for an organization with a short-notice response mission anywhere in the world.

- Am widely recognized as an expert in the installation, operation, and maintenance of commercial and military HF, UHF, VHF, and satellite communications equipment and associated cryptographic components.
- Work closely with vendors during the development stages of networks and packages and am familiar with applications for off-the-shelf equipment from such suppliers as Motorola and their Quantar and Spectra product lines.
- Have been credited with saving the government thousands of dollars in R&D costs and keeping within tight budget constraints through the creative use of available technology.
- Contributed ideas and valuable input during fielding of new PRC/117-F and PSC-5 satellite communications radio, a new 64K voice and video system, the Motorola LST-5E satellite communications radio, and the Racal, MHSR and MBITR radio.
- Developed programs praised for their results in producing knowledgeable and well-trained technicians who achieved 100% passing scores in exercises and inspections.
- Created a tracking database which allowed 100% accountability for $2 million in assets.
- Was handpicked over 25 peers as the communications specialist for a reconnaissance team.

SENIOR SIGNAL SUPPORT SUPERVISOR. Ft.Benning, GA (1992-94). Earned respect for my high standards and concern for others while supervising 14 people and controlled a $3 million inventory of communications systems, power generation equipment, and vehicles.

- Provided leadership which allowed the section to achieve a 97% readiness rating for six consecutive months and exceed standards during numerous exercises and inspections.
- Was promoted to this job in 1993 after excelling as Team Chief of a five-person section operating an FM retransmitting system.

PERSONAL

FAA Private Pilot license, single-engine land and FAA parachuting license.

Date

Exact Name of Person
Exact Title
Exact Name of Company
Address
City, State, Zip

Dear Exact Name of Person (or Dear Sir or Madam if answering a blind ad):

With the enclosed resume, I would like to make you aware of my technical expertise and skills related to fiber optics cable splicing and installation as well as my reputation as an effective and productive leader, trainer, and supervisor.

As you will see from my resume, I have proudly served my country in the U.S. Army where I have earned a reputation for my positive attitude, dedication to achieving results, and effectiveness in training and advising others. In my present assignment as a Special Forces Communications Supervisor, I have been selected ahead of my peers as the Communications Supervisor for several task force missions and large-scale exercises. One of the areas of emphasis in this job is training and I have been involved in instructing personnel from numerous South and Central American countries in communications procedures and equipment.

Earlier as a cable and wire systems installer and supervisor, I directed the performance of and trained technicians while personally installing, operating, and maintaining communications systems. In one job, I oversaw a cable and wire section in a switching node company which provided contingency circuit and record switch capabilities at the Joint Chiefs of Staff level. Previously I directed the installation of wire and telephone systems for a tactical signal company.

During my military career, I have been singled out for numerous honors and awards which have included two Joint Meritorious Unit Awards, three Army Commendation Medals, two Joint Service Achievement Medals, and seven Achievement Medals.

If you can use a technically proficient individual with a high level of enthusiasm, energy, and drive, I hope you will contact me to suggest a time we might meet to discuss how I could contribute to your organization. I can provide excellent professional and personal references at the appropriate time. Thank you in advance for your time.

Sincerely,

Henry Sprague

HENRY SPRAGUE

1110½ Hay Street, Fayetteville, NC 28305   •   preppub@aol.com   •   (910) 483-6611

OBJECTIVE

To offer a strong technical background and extensive experience with fiber optics cable splicing and installation to an organization that can use a skilled professional with a reputation as a dedicated and self-motivated professional with a high degree of initiative.

EDUCATION & TRAINING

Received extensive advanced leadership and technical training which included programs in fiber optics transmission and operations, Spanish, communications systems supervision, and airborne operations as well as the following specialized programs:
- Laser Tech Int. Fiber Optics Splicing School, 1999 (splicing, connecting, and testing)
- Communications Electronics Installers Course, (mainframe installation, connecting, testing)
- Basic and Advanced Cable Splicing Installation and Maintenance Courses, 1998
- Telephone Pole Climbing Course, 1997

EXPERIENCE

Have built a reputation as a positive thinker and enthusiastic leader, U.S. Army:
COMMUNICATIONS SUPERVISOR. Ft. Campbell, KY (2001-present). Am sought out by other communications specialists for my expertise and knowledge while operating, installing, maintaining, and accounting for more than $250,000 worth of equipment and advising the general manager on communications matters.
- Selected ahead of 17 peers as Communications Supervisor for task forces in Ecuador and Peru as well as exercises in Texas and Panama; achieved 100% success rates for secure satellite and high frequency communications.
- Applied Spanish-language skills while training technicians from numerous Central and South American countries including one group of 50 Honduran managers/supervisors.

CABLE AND WIRE SECTION SUPERVISOR. Ft. Huachuca, AZ (1998-01). Supervised and trained eight technicians in a major switching node company which provided Joint Chiefs of Staff-level contingency circuit and record switching capabilities.
- Controlled a $4 million inventory of high-tech communications equipment in the cable and wire section of a switch and control unit.
- Supervised five people who wired a major node signal company during an exercise.

WIRE SYSTEMS INSTALLER AND SECTION SUPERVISOR. Korea (1995-97). Supervised and trained five people while overseeing the installation and operation of wire and telephone systems for a tactical signal company with $250,000 worth of equipment.
- Directed the maintenance of equipment including trucks and trailers; ten analog, 33 secure, and 33 digital telephones; and 26 reels of 26-pair cable.
- Personally wired the telephone center for secure phones for a large-scale exercise.

WIRE SYSTEMS INSTALLER. Ft. Gordon, GA (1993-95). Cited for "tremendous technical knowledge," supervised and assisted two subordinates installing and operating wire and cable systems in an organization capable of two-hour worldwide relocation.
- Directed preventive and unit-level maintenance on wire and cable, and cargo vehicles.

AUTOMATIC SWITCHBOARD TEAM SUPERVISOR. Ft. Ord, CA (1989-92). Supervised four people operating and maintaining one communications assemblage as well as support equipment including four generator sets, two vehicles, and a cargo trailer.
- Was promoted after excelling as a Switchboard and Cable Section Supervisor (1991-92) and Wire Team Supervisor (1989-90) in support of a rapid-response force.

PERSONAL

Earned honors including 15 prestigious medals and awards for exemplary performance.

Date

Exact Name of Person
Exact Title
Exact Name of Company
Address
City, State, Zip

Dear Sir or Madam:

With the enclosed resume, I would like to make you aware of my background in the troubleshooting, repair, and maintenance of digital electronic systems and radio communications equipment and my track record of success in the supervision and training of technical personnel.

As you will see, I am completing an Associate's degree in General Studies, with a concentration in Electronics. I have completed numerous courses related to electronics repair, including communications electronics, electrical maintenance, digital electronics, microprocessor systems, and computer repair. In addition to my college course work, I excelled in numerous technical courses.

In my current position as a Computer Center Supervisor with the Department of Defense, I manage sophisticated laser targeting systems as well as digital and radio communications equipment used to make precise calculations for live-fire training projects. I supervise and train four employees, including one more-junior supervisor. My training efforts have resulted in 100% first-time pass rates for personnel under my supervision.

In an earlier job as a Electronics Equipment Operator, I supervised three employees and trained six personnel in the use of oscilloscopes, multimeters, signal generators, and logic probes to locate faults and troubleshoot malfunctions in a wide variety of digital and analog electronic equipment. I was responsible for the repair of single- and multi-channel radios, generators, radar equipment, and weapons control systems on AH-64 Apache helicopters, as well as other types of electronics equipment, microprocessors, and computer systems.

If you can use a motivated, experienced technician with exceptional trouble-shooting and repair skills along with a the proven ability to train, supervise, and motivate others, then I hope you will contact me. I can assure in advance that my integrity is beyond reproach, and I could quickly become a valuable asset to your organization.

Sincerely,

David Ensor

DAVID ENSOR

1110½ Hay Street, Fayetteville, NC 28305   •   preppub@aol.com   •   (910) 483-6611

OBJECTIVE

To benefit an organization that can use an experienced technician who offers a background in the troubleshooting, repair, and maintenance of a wide range of digital electronics and radio communications equipment as well as the training and supervision of personnel.

EDUCATION & TRAINING

Completing **Associate's degree** program in **General Studies** at Austin College, Sherman, TX. Completed one year of college course work, Cape Cod Community College, Barnstable, MA. Have completed a number of college-level courses related to electronics repair, including:

Communications Electronics   Electrical Maintenance   Microprocessor Systems

Digital Electronics   Introduction to Computers   Computer Repair

In addition to my college course work, completed military training in the use of digital communication equipment, laser range finders, and radio communications.

Graduated from the Army's Automatic Testing Equipment Operator/Maintainer School.

- Developed knowledge and skill in troubleshooting and repair of digital electronics, microprocessor and computer systems, and other electronic equipment.

TECHNICAL SKILLS

Troubleshoot and repair a wide variety of electronics equipment.

Read and interpret wiring diagrams, blueprints, and schematics.

EXPERIENCE

COMPUTER CENTER SUPERVISOR. Department of Defense, locations worldwide, (2001-present). Now working at a classified location in Nevada, supervise and train four employees, including one more-junior supervisor, in the daily functions of the Operations Center and in the management of digital communications equipment, laser range finders, and radio communications used to calculate precise measurements used in live-fire training projects.

- Personally account for the security and maintenance of more than $150,000 worth of digital and radio communications equipment and laser targeting systems.
- Organize and monitor all training for the unit, resulting in a 100% first-time pass rate for all personnel under my supervision; maintain complete and accurate training records.
- Collect data and prepare precise mathematical calculations to ensure safety and accuracy in the use of live ammunition for training exercises.
- Am responsible for in-processing of new staff, scheduling, and setting up target ranges for training exercises.

SENIOR AUTOMATIC TEST EQUIPMENT OPERATOR. Department of Defense, Italy and Germany (1995-01). Trained a staff of six personnel and directly supervised three employees using oscilloscopes, multimeters, signal generators and logic probes to troubleshoot, repair, and maintain digital electronic equipment, microprocessors, and computer systems.

- Solely accountable for the security of $1.5 million dollars worth of electronics testing and repair equipment, maintained organizational equipment with zero discrepancies.
- Received a rating of **excellent** in official evaluations for my skill in training personnel; each of the six operators that I trained passed annual testing on the first try.
- Repaired radar and weapons control systems on AH-64 Apache helicopters, single- and multi-channel radios, generators, and infrared vision equipment.
- Took on additional responsibility, learning the SAMS system on my own time in order to serve as Detachment Administrative Specialist; received a Defense Department Medal for my initiative.

PERSONAL

Received a number of prestigious awards, including the National Defense Service Medal, Commendation Medal, and Achievement Award. Excellent references on request.

Exact Name of Person
Exact Title
Exact Name of Company
Address
City, State, Zip

COMPUTER CENTER SUPERVISOR

Dear Exact Name of Person (or Dear Sir or Madam if answering a blind ad):

With the enclosed resume, I would like to make you aware of my interest in seeking employment with your organization.

As you will see from my resume, I have excelled in a career field which required excellent problem-solving and decision-making skills. While managing a complex computer center used to compute precise measurements for live-fire utilization, I became respected for my "leadership by example" and for my attention to detail in all matters. Since people's lives and multimillion-dollar assets depended upon my judgments and decisions, I have become accustomed to working in an environment in which there is "no room for error."

In addition to managing up to 9 employees, I have been accountable for half a million dollars in assets with a record of perfect accountability. During the live-fire projects under my direction, I have maintained a perfect safety record.

If you can use an honest, reliable, and hard-working young professional who could make significant contributions to your organization, I hope you will contact me to suggest a time when we might meet to discuss your needs. I can assure you in advance that I could rapidly become an asset to your organization.

Sincerely,

Marty Fish

MARTY FISH

1110½ Hay Street, Fayetteville, NC 28305   ·   preppub@aol.com   ·   (910) 483-6611

OBJECTIVE

To offer my proven management and problem-solving skills to an organization that can use a hard-working young professional with excellent technical and computer skills along with knowledge of computer and telecommunications equipment operations.

EDUCATION & TRAINING

Completed approximately a year of college course work, Centre College, Danville, KY.
Excelled in National Security Agency-sponsored training which included courses in emergency lifesaving, safety, and hazardous material handling procedures, an Equal Opportunity Course, and the Primary Leadership Development Course.

SPECIAL SKILLS

Offer proficiency in utilizing computers with popular software; am knowledgeable of the LCU lightweight computer and BCT Briefcase Terminal Computer with touchscreen.
Am familiar with the SINCGARS radio and operation of vehicles up to 2-1/2 ton trucks.
Was entrusted with a Secret security clearance.

EXPERIENCE

Became recognized as a results-oriented, technically proficient young professional while serving as a Computer and Telecommunications Operator with the National Security Agency:
COMPUTER CENTER SUPERVISOR & SENIOR RADIO OPERATOR. Los Angeles, CA (1998-present). Was specially selected to manage a state-of-the-art computerized facility used to calculate precise measurements used in live-fire projects during which human lives and multimillion-dollar assets depended upon the reliability of our judgments.

- **Personnel supervision:** Supervised nine people in a center which was called on to provide immediate response to crisis situations anywhere in the world.
- **Quality control:** Supervised the transmission of requests for data and made computations of complex and highly technical data of others to ensure their accuracy and completeness; provided the leadership which resulted in the unit's receiving certification on their first attempt
- **Assets management:** Controlled more than $500,000 worth of computer/radio equipment and a mobile van.
- **Awards and honors:** Supervised an operations center rated as one of the very best at the Joint Readiness Training Center during training in small guerilla forces and antiterrorism activities; personally received three prestigious medals for my exceptional performance.
- **Leadership:** Earned a reputation for being the best of all the professionals in my field, and was handpicked to coordinate projects involving people from all branches of the service; managed gunfire for units from all the military services during a special project at the National Training Center.

COMPUTER OPERATOR and **INVENTORY CONTROLLER.** Germany (1996-98). Received commendable ratings during major inspections of operational readiness and proficiency while accounting for more than 100 weapons and the operation of a track vehicle in addition to major responsibilities for completing automated and manual computations.

- Earned praise for technical proficiency and speed with special-use computers.

COMPUTER OPERATOR. Germany (1994-96). Cited as a key player in the success of the technical operations center during a major field training exercise, provided support by receiving radio transmissions and operating computer systems used to ensure the accuracy and timeliness of technical data.

PERSONAL

Am knowledgeable of Quality Assurance and safety standards for the workplace.

Exact Name of Person
Exact Title
Exact Name of Company
Address
City, State, Zip

COMPUTER PRODUCTS SALES

Dear Exact Name of Person (or Dear Sir or Madam if answering a blind ad):

With the enclosed resume, I would like to express my interest in exploring employment opportunities with your organization.

As you will see from my resume, I have excelled in a track record of promotion during 14 years with Mayfair Corporation, which led to my present position as Director of Sales in the Santa Fe regional office. I have achieved spectacular results related to product sales and support with this major high-tech telecommunications company providing support to corporate giants including Sprint and Bell Communications.

In my current position since 1998, I direct regional sales and support services while managing 11 consultants involved in product introduction and customer training. I was promoted based on my effectiveness as an Area Sales Manager. I earned the distinction of **"National Sales Manager of the Year"** for achieving an unprecedented 300% of the corporate goal and six new product approvals.

Although I am held in the highest regard by my current employer and can provide an outstanding reference at the appropriate time, I have decided to selectively explore opportunities in companies which can utilize a dynamic high achiever who can produce outstanding bottom-line results. I would appreciate your holding my expression of interest in your company in confidence until after we speak.

If you can use a results-oriented and technologically knowledgeable producer with an astute understanding of sales, marketing, and product introduction, I hope you will contact me soon to suggest a time when we might meet to discuss how I could contribute to your organization. I will provide excellent professional and personal recommendations at the appropriate time. Thank you in advance for your time.

Sincerely,

Edward Grimes III

EDWARD GRIMES III

1110½ Hay Street, Fayetteville, NC 28305 • preppub@aol.com • (910) 483-6611

OBJECTIVE	To offer a background of success in managing the full process of product introductions through product approvals while providing quality customer support of cable and electronics equipment to an organization that can benefit from my leadership, team-building, and analytical abilities.
EDUCATION & TRAINING	**B.S. in Engineering Technology (BSET),** University of Texas at Houston, 1986. **A.A.S. in Electronics,** Central Texas Technical College, Houston, TX, 1984. Completed training programs sponsored by Global Knowledge: Understanding Network Fundamentals (2000) and ATM, Converging Voice, and Data Networks (1999).
HONORS	Received the honor of **"National Sales Manager of the Year" for North America** in recognition of achieving the largest sales growth and new product approvals for the Mayfair Telephone digital carrier system.
EXPERIENCE	Have advanced in the following track record with the Mayfair Corporation: **DIRECTOR OF SALES.** Mayfair Communications, Santa Fe, NM (1998-present). For this company which was formerly the Lightning GTM Division, direct all phases of sales and support services for access electronics to major telecommunications companies.

- Manage the new product approval process, from concept to compliance with company standards.
- Consistently exceed sales goals as products are integrated into customer operations.
- Develop and maintain strong and mutually respectful relations with support staff at the customer telephone companies in order to support continued growth as well as to meet their needs with new products.
- Manage 11 consultants who assist in product introduction and customer training.
- Contribute as an active member of the internal sales and marketing team involved in product development and the rollout of new products.
- Am recognized as a detail-oriented manager who applies excellent written and verbal communication skills while listening to customers and understanding their requirements.

AREA SALES MANAGER. Mayfair Corporation, Charlotte, NC and Richmond, VA (1990-98). After 1-1/2 years in Charlotte, was promoted to the Richmond location to direct sales of telephone and cable television products.

- Held direct responsibility for sales to the headquarters of these major customers as well as to independent telephone and broadband companies.
- Acted as liaison between other sales regions and the corporate product development and manufacturing activities.
- As **U.S. Account Team Manager**, developed and made presentations on new product ideas to headquarters management staff.
- Achieved sales records leading to recognition as "Sales Manager of the Year" in 1996 including an unprecedented 300% of corporate goals and six new product approvals.
- Developed a thorough understanding of the telephone industry and its organization.

APPLICATIONS ENGINEER. Fuquay-Varina, NC (1986-90). In my first assignment at the company headquarters, assisted in development and functional testing of three new product lines. Provided field support for sales and marketing and for customer training aids.

- Quickly earned recognition for my emphasis on quality and customer satisfaction.

PERSONAL	Am known for my open mind, willingness to listen to the customer, and manage sales to meet goals and objectives as well as customer needs. Outstanding references on request.

Exact Name of Person
Exact Title
Exact Name of Company
Address
City, State, Zip

COMPUTER PROGRAMMER

Dear Exact Name of Person (or Dear Sir or Madam if answering a blind ad):

With the enclosed resume, I would like to express my interest in exploring employment opportunities with your organization.

Since graduating from Yale University, I have worked for only four companies while acquiring vast experience in accounting and computer operations. As a Controller for a CBS, Inc. company in New York City prior to relocating to Miami, I created and maintained computer models that accurately forecast revenues, expenses, and cash flows in a dynamic environment. In a subsequent position in Miami as a Controller for a privately held company, I designed, implemented, and managed a microcomputer accounting and financial reporting system which replaced a manual process.

Most recently while working in the securities industry, I have become skilled in utilizing WatcherPlus software and Mach123 software. However, because of the temperamental nature of the securities industry, I have decided to resign from my current position and seek full-time employment in a company which can utilize my strong computer and accounting expertise. Highly regarded by my previous employer, for whom I have worked first as a full-time Controller and then as a part-time Consultant, I have been offered full-time employment with that company. However, I am seeking a position which will allow me greater opportunity to use and expand on my already-strong base of knowledge of computer operations and computer programming.

An astute mathematician and data manager with extensive experience in financial management, I offer a proven ability to rapidly master new software, programming languages, and technical knowledge. For example, in 1997 I embarked on a program of self-study for the CPA exam and I passed all four sections of the CPA exam on my first attempt. Considered an effective manager of human resources, I have supervised up to 25 individuals.

If you can use a highly respected analyst and problem solver with an aggressive bottom-line orientation along with a proven ability to work well with others at all organizational levels, I would enjoy an opportunity to meet with you to discuss your needs. I can provide outstanding personal and professional references.

Sincerely,

Mason Jenkins

MASON JENKINS

1110½ Hay Street, Fayetteville, NC 28305　　•　　preppub@aol.com　　•　　(910) 483-6611

OBJECTIVE
To contribute to an organization that can use a versatile professional with expertise in financial reporting, forecasting, analysis, and information management along with extensive knowledge of computer software and computer programming abilities.

EDUCATION & TRAINING
Yale University, Bachelor of Science, 1983.
Computer Programming: Pursuing studies in Java; previously studied Oracle.
- Skilled mathematician and data manager with proven ability to rapidly master new computer programs and languages.

Accounting: Vast knowledge of accounting software and exposure to accounting packages; expert in using microcomputer spreadsheets and database programming.
- On my own initiative, prepared for the CPA exam through self-study and passed all four parts of the CPA on my first attempt.

EXPERIENCE
FINANCIAL CONSULTANT. Solomon Smith Barney, Miami, FL (1999-present). Have become knowledgeable of the securities industry while trading Nasdaq Exchange equities using WatcherPlus software and Mach123 software.
- Continue to work part-time as a Consultant for XYZ Co. (previous employer).

CONTROLLER. XYZ Company, Miami, FL (1991-99). Joined this company in its start-up phase and supervised accounting, financial reporting, and administrative functions. Reported to the CEO of this privately held manufacturer with customers worldwide.
- Designed, created, implemented and managed a microcomputer accounting and financial reporting system to replace a manual system.
- Supervised two employees. Produced financial statements, tax returns, audit trail documentation, and management reports for four corporations with $2 million of annual expenditures.
- Negotiated and managed comprehensive business insurance policies and employee group benefits policies (20 employees).
- Negotiated and managed past due accounts payable.

CONTROLLER. BRS/Saunders, New York, NY (1988-91). For this CBS, Inc. company which distributed on-line medical information, managed budgeting, accounting, financial reporting, and analysis. Reported to VP of Finance and Administration.
- Created and maintained computer models that accurately forecast revenues, expenses and cash flows in a fast-growth environment.
- Prepared and managed the annual budget that increased from $1.5 million in 1984 to $8 million in 1986.
- Analyzed financial results. Planned pricing and spending strategies to successfully achieve the desired profit goals.
- Supervised three employees. Implemented complete microcomputer automation of financial reporting procedures.

DIRECTOR OF OPERATIONS. Westin Testing Institute, New Haven, CT and Atlanta, GA (1983-88). Oversaw the operation of professional school entrance exam prep courses offered in 50 locations nationwide. Supervised 25 Instructional Coordinators. Wrote curriculum materials for math and analytical reasoning, and taught classes.

PERSONAL
Resourceful problem solver. Strong personal initiative. Excellent references.

Exact Name of Person
Exact Title
Exact Name of Company
Address
City, State, Zip

**COMPUTER
PROGRAMMER**

Dear Exact Name of Person (or Dear Sir or Madam if answering a blind ad):

With the enclosed resume, I would like to make you aware of my interest in seeking employment with your organization. Single and flexible as to corporate needs for travel, relocation, and further training, I am currently in the process of relocating to the Raleigh area.

As you will see, I am becoming proficient in numerous aspects of computer programming and operation. I have recently completed training conducted by Sun Micro Systems related to computer programming and Java, and I have also completed training related to HTML. Knowledgeable of PhotoShop and Microsoft Office, I have studied Solaris, Java, and Javascript.

Although I am only 22 years of age, I already have been highly successful as a restaurant owner and as a sales representative. Although I am confident that I could establish a successful career in many different fields, I decided last year that my ultimate professional goal is to become a senior programmer and expert Java architectural developer, perhaps one day managing a team of programmers. As a highly focused and goal-oriented individual, I have completed extensive training related to Java and HTML, and I am preparing to take the Certification exam for Java in September 2004.

Although I am untested in the computer programming field, you will see from my resume that I have a habit of making a success out of everything I take on. I left college to buy and manage a restaurant, and I transformed a run-down family eating establishment into a "happening place" while increasing profitability from $30,000 to $100,000 weekly. I was recruited for my current position, and I have excelled in managing a territory. I have also made the largest equipment sale in my company's history.

If you are seeking individuals with a keen determination to make a career in Java programming and the computer field, I hope you will contact me to suggest a time when we might meet to discuss your needs. Although I can provide outstanding references at the appropriate time, I would appreciate your not contacting my current employer until after we talk. Thank you in advance for your time.

Sincerely,

Timothy Mays

TIMOTHY MAYS

1110½ Hay Street, Fayetteville, NC 28305   •   preppub@aol.com   •   (910) 483-6611

OBJECTIVE

To benefit an organization that can use a highly motivated young professional with knowledge of Java and computer programming whose professional goal is to eventually be a senior programmer and expert Java architectural developer managing a team of programmers.

EDUCATION

Completed nearly two years of college course work, University of Florida, Gainesville, FL, 1996-98.
- Left college in good standing in order to buy and manage a business, which became very successful; I plan on completing my degree in my spare time.

Graduated from Sidpers High School, Sidpers, FL; played varsity golf and volunteered as a Peer Mentor counseling troubled youth.

COMPUTERS

Earned Certificates of Completion from training related to programming sponsored by Sun Micro Systems which included the SL-210 and SL-275 courses, Ft. Lauderdale, FL, 2000-01.
- Am preparing to take the Certification exam for Java in September 2001.

Knowledgeable of PhotoShop 5.5 and Microsoft Office including Word and Excel.

Completed training related to HTML, Code Warrior University.

Through formal training and independent study, studied Solaris, Java, Javascript, HTML.

EXPERIENCE

SALES REPRESENTATIVE & TERRITORY MANAGER. U.S. Food Service, Ft. Lauderdale, FL (2001-present). Was aggressively recruited by this company when I was a restaurant owner; began as a trainee in Boca Raton and, in only one month, moved sales in that area from $8,000 per week to $20,000 per week while growing the territory 30%; was immediately given my own sales territory.
- In Ft. Lauderdale, have excelled in prospecting for the most difficult accounts; produced the largest equipment sale in the company's history.
- Have developed accounts which include cafeterias, restaurants, day care facilities, hospitals, nursing homes, schools, and others.
- Am skilled in managing all aspects of running a small business, which includes handling collections and bank deposits and determining delivery routes.

OWNER & OPERATOR. Freshest Ever Seafood, Boca Raton, FL (1998-01). Left college in order to buy this restaurant when I was 19 years old; turned a run-down restaurant into a "happening place" by remodeling the restaurant, changing menus, making aggressive use of large upstairs banquet facilities, and changing advertising.
- Revitalized the business; grew sales from $30,000 to $100,000 a month.
- Sold the business in 2001 when I went to work for U.S. Food Service.

SALES REPRESENTATIVE & SITE MANAGER. Gainesville Remodeling Group, Gainesville, FL (1996-98). While I was attending college, completely financed my college education by working for this company full-time; began as a door-to-door canvasser and was promoted into sales; quickly excelled in sales and produced sales of $120,000 per month compared to the $40,000 monthly average.
- Was specially selected to open a new facility in Gainesville; established a home improvements business specializing in items such as windows and doors, and developed sales of $200,000 to $300,000 in the first month of operation.

PERSONAL

Excellent references on request. Offer strong skills in both people management and money management. Am very confident of my ability to take on any activity or technical subject and rapidly gain expert knowledge. Extremely self-motivated and focused individual.

Date

Exact Name of Person
Title or Position
Name of Company
Address (number and street)
Address (city, state, and zip)

Dear Exact Name of Person: (or Sir or Madam if answering a blind ad.)

With the enclosed resume, I would like to express my interest in exploring employment opportunities with your organization.

As you will see, I served my country in the U.S. State Department where I built a reputation as a highly adaptable individual with a special ability for quickly learning and mastering new concepts and technology. My expertise has been developed while becoming proficient in management information systems, administrative support operations, desktop publishing, and office computer applications.

Presently pursuing a B.S. in Computer Information Systems, I earned an A.A.S. degree in Administrative Management while excelling in supervisory roles in both Europe and the U.S. Through experience and training, I have become highly knowledgeable and skilled with operating systems and software including MS-DOS; Microsoft Excel, Access, PowerPoint, and Word for Windows 7.0; Harvard Graphics; and dBase III Plus.

Throughout my career I have been selected for special assignments where I have been credited with accomplishments which have included reducing budget requirements with no loss of services, overcoming a 30% staff reduction by streamlining procedures, and developing new methods for applying technology for increased productivity. As just one example, during my most recent assignment, I was cited for making "an immediate impact" in the contracting office of an electronics systems center by identifying requirements which resulted in installation of new systems and by designing a new computer spreadsheet for tracking budget expenditures in an organization with more than $3.7 million in 500,000 contractual documents.

If you can use a creative, innovative professional who offers special skills as a writer along with technical expertise in computer applications, I hope you will contact me to suggest a time when we might meet to discuss your needs. I can provide outstanding references at the appropriate time.

Sincerely,

Casey Holtz

CASEY HOLTZ

1110½ Hay Street, Fayetteville, NC 28305 • preppub@aol.com • (910) 483-6611

OBJECTIVE

To offer expertise in management information systems, administrative support operations, desktop publishing, and office computer applications to an organization that can use a highly adaptable professional with a reputation for creativity, innovation, and an eye for detail.

EDUCATION & TRAINING

Pursuing a **B.S. in Computer Information Systems,** Western New England College, MA.
A.A.S., Administrative Management, Community College of the Air Force, 1992.
Excelled in extensive computer courses as well as in Air Force training in Total Quality Management (TQM), security program management, and leadership development.

COMPUTER EXPERTISE

Through experience and training, am highly knowledgeable and skilled with the following:

Microsoft Excel	MS PowerPoint	MS Word	Windows 7.0
MS Access	Harvard Graphics	dBase III Plus	MS-DOS

EXPERIENCE

Built a track record of advancement and was consistently singled out for my ability to quickly learn and master new concepts and improve productivity, U.S. State Department:

SUPERVISOR, INFORMATION MANAGEMENT AND EXECUTIVE SERVICES. Italy (2001-present). Cited as a "dynamic problem solver" who made an immediate impact in the contracting office of an electronics systems center, directed the annual distribution of more than $3.7 million in 500,000 contractual documents.

- Managed an Information Technology Equipment (ITE) account valued in excess of $1 million as well as a $260,000 travel, supply, and MIS funding budget.
- Reduced budget requirements 10% with no resulting reduction in the quality of services.
- Designed a spreadsheet for tracking budget expenditures which provided the director with vital data needed to make sound business decisions and meet critical requirements.
- Was instrumental in identifying ITE requirements which resulted in 117 new systems being installed with Standard Procurement System software and Windows NT migration.

CHIEF OF OPERATIONS. Germany (1998-00). Excelled in a two-year special assignment supervising as many as 56 people and coordinating transportation issues and delivery schedules with representatives at more than 40 geographically dispersed facilities.

- Described as "the best writer in the unit," edited and rewrote more than 100 performance evaluations and award narratives while also applying research and interviewing skills.

SUPERINTENDENT FOR AUTOMATION AND ADMINISTRATION. Italy (1995-98). Handled multiple simultaneous responsibilities while providing guidance and training in a multinational, joint services headquarters to include overseeing automation support, publication, and the preparation of studies, operating concepts, and plans and procedures.

- Analyzed more than 100 computer user requirements and justified procurement of 13 computers, LAN hook ups, and hardware/software upgrades despite severe budget cuts.
- Was a key figure in the development of a database which tracked transportation, housing, and food service needs for 500 exercise participants from 11 NATO nations.

CHIEF FOR INFORMATION MANAGEMENT. Belgium (1992-95). Was credited with overcoming a 30% staff reduction by streamlining and reorganizing procedures as well as more effectively utilizing ADP capabilities while managing office automation in support of 450 people in an international logistics center.

PERSONAL

Was entrusted with a Top Secret security clearance. Am a skilled writer.

Exact Name of Person
Exact Title
Exact Name of Company
Address
City, State, Zip

COMPUTER
OPERATOR

Dear Exact Name of Person (or Dear Sir or Madam if answering a blind ad):

With the enclosed resume, I would like to make you aware of my interest in offering experience, knowledge, and skills to an organization that can benefit from my creativity and innovative manner of finding effective ways of improving the quality and timeliness of administrative office operations.

As you will see from my resume, I have built a reputation as a self-starter with a high level of initiative and drive while serving my country in the U.S. Army. Through experience and training I have become proficient with automated systems and with finding the methods for maximizing available resources. I am experienced in utilizing Harvard Graphics, dBase IV, Lotus Notes, Delrina FormFlow, and the Microsoft Office software and in creating presentations using PowerPoint. I am also familiar with systems used to analyze, track, and record human resources trends and activities.

In my most recent position as an Executive Assistant at the headquarters of an 87,000-person organization, I became known for my eye for detail and organizational skills displayed while maintaining records for personnel located throughout the world. A main area of focus was analyzing and integrating updated data into reports before forwarding them to a higher headquarters. Throughout my military service, I was selected for positions requiring strong office automation, fiscal management, and personnel administration knowledge and was consistently described as "invaluable" and "an exceptional performer."

Although I was strongly encouraged to remain in military service and assured of continued rapid advancement, I decided to leave the U.S. Army and enter the civilian workforce. I am single and could relocate as your needs require.

If you can use an excellent communicator with high degrees of enthusiasm, energy, and drive, I hope you will contact me soon to suggest a time we might meet to discuss how I could contribute to your organization. I can provide excellent professional and personal references at the appropriate time. Thank you for your time and consideration.

Sincerely,

Susan West

SUSAN WEST

1110½ Hay Street, Fayetteville, NC 28305 • preppub@aol.com • (910) 483-6611

OBJECTIVE   To contribute to an organization in need of a mature self starter who quickly masters new procedures and offers a strong ability to develop ideas which increase productivity and efficiency as well as excellent office administration and automation skills.

EDUCATION   Studied Business at Hawaii Pacific University, Honolulu, HI.
& TRAINING   Excelled in training for administrative specialists as well as courses emphasizing the development of leadership skills and applications for automated systems.

SPECIAL   Have developed proficiency with computer programs and applications including:
KNOWLEDGE

Microsoft – Word, Excel, PowerPoint, and Access		Lotus Notes
Delrina FormFlow	Harvard Graphics	dBase IV
Exchange	Outlook	the Internet

proprietary U.S. Army personnel administration and tracking programs

EXPERIENCE   **Was respected for attention to detail, expert organizational skills, and my innovative ideas displayed while supporting executive and administrative functions, U.S. Army:**
COMPUTER TECHNICIAN & EXECUTIVE ASSISTANT. Ft. Shafter, HI (2001-present). Maintained personnel accountability records for 87,000 people geographically dispersed throughout the world while providing administrative support.

- Utilized PowerPoint to develop monthly slide presentations for the senior general officer; integrated database upgrade programs from the Department of the Army.
- Analyzed reports and integrated accurate and updated data into them before consolidating and forwarding them to an Atlanta, GA, regional headquarters.
- Determined career fields and experience levels related to the most serious personnel shortages and prepared spreadsheets tracking these trends.

EXECUTIVE ASSISTANT. Ft. Shafter, HI (1999-01). Supervised three personnel specialists while handling a wide range of purchasing, office operations, records maintenance, and data processing actions in an executive staff office environment.

- Handpicked for a three-month special project assisting the chief executive in revamping policy guidelines; typed and distributed the new guidelines and also developed a record management system using the MARKS system for rapid retrieval of information.
- Created a Standard Operating Procedures (SOP) manual and a well-received system of screening, prioritizing, and classifying messages for executives.
- Designed three pewter memento coins used by two general officers to personally recognize instances of exceptional performance.
- Coordinated schedules, office meetings, and travel arrangements for senior executives.

ADMINISTRATIVE SPECIALIST. Guantanamo Bay, Cuba (1998-99). Officially evaluated as "indispensable" to the success of administrative support, was selected to process performance evaluations, accountability records, and mail for personnel from all the military services—Army, Navy, Air Force, Coast Guard, and Marines—for a task force.

Highlights of other experience: Refined time management and organizational skills in temporary jobs (simultaneous with military service) which included **Tax Clerk, Credit Investigator**, and **Customer Service Representative** for a bank and a loan company.

PERSONAL   Received numerous awards and medals for exemplary performance.

Date

Exact Name of Person
Title or Position
Name of Company
Address (number and street)
Address (city, state, and zip)

COMPUTER PROGRAMMING
STUDENT

This is an example of a
resume and cover letter
targeted specifically to
the computer industry.
Notice that this individual
served in the U.S. Army
and then went back to
college, so he used the
G.I. Bill to finance his
college education.

Dear Exact Name of Person: (or Sir or Madam if answering a blind ad.)

I would appreciate an opportunity to talk with you soon about how I could contribute to your organization through my degree in Computer Programming as well as through my technical computer skills and proven background of expertise in training program development and management.

With a reputation as a talented instructor, technical writer, and specialist in planning and developing course requirements, I was promoted ahead of my peers to leadership positions in the U.S. Army. Since leaving military service, I have completed degree requirements for an Associate in Applied Science (A.A.S.) degree from Cortland Technical Community College, NY. My skills include repairing and upgrading computers, programming in various languages, and utilizing DOS, Windows, and UNIX operating systems.

I hope you will welcome my call soon to arrange a brief meeting to discuss your current and future needs and how I might serve them. Thank you in advance for your time.

Sincerely,

Charles Harding

Alternate last paragraph:
I hope you will call or write me soon to suggest a time convenient for us to meet and discuss your current and future needs and how I might serve them. Thank you in advance for your time.

CHARLES HARDING

1110½ Hay Street, Fayetteville, NC 28305   •   preppub@aol.com   •   (910) 483-6611

OBJECTIVE To offer my education and skills related to computer analysis, design, and programming; systems administration/networking; and equipment repair/upgrade coupled with my experience in performance-based computer instruction and training management.

EDUCATION & TRAINING Completed **Associate in Applied Science degree in Computer Programming,** Cortland Technical Community College, NY, 2001.
- Completed specialized course work including the following:

systems analysis	operating systems	UNIX
financial accounting	network technology	statistics
database management	data communications	data access

- Excelled in more than 6,600 hours of courses emphasizing training development and management as well as a Spanish language course.
- Completed rigorous Special Forces training.

COMPUTERS Experienced in repairing, upgrading, and networking IBM-compatible PCs with Windows and UNIX operating systems using software including:

Windows 2000	WordPerfect	MS Word
dBase IV	Micro Focus	Novell Netware
Visual BASIC 4	Harvard Graphics	COBOL

EXPERIENCE **FULL-TIME STUDENT.** Cortland Technical Community College, NY (1999-2001).

Advanced to the rank of Sergeant in the U.S. Army:
TRAINING PROGRAM MANAGER. Ft. Stewart, GA (1997-99). Handled activities ranging from supervising six people carrying out short- and long-term training management, to assisting in the development of one- and two-year training plans, to developing and consolidating weekly training schedules.
- Conducted weekly training meetings which focused on problem solving, directing the best utilization of resources, and keeping a senior executive informed of events.
- Coordinated administrative and medical support and resources for an 83-person company with an extensive inventory of communications equipment and 11 trucks.

SENIOR INSTRUCTOR and **OPERATIONS MANAGER.** Ft. Campbell, KY (1994-98). As senior course developer and administrator for numerous types of courses, provided subject matter expertise for the U.S. Army's Special Warfare Center and School.
- Monitored the performance of eight classroom instructors teaching groups of 20 students in dozens of different specialized areas.
- Taught performance-based instruction and the lecture method of instruction in a two-week Instructor Training Course which produced effective professional instructors.
- Served as Senior Instructor for the Training Developer Course in which instructors were taught how to develop training products in their specialized areas.
- Wrote instructional material for numerous courses and reviewed more than 150 training documents for sound doctrine and made recommendations for changes.
- Implemented a software program that facilitates training management by tracking expenses, generating calendars, and automating training resources.

PERSONAL Was entrusted with a Top Secret security clearance. Was honored with one Humanitarian Service, one Meritorious Service, and two Commendation Medals.

**COMPUTER SALES
REPRESENTATIVE**

Dear Sir or Madam:

I am writing to express my strong interest in the position of **Country Manager —Korea**, which was recently posted in the career opportunities section of the Adobe web site. With exceptional leadership and personnel management experience along with an extensive sales and marketing background related to software sales and distribution, I feel I am ideally suited to your needs. I was born in Seoul, Korea, speak both English and Korean fluently, and have previously worked in various overseas locations, including Korea.

As you will see from my resume, I am currently excelling as the President and Sales Manager of B & B Softmart, a busy local software reseller with annual sales of nearly a million dollars. In this position and a previous job as Executive Vice President of Ace Software Express, I have interacted closely with vendors, manufacturers, distributors, and sales representatives within the software industry on a daily basis. While directing the sales and marketing efforts at each of these businesses, my exceptional leadership and motivational skills have resulted in growth of market share and strong annual sales increases despite fierce competition. In my current entrepreneurial role, I have developed all the company's accounts "from scratch."

You will notice that I also served my country in the Peace Corps, and I refined my Korean language skills while working in Seoul.

If you can use an articulate professional who is extremely familiar with Korean language and culture and who possesses proven management and entrepreneurial skills along with practical experience in software distribution, I hope you will write or call me soon to suggest a time when we might meet to discuss your needs. I can provide outstanding references at the appropriate time.

Sincerely yours,

John Jarcho

JOHN JARCHO

1110½ Hay Street, Fayetteville, NC 28305   •   preppub@aol.com   •   (910) 483-6611

OBJECTIVE   To contribute to an organization that can use an articulate professional with outstanding communication and sales skills along with a strong bottom-line orientation who has excelled in management positions in the software industry and in the Peace Corps.

LANGUAGES   Speak, read, write, and translate **Korean** and **English** fluently (born in Seoul, Korea).

EDUCATION   **Bachelor of Arts** in **International Relations** with minors in Political Science and History, Winston College, Winston, PA, 1990.
Completed extensive formal and on-the-job training in **sales** and **marketing.**
Excelled in numerous **leadership** and training courses sponsored by the Peace Corps; graduate of the eight-month Peace Corps Manager's Course as well as other courses designed to refine **management** and **communication** skills.

SOFTWARE   Proficient with Mail Order Manager (MOM) Program, MS Office, and working knowledge of many of the Adobe products to include PageMaker and Photoshop.

EXPERIENCE   **PRESIDENT** and **SALES MANAGER.** B & B Softmart, Cliffside Park, NJ (2001-present). Manage all operational aspects of this local software reseller with annual sales of $950,000; manage human, fiscal, and material resources; sales and marketing; and performing liaison with vendors, manufacturers, and distributors; have developed all accounts "from scratch."
- Despite strong competition from other software resellers in the area, have led the company to continuously achieve **25% sales increases annually** since the founding of the business.
- Supervise six employees, directing marketing, sales, and customer service efforts.
- Interact with software vendors, manufacturers, distributors, and sales representatives on a daily basis, acquiring vital information concerning new products, pricing, and shipping.
- Track sales of current titles by manufacturer, category, and type of software in order to anticipate potential growth areas and ensure a strong in-stock position on fast-moving titles.
- Interview, hire, and train all personnel, instructing them in company policies and procedures, customer service, inventory control, and product knowledge.

EXECUTIVE VICE PRESIDENT. Ace Software Express, Inc., Clifton, NJ (1997-01). Was instrumental in the successful growth of this software reseller; managed the operation of this company while quickly mastering all aspects of the software resale industry.
- Formulated and developed long- and short-term sales projections, analyzing sales figures from previous years and sales trends for the current fiscal year.
- An articulate communicator and talented motivator, inspired the sales force to excel, producing increases in sales and market share; supervised 12 employees in areas which included sales and customer service, inventory, and shipping.

Was promoted ahead of my peers and excelled in leadership roles, U.S. Peace Corps, various locations worldwide, 1990-97: Provided assistance to organizations scattered throughout the Pacific region (the Hawaiian Islands, Guam, and Saipan). Supervised a 12-person administration section providing support to a 500-person organization. Advanced to a position as Project Manager in Korea.

PERSONAL   Am an adaptable professional with a reputation for unquestioned loyalty and honesty.

Date

Exact Name of Person
Exact Title
Exact Name of Company
Address
City, State, Zip

COMPUTER SALES SPECIALIST

Dear Exact Name of Person (or Dear Sir or Madam if answering a blind ad):

With the enclosed resume, I would like to make you aware of my interest in exploring employment opportunities with your organization and introduce you to my talents and skills.

As you will see from my enclosed resume, I am recognized as a hard-working young professional who is effective in prioritizing tasks, managing time effectively, and handling multiple simultaneous activities. I am relocating back to Columbus, where I worked previously, so that I can work full time while attending Columbus State University in my spare time in order to complete my degree.

I relocated from Columbus to Atlanta nearly two years ago in order to live nearer to my mother, who was experiencing serious health problems, and I became employed by a newly opened Dell Computer store. I have earned a reputation as an efficient and knowledgeable Computer Sales Specialist while assisting customers in having their computer systems configured to their particular user needs. Since making Dell aware of my decision to return to Columbus to work and attend college, Dell has offered me employment in a Columbus store. I have decided, however, to explore employment opportunities with other Columbus companies, and I am selectively approaching organizations which could use my customer service, technical support, and administrative background.

I am a hard worker who excels in dealing with people in a gracious and helpful manner while troubleshooting problems and finding solutions. I work well independently or while contributing to the efforts of team. Fluent in Spanish, I have volunteered with Special Olympics as a translator. I can provide outstanding references.

If you can use a cheerful and adaptable individual who offers a proven ability to work well with others, I hope you will contact me to suggest a time when we might discuss your needs.

Yours sincerely,

Samantha Love

SAMANTHA LOVE

1110½ Hay Street, Fayetteville, NC 28305   •   preppub@aol.com   •   (910) 483-6611

OBJECTIVE

To offer excellent customer relations and communication abilities as well as technical computer skills and knowledge to an organization that can use a self-motivated and enthusiastic young professional who excels working independently and as a contributor to team efforts.

EDUCATION & TRAINING

Have completed **30 hours of course work in pursuit of an A.A. degree,** Columbus State University, Columbus, GA.

- Demonstrated my ability to prioritize tasks and manage time effectively while attending college in the mornings and working from approximately noon to 9 p.m.
- Volunteer with the Red Cross and have applied **Spanish language** skills as a **Translator** for Special Olympics events and with the School of the Americas.

Graduated from Spencer High School, Columbus, GA.

- Was a member of the National Honor Society throughout high school.

Completed a Dell Computer **technical computer, sales, and customer service course.**

Completed **customer service training** program sponsored by Teleservice.

SPECIAL SKILLS

Language: Speak, read, and write Spanish fluently.

Computers: Familiar with software which includes Word, Excel, PowerPoint, Novell, and other commonly used programs as well as with hardware and peripheral equipment.

EXPERIENCE

COMPUTER SALES SPECIALIST. Dell Computer. Atlanta, GA (2000-present). Have quickly earned recognition for my ability to relate technical applications to a common sense approach while assisting customers in this newly opened store which specializes in configuring computer systems and designing them to meet users' needs and requirements.

- Have been cited as a dedicated young professional with a knack for helping customers through my knowledge of the company's products and system capabilities.
- Patiently yet aggressively resolve client issues when shipments are delayed due to inventory or configuration problems.
- Work extensively with the ordering system (AS-400) while creating and updating configurations.
- Was officially rated as excellent in all areas of performance with special attention given to my ability to follow through and solve client issues.
- Based on my excellent performance in this job, have been offered a position with Dell in Columbus, GA, where I will be attending Columbus State University.

CUSTOMER SERVICE TRAINEE. Dell Computer, Columbus, GA (1998-00). Selected to receive training in handling customer service calls and updating account information, was recognized for my patient, professional, courteous style of dealing with callers in a center which processed credit cards.

- Worked with several financial institutions on many aspects of financing clients.

ADMINISTRATIVE ASSISTANT. Spencer County School System, Columbus, GA (1996-98). While still in high school, became familiar with professional office procedures and functions while answering phones, making copies, and updating files and transcripts.

PERSONAL

Offer well-developed decision-making and problem-solving skills. Am a positive, energetic, and enthusiastic individual who can be counted on to get the job done.

Date

Exact Name of Person
Title or Position
Name of Company
Address (no., street)
Address (city, state, zip)

Here we have another example of a student with previous military experience. He has a Computer Expertise section on his resume since he figures one of his key areas of strength is his computer knowledge.

Dear Exact Name of Person: (or Dear Sir or Madam if answering a blind ad.)

With the enclosed resume I would like to introduce you to the strong computer skills and software knowledge which I could put to work for you.

With a degree in Computer Science, I offer previous experience as a Computer Operator while serving in the U.S. Navy. In fact, my military experience revealed that I have a knack for computer technology, as I rapidly mastered the software used by the Navy at a central operations center. Even prior to earning my B.S. degree at Emory, I excelled in numerous technical training programs. I was entrusted with one of the nation's highest security clearances: Top Secret.

Throughout my life, I have become known for my resourcefulness and creativity. I am eager to combine my strong computer knowledge with my innate problem-solving ability in order to benefit a company that can use a highly motivated hard charger.

I hope you will welcome my call soon to determine if there is a time when we could meet in person so that I could show you that I am a dedicated and ambitious person who could become a valuable part of your team. Thank you in advance for your time.

Sincerely yours,

Adam Henke

ADAM HENKE

1110½ Hay Street, Fayetteville, NC 28305 • preppub@aol.com • (910) 483-6611

OBJECTIVE

To offer extensive knowledge of computer software operations and systems maintenance to an organization that can use a skilled young professional with an aptitude for quickly learning and applying new technology.

EDUCATION & TECHNICAL TRAINING

B.S. in Computer Science, Emory University, Atlanta, GA; degree anticipated June, 2001. Excelled in military training programs emphasizing the following:

basic electricity	records processing	tape libraries
quality assurance	basic test equipment	system design
system tape backup	system configurations	LAN hardware
peripheral operations	system error messages	system diagnosis
message format	communications security	radio/phone procedures

COMPUTER EXPERTISE

Offer exceptional computer skills gained through formal training related to:

Windows 2000	DOS	WordPerfect
Harvard Graphics	Harvard FX	Picture Publisher
Word Scan	Novell	UNIX

Microsoft Office (entire package including Excel and Word)

EXPERIENCE

FULL-TIME COLLEGE STUDENT. Emory University, Atlanta, GA (2000-present). Attend Emory University in the Computer Science degree program.

Advanced on the basis of technical proficiency, natural aptitude, and attention to detail as a
DATA PROCESSING TECHNICIAN *in the U.S. Navy:*
SHIFT SUPERVISOR. The USS Guam, Norfolk, VA (1997-99). Was promoted to supervise operation of the specialized ADP system used to support supply and operational activities.
- Officially described as a "superb performer" and awarded a service medal and citation, was recognized for technical expertise and a positive attitude.

MEDIA LIBRARIAN. The USS Guam, Norfolk, VA (1996-97). In recognition of my attention to detail and knowledge, was given the responsibility of managing and keeping detailed records of an inventory of electronic data tapes generated by the SNAP system.
- Ensured a "discrepancy free" rating for the supply department in a major assessment of logistics operations which resulted in an overall 98.4% rating.
- Assisted in removing more than 450 excess ADP electronics items: as a result, storage space was maximized and inventory control simplified.
- Was the supply department "Employee of the Month," February 1996.

COMPUTER OPERATOR. Office of Naval Intelligence, Suitland, MD (1993-95). Operated VAX 600, VAX 8810, Filenet system, and Network Control microcomputers at a central operations center.
- Was cited for expert handling of more than 50 "hot line" calls a day which required that all information was properly documented and transferred so that problems were solved and users achieved maximum production time.
- Officially described as "having unlimited potential," was praised for being industrious and self motivated and for setting the standard for my peers.

PERSONAL

Was entrusted with a Top Secret security clearance. Accurately type at least 45 words per minute. Am in excellent physical condition. High level of determination and initiative.

Date

Exact Name of Person
Exact Title
Exact Name of Company
Address
City, State, Zip

Dear Exact Name of Person (or Dear Sir or Madam if answering a blind ad):

With the enclosed resume, I would like to express my interest in exploring employment opportunities with your organization.

As you will see from my resume, I hold a degree in Computer Science and previously completed extensive coursework at the University of Georgia in Electrical Engineering. After the University of Georgia, I became employed by the Case Company and worked for that corporation for 14 years as a Product Support Manager. I resigned from my position with the Case Company and became a full-time Computer Science student in 2000 when the company asked me to accept a promotion which required relocation to their home office in Wisconsin. At that point, I decided to complete the college degree which I had begun many years earlier, and I have worked part-time as a business consultant while completing my B.S. I have completed courses related to HTML, Java, Visual Basic, C and C++, UNIX, and Interfacing, and I am making plans to pursue Oracle in my spare time.

While providing all types of wholesale support and sales to 20 retail dealers in my job as a Product Support Manager with the Case Company, I was extensively involved in training the dealers' employees in computer operations. The Case Company decided in 1994 that it would require its dealer-customers to communicate with the company through online methods, so it became a major part of my job to work with dealers' platforms which included UNIX, AS 400, and Windows NT. I trained the dealers' employees in computer operations, and I also trained technicians to perform troubleshooting using high-tech computer equipment.

A key part of my job was helping dealers maximize the profitability of their retail businesses, so I became very skilled at interpreting financial documents including proformas, balance sheets, and other paperwork. I take pride in the fact that I helped all my dealer customers improve their bottom line through my recommendations related to market share, product line conversions and product mix, warranty policies and procedures, and stock ordering. I was consistently in the top 5% of the company's managers in a variety of areas including customer satisfaction.

If you can use a versatile professional who offers a versatile background which includes extensive customer service experience as well as computer knowledge, I hope you will contact me soon to suggest a time we might meet. Thank you for your time.

Sincerely,

David Curtins

DAVID CURTINS

1110½ Hay Street, Fayetteville, NC 28305　　•　　preppub@aol.com　　•　　(910) 483-6611

OBJECTIVE

I want to contribute to an organization that can use a resourceful professional with an extensive technical background in electrical engineering and computer science along with vast experience in business consulting, operations management, and sales.

EDUCATION

B.S. degree in Computer Science, Phillips College, Weston, GA, 2001.
- Completed course work related to Java, Visual Basic, C and C++, UNIX, Interfacing, and other subjects. Will pursue Oracle studies in my spare time.
- **Previous course work in Electrical Engineering:** Began college with a major of pre-med and changed to Electrical Engineering, University of Georgia.

Technical computer training: Extensive training related to UNIX, AS 400, Windows NT, and other platforms sponsored by the Case Corporation.
- Skilled at interpreting schematics, diagrams, and blueprints; highly proficient in working with electrical circuitry. Highly skilled with Word, PowerPoint, Excel.

Financial training: Am skilled at reading profit-and-loss statements, pro formas, balance sheets, and other financial documents.

Graduated from Jeff Davis High School, Hazlehurst, GA, 1983.
- Was a school leader: was voted "Mr. Junior" and "Mr. Senior."

EXPERIENCE

BUSINESS CONSULTANT & FULL-TIME COMPUTER SCIENCE STUDENT. (2000-present). After working for the Case Company for 14 years, I resigned from the corporation when the company wanted me to accept a promotion and relocation to its home office in Racine, WI; I decided to resign and complete my college degree.

PRODUCT SUPPORT MANAGER. Borders Company, Racine, WI (1988-2000). Was responsible for 20 retail dealers and served as their wholesale source of supply for agricultural items such as plow tools.
- Became skilled in all aspects of business consulting as I worked with retailers to improve their profitability and merchandising mix; developed plans to foster better relationships between dealers and their customers.
- Developed innovative plans to help dealers increase the service part of their business.
- Utilized PowerPoint to make presentations and conduct training.
- Functioned as a business consultant; was trained to read financial statements and profit-and-loss statements.
- In 1994, after the company made the decision to require dealers to communicate their orders and other matters online, was extensively trained in computer operations related to UNIX, AS 400, Windows NT, and other platforms. Became skilled in assisting customers in their networking needs, and trained the dealers' employees in computer use and troubleshooting.
- Trained technicians to perform troubleshooting using high-tech computer troubleshooting equipment.

Highlights of achievements:
- Increased parts sales from $3.9 million in 1991 to $6.8 million in 1999.
- Boosted customer satisfaction rating from 62% in 1997 to 84% in 1999.
- Developed effective business plans which established goals for numerous product lines and which established objectives for operating income, market share, product line conversions, warranty policies and procedures, customer complaints, service reports, stock order goals, and claim audits.

PERSONAL

Outstanding references on request. Extremely resourceful and effective problem solver.

  Date

                    Exact Name of Person
                    Exact Title
                    Exact Name of Company
                    Address
                    City, State, Zip

COMPUTER SCIENCE   Dear Exact Name of Person (or Dear Sir or Madam if answering a blind ad):
STUDENT

                    With the enclosed resume, I would like to make you aware of my background as
                    a versatile and experienced professional with a history of success in areas which
                    include computer operations, logistics and supply, production control, and employee
                    training and supervision.

                    As you will see, I am completing requirements for my bachelor's degree in Computer
                    Science from Methodist College which I expect to receive this winter. I am proud of my
                    accomplishment in completing this course of study while simultaneously meeting the
                    demands of a career in the U.S. Army. In my current military assignment as a
                    Technical Inspector, I ensure the airworthiness of aircraft which is required to relocate
                    anywhere in the world on extremely short notice in response to crisis situations.

                    Throughout my years of military service I have been singled out for jobs which
                    have required the ability to quickly make sound decisions and have continually maximized
                    resources while exceeding expected standards and performance guidelines. I have been
                    responsible for certifying multimillion-dollar aircraft for flight service, training and
                    supervising employees who have been highly productive and successful in their own
                    careers, and applying technical computer knowledge in innovative ways which have
                    further increased efficiency and productivity.

                    I offer a combination of technical, managerial, and supervisory skills and a level
                    of knowledge which will allow me to quickly achieve outstanding results in anything I
                    attempt. Known for my energy and enthusiasm, I am a creative professional with a
                    strong desire to make a difference in whatever environment I find myself.

                    I hope you will contact me to suggest a time when we might meet to discuss your
                    needs. I can assure you in advance that I could rapidly become an asset to your organization.

                                                                    Sincerely,

                                                                    Kyle Sweeney

KYLE SWEENEY

1110½ Hay Street, Fayetteville, NC 28305   •   preppub@aol.com   •   (910) 483-6611

OBJECTIVE

To offer a versatile background emphasizing computer operations, logistics, inventory control, production control, and security to an organization that can benefit from my experience as a supervisor and manager with a reputation for creativity.

EDUCATION & TRAINING

Will receive a **B.S. in Computer Science,** Elon College, Elon College, NC, winter 2002. Selected for extensive training, including courses for security managers and computer operations and applications as well as technical courses in aircraft repair and maintenance, professional leadership development, equal opportunity practices, and Airborne School.

COMPUTER SKILLS & CLEARANCE

Am highly computer literate and offer skills related to the following:

ScanPro   Novell   LAN systems   Lotus   Excel   Access   dBase III/IV   e-mail

Was entrusted with a Top Secret security clearance.

EXPERIENCE

Earned a reputation as a focused and goal-oriented professional, U.S. Army:

TECHNICAL INSPECTOR. Ft. Bragg, NC (2001-present). Officially cited for my in-depth knowledge of aviation maintenance and logistics issues, conduct technical inspections on 24 helicopters while also providing training, guidance, and supervision.

- Transformed a substandard quality control section into one which sets the example.
- Received the NATO Medal for Service for my contributions during operations in the former Yugoslavia in 2002.

SUPERVISOR FOR AVIATION MAINTENANCE AND SUPPLY. Ft. Bragg, NC (1999-00). Made numerous important contributions while coordinating supply, maintenance, and readiness issues for units throughout the 18th Airborne Corps.

- Received a letter of commendation from a three-star general for my expertise demonstrated as the Security Manager for the corps headquarters and for personally revitalizing the physical security program which received "commendable" ratings.
- Developed a data base for managing aircraft maintenance histories which greatly increased the reliability of information about the organization's 968 assigned aircraft.
- Created and presented effective training on physical security and ADP operations.

MAINTENANCE SUPERVISOR. Ft. Bragg, NC (1998-99). Provided oversight for a $6 million annual operating budget and ensured the quality and timeliness of all phases of support for a fleet of 104 aircraft while reviewing daily/monthly status reports, coordinating supply up to the wholesale level, and recommending procedural changes.

- Consistently exceeded Department of the Army standards for aircraft availability and was singled out for praise for my expertise as a trainer, mentor, and leader.

MAINTENANCE SUPERVISOR. Germany (1995-98). Cited as directly responsible for a high level of achievement and productivity; collected and processed maintenance data on 123 aircraft while controlling flight safety information and support for four divisions.

- Selected to oversee a project during which new equipment and automation assets were integrated into use; achieved a smooth transition.
- Was a member of the team which first fielded the ULASS computer system which is a tool for managing production, maintenance hours, and supplies.

PERSONAL

Am known for my enthusiastic style of leadership and reputation for unwavering moral and ethical standards. Was honored with numerous medals in recognition of my contributions.

Exact Name of Person
Exact Title
Exact Name of Company
Address
City, State, Zip

COMPUTER SPECIALIST   Dear Exact Name of Person (or Dear Sir or Madam if answering a blind ad):

I would like to take this opportunity to introduce you to a detail-oriented and highly motivated young professional who offers exceptional technical and leadership abilities refined while working in the Department of Defense.

As you will see from my enclosed resume, I am a technically knowledgeable and skilled individual with strong abilities in troubleshooting and problem solving along with a thorough understanding of the latest technological advances. I am applying time management skills while excelling in demanding jobs and pursuing a degree in Computer Science on my own time. My training has included a professional leadership development program in addition to technical programs in intelligence analysis, LAN administration and management, and multichannel transmission systems operations.

After earlier success in telecommunications system repair, maintenance, and operation, I was selected for advanced training as an Intelligence Analyst. In my most recent assignments I have been combining my technical expertise with analytical, research, and communication skills to excel in jobs as an analyst and inspector of information, physical, and personal security plans and programs.

Entrusted with a Top Secret/SBI security clearance, I have consistently been recognized as a mature young professional who can be counted on to work well as a team leader or independently. I am an innovative and creative thinker who offers superior troubleshooting skills and the ability to quickly master technological advances.

If you can use a dedicated, self-motivated, and technically knowledgeable leader, I hope you will contact me soon to suggest a time when we might have a brief discussion of how I could contribute to your organization. I will provide excellent professional and personal references at the appropriate time.

Sincerely,

Stephen Klink

STEPHEN KLINK

1110½ Hay Street, Fayetteville, NC 28305   •   preppub@aol.com   •   (910) 483-6611

OBJECTIVE

I offer exceptional technical and leadership skills to an organization that can use a dedicated team player and creative problem solver knowledgeable of state-of-the-art technology with automated systems, intelligence gathering/analysis, and telecommunications.

EDUCATION & TRAINING

Pursuing a degree in **Computer Science** with Madison Technical Community College and Central Texas College.

Received **Department of Defense technical and leadership training** which included:
Local Area Networks (LAN) Design, Administration, and Management
Basic UNIX and Advanced UNIX
Multichannel Transmission Systems Operation
Basic Noncommissioned Officer and Professional Leadership Development Courses
Intelligence Analyst Course
Jumpmaster training

TECHNICAL EXPERTISE

Equipment and systems: troposcatter, JDISS, Warlord, ASAS (All Source Analysis System), Group Modems, Trunk Group Modems; radios: HF, FM, UHF, and SINCGARS; and KY68, and KIK-13.
Operating systems: UNIX/SOLARIS, LINUX, Windows NT work station/server, Windows.
Software: HTML, Internet Explorer 5.0, Netscape, WordPerfect, Front Page, AMHS, INTEL LINK, Microsoft Exchange Server; MS Word, Excel, Access, Works, PowerPoint.

EXPERIENCE

Advanced to supervisory roles in the Department of Defense:
INTELLIGENCE ANALYST. Washington, DC (2001-present). Utilize analytical skills and automated databases to produce detailed intelligence reports, briefings, and visual aids for organizations involved in counternarcotics actions in Central and South America.

INTELLIGENCE ANALYST and **INFORMATION, PERSONAL, AND PHYSICAL SECURITY PROGRAM INSPECTOR.** Italy (2000-01). Handled dual roles in a Special Forces Group Headquarters: advised and inspected subordinate units for compliance with rules/regulations and further refined briefing skills while also ensuring security and timely production of classified reports and briefings.
• Received superior ratings during numerous inspections while carrying out the error-free processing of more than 1,000 passports, visas, and security clearances.

SUPERVISORY INTELLIGENCE ANALYST. Korea (1998-00). Directly trained, supervised, and mentored subordinates while directing the production, editing, filing, and processing of classified information; indirectly oversaw the same activities for three subordinate units.
• Refined communication skills preparing and presenting briefings to high-level staff officers.
• Applied troubleshooting and technical skills while maintaining LANs, installing and conducting inventories of software, and making hardware repairs.

TELECOMMUNICATIONS TEAM CHIEF. Ft. Gordon, GA (1996-98). Was honored with numerous awards for my accomplishments while supervising and training four people in the installation and maintenance of tropospheric scatter equipment including COMSEC (communications security) devices and equipment.
• Was handpicked to assist in the installation and maintenance of a LAN system.

PERSONAL

Have been entrusted with a **Top Secret/SBI** security clearance. Received awards which included eight cash bonuses for exceptional performance.

Exact Name of Person
Exact Title
Exact Name of Company
Address
City, State, Zip

COMPUTER SPECIALIST

Dear Exact Name of Person (or Dear Sir or Madam if answering a blind ad):

With the enclosed resume, I would like to make you aware of my background as a motivated young professional with exceptional technical and computer skills who offers a track record of accomplishment in the troubleshooting, maintenance, operation, and repair of telecommunications equipment and computer hardware.

Currently excelling as an Operations Specialist with the Department of State in Richmond, VA, I provide computer hardware and software support in addition to my regular duties of scheduling unit training and special events. Earlier as a Systems Support and Automation Specialist, I was cited for efforts in providing communications reliability, described as "vital in maintaining communications during a major exercise." In the same award recommendation, I was recognized for my work in maintaining and repairing computers and for possessing "unsurpassed technical competence."

Prior to joining the military I worked as an Electronics Specialist for Innovative Concepts in Electronics, where I refined my skills related to electronic systems testing and diagnosis while troubleshooting and manufacturing circuit boards and other parts for computer games.

Although many of my technical abilities have been self-taught, I have completed State Department training in the operation, troubleshooting, maintenance, and repair of telecommunications equipment, and I am pursuing a Bachelor of Science in Computer Science.

If you can use a talented telecommunications professional whose technical and computer skills have been proven in challenging environments, I look forward to hearing from you soon. I assure you in advance that I have an excellent reputation and would quickly become an asset to your organization.

Sincerely,

Kyle Myslinsky

KYLE MYSLINSKY

1110½ Hay Street, Fayetteville, NC 28305　•　preppub@aol.com　•　(910) 483-6611

OBJECTIVE

To benefit an organization that can use a motivated and experienced young professional with exceptional technical skills who offers a background in troubleshooting, maintenance, and repair of telecommunications equipment and computers.

EDUCATION

Pursuing a **Bachelor of Science in Computer Science**; have completed one year of this program at Richmond State University, Richmond, VA.

Completed numerous technical and leadership development courses as part of my Department of State training, including telecommunications training as well as a leadership workshop.

COMPUTERS

Familiar with many of the most popular computer operating systems and software, including Windows 95; Microsoft Word, Excel, Access, and PowerPoint; Delrina FormFlow, Calendar Creator, and Anti-virus.

Skilled at troubleshooting, upgrading, and repairing computer hardware, as well as configuring software to work with other programs on the system.

TECHNICAL SKILLS

Skilled in the operation of a number of advanced computer and telecommunications systems including Local Area Networks (LANs), SINCGARS, MSRT, Mobile Subscriber Equipment (MSE), ANCD, Antennas (OE254), and Secure/Unsecure Telephone Systems.

EXPERIENCE

With the Department of State, advanced to positions of increasing responsibility, playing a key role in providing computer and telecommunications service:

1998-present: **OPERATIONS SPECIALIST.** Richmond, VA. Promoted to this position from Systems Support Specialist; provide computer hardware and software support in addition to monitoring and overseeing document control and dispensation and creating, updating, and maintaining personnel files within the organization.

* Developed training schedules, verifying availability of training materials and facilities.

1995-1998: **SYSTEMS SUPPORT & AUTOMATION SPECIALIST.** Baltimore, MD. In addition to troubleshooting, maintaining, and repairing various types of telecommunications equipment, oversaw the proper operation of the organization's 75 computer systems.

* Maintained and repaired a wide variety of radio and telecommunications equipment, to include troubleshooting to the component level, repair, and replacement of defective parts.
* Performed set-up, maintenance, and operation of Local Area Networks (LANs) for the organization, as well as handling software and hardware support.
* Without any formal training, developed a thorough working knowledge of computer hardware and software troubleshooting, repair, maintenance, and configuration.
* Ordered replacements for defective computer components; removed old parts and installed upgrades, new peripherals, or replacements.
* Recognized in an official recommendation for "working more than 32 hours to ensure that the Battle Simulation Center's computers were fully operational . . . as a result, the battalion established the division's first ever HUMINT TACLAND network."

ELECTRONIC SPECIALIST. Innovative Concepts in Electronics (ICE), Tondawanda, NY (1994). Performed troubleshooting and manufacturing of printed circuit boards and other computer parts for commercial video games; developed skills related to the testing of electronic systems and diagnosis of circuit-related malfunctions.

PERSONAL

Entrusted with a Secret clearance. Recognized with several prestigious awards.

Exact Name of Person
Exact Title
Exact Name of Company
Address
City, State, Zip

COMPUTER SPECIALIST

Dear Exact Name of Person (or Dear Sir or Madam if answering a blind ad):

I would appreciate an opportunity to talk with you soon about how I could contribute to your organization through my knowledge of computer hardware and software along with my technical troubleshooting and maintenance skills.

Presently serving the State of New York as a Supervisory Computer Specialist, I supervise four PC Technicians while overseeing computer system maintenance and operations. In this job I am involved in multiple activities in support of LANs (Local Area Networks), personal computers, operating systems, and servers. One of my previous projects was participating in Y2K compliance actions. I analyzed 900 systems, made recommendations and decisions on needed upgrades, and ordered approximately $500,000 worth of equipment needed to ensure all systems met compliance requirements.

As you will see from my enclosed resume, I earned a prestigious award in an earlier job while working on a project for NATO. As a member of a task force sent to Bosnia, I applied my expertise with the ULLS (Unit Level Logistics System) in an automation repair facility where I solved more than 300 software problems. In this job I was singled out to receive two Certificates of Appreciation for my assistance while upgrading computer systems and helping another unit solve its computer problems.

If you can use a self-disciplined professional who can be counted on to provide technical expertise and a high level of knowledge, I hope you will contact me to suggest a time when we might meet to discuss your needs. I can assure you in advance that I could rapidly become an asset to your organization.

Sincerely,

Wayne Luke

WAYNE LUKE

1110½ Hay Street, Fayetteville, NC 28305   •   preppub@aol.com   •   (910) 483-6611

OBJECTIVE

To offer my expertise at troubleshooting computer hardware and software problems and my strong technical abilities to an organization that can use a well-trained and knowledgeable young professional with a reputation as a hard worker and quick learner.

TRAINING

Am attending training courses at Rayford's Computer Services, Falmouth, NY:

Introduction to LAN NT Server 4 "Enterprise"	Windows NT Workstation
Windows NT Server 4 TCP/IP	UNIX Operating System
Internet Information Server MS Exchange E-mail Server	Web Publishing

Excelled in military training for computer programmers in a course which emphasized database programming and development, computer application development and processing, and software troubleshooting techniques, Ft. Gordon, GA, 1997.

MCSE Certification: will test soon for Microsoft Certified Systems Engineer certification.

COMPUTER

Offer experience with the following computer systems, programs, and operating systems:

Windows NT200 4.0 Workstation and Server	UNIX
MS Word, Excel, PowerPoint, and Access	dBase 4
DOS through version 6.22	Harvard Graphics
military supply systems: SAMS, ULLS, and SARSS	WordPerfect

Supervise, install, operate, and perform unit-level maintenance on network servers, multi-function and/or multi-user information processing systems, peripheral equipment, and associated devices in mobile and fixed facilities.

Perform systems analyst, system administrator, and LAN management functions.

Conduct data system studies; prepare documentation and specifications for proposals.

EXPERIENCE

Am earning a reputation for my technical proficiency and knowledge while working for the State of New York:

SUPERVISORY COMPUTER SPECIALIST. New York, NY (1999-present). Supervise four PC Technicians while handling multiple duties which relate to the maintenance and operation of military computer systems.

- Apply technical skills while supervising and personally troubleshooting to the component level, repairing, upgrading, and maintaining PCs.
- Install peripheral equipment and repair printers and notebooks; install software on client systems using Windows NT Server.
- Assist in the design, installation, implementation, and administration of LANs (Local Area Networks), personal computer systems, operating systems, and servers.
- Contributed to the success of unit Y2K compliance actions—analyzed 900 systems, made decisions on what was needed to ensure compliance, and ordered approximately $500,000 worth of equipment needed for upgrades.
- Provide access to new users and assign them a security level which permits them to access information and applications necessary to perform the functions of their job.
- Investigate reports of problems with hardware, software, and peripherals, then coordinate repairs and ensure problems are resolved; provide daily support for services such as printing, e-mail, system backups, disk and printer management, e-mail administration.

COMPUTER PROGRAMMER and **SOFTWARE ANALYST.** Belgium (1997-99). Was recognized as an "exemplary performer" and skilled technician for my expertise shown while troubleshooting software problems in NATO software; upgraded nine computer systems.

PERSONAL

Am self disciplined and can be counted on to follow through and complete the job.

Date

Exact Name of Person
Exact Title
Exact Name of Company
Address
City, State, Zip

COMPUTER TECHNICIAN   Dear Exact Name of Person (or Dear Sir or Madam if answering a blind ad):

With the enclosed resume, I would like to make you aware of my interest in exploring permanent employment opportunities with your organization.

Currently a Technician with Nortel through Manpower Services, I manage the company's enhanced network spares testing for the second shift. I am continuously involved in testing, troubleshooting, and quality assurance as I test, troubleshoot, and monitor finished packs utilizing system test procedures. I have become skilled in working with documentation related to conducting testing according to company protocols.

During the past ten years while working in full-time jobs, I used my spare time to gain knowledge and certifications related to the computer software and hardware field. I am currently CompTIA A+ Certified and am working toward my Certified CISCO Network Associate (CCNA) certification. With long-range plans to earn credentials as a network engineer, one of my immediate goals is to obtain the Microsoft Certified Systems Certificate (MCSE).

I recently completed an Associate of Science degree in Media Integration Technology, and I took courses related to web site design and management, COBOL programming, HTML, software selection and installation, and hardware installation and maintenance. Prior to earning my college degree, I completed college training related to microcomputer troubleshooting and repair as well as television, VCR, and camcorder repair.

Although I am comfortable working in technical environments which require strong technical problem-solving skills, I also offer exceptional communication and management abilities which have been refined in leadership positions. I can provide outstanding personal and professional references.

Yours sincerely,

Rachel Clinton

RACHEL CLINTON

1110½ Hay Street, Fayetteville, NC 28305 • preppub@aol.com • (910) 483-6611

OBJECTIVE

I want to contribute to the growth and profitability of a company that can use a versatile professional with extensive knowledge related to the operations of computer hardware and software along with strong troubleshooting and problem-solving skills.

EDUCATION

Completed *with honors* an **Associate of Science degree in Media Integration Technology,** Western Technical Community College, 2000; completed this degree in my spare time while excelling in my full-time job. Courses included these:

Advanced and Basic Video Concepts   Advanced and Basic Audio Integration
Programming and Logic   Introduction to COBOL Programming
Introduction to HTML   Hardware Installation and Maintenance
Software Selection and Installation   Web Site Design and Management
Multi-Media Presentation Software   Distance Learning & Video Conferencing

Completed **Basic Microcomputer Troubleshooting and Repair;** completed **Advanced Microcomputer Troubleshooting and Repair;** and completed **Television, VCR, and Camcorder Repair,** 1994.

CERTIFICATIONS

Hold the following certification and am pursuing others:
- **CompTIA A+ certified,** Advanced Technologies: June 2000.
- Currently working toward Certified CISCO Network Associate (CCNA).
- Am making plans to work toward the Microsoft Certified Systems Certificate (MCSE).

COMPUTERS

Knowledgeable of operating systems including DOS, WIN3.x, WIN 95, and WIN 98.
Familiar with programs for multi-media applications including Cool Edit for audio editing, Adobe Premier 5.1 for video editing, FrontPage 2000 for web design and management, Excel spreadsheets, Word, and PowerPoint.
Offer training/experience related to Networking Essentials, Windows NT server, Workstation.

EXPERIENCE

COMPUTER TECHNICIAN. Nortel, Charlotte, NC (2000-present). Manage the company's enhanced network spares testing for second shift; perform tests on finished packs utilizing system test procedures.
- Monitor products during heat cycles; run store files and am involved in the process of identifying failures. Test DMS 10/100 equipment per store files.
- Have become skilled in troubleshooting and quality assurance.
- Test, troubleshoot, and monitor spares.
- Have mastered the job of tester and have become skilled in duties performed by a technician; work with technicians, senior technicians, and technical support specialists.
- Utilize multimeters to test voltage; cable and de-cable frames.
- Have become skilled in working with documentation related to conducting testing per STPs, QOPs, and NTPs.
- Have become familiar with the LINUX and ISUS software used by Nortel; have become knowledgeable of the system commands and utilities used in the testing process.

ELECTRONICS REPAIR TECHNICIAN. (1990-99). During the 1990s, pursued college-level training related to software and hardware repair and was self-employed as a repair technician for electronics equipment.

PERSONAL

Highly motivated individual. Excellent references on request. Excellent communication skills.

Exact Name of Person
Title or Position
Name of Company
Address (number and street)
Address (city, state, and zip)

ELECTRICAL ENGINEER

Dear Exact Name of Person: (or Sir or Madam if answering a blind ad.)

With the enclosed resume, I would like to express my interest in exploring employment opportunities with your organization.

As you will see, I am currently serving my country as Foreign Service Officer and am building a track record of superior results and accomplishments while consistently being handpicked for high-visibility managerial roles in telecommunications and automated systems environments. In my present job as Signal Communications Manager, I have led a team of 12 communications specialists to "no faults noted" ratings in four consecutive high-level inspections. In this capacity, I provide oversight for automation architecture, upgrades, and repairs.

I was handpicked for this job from a pool of well-qualified managers on the basis of my accomplishments as manager of a 31-person department which provided uninterrupted signal communications support in real-world emergencies, during training, and in day-to-day operations. For an organization with equipment valued more than $11 million, I managed one of only three teams which passed a major inspection with no deficiencies—on our first attempt.

In my first assignment as a Foreign Service Officer, I quickly earned advancement ahead of my peers based on my strong skills while training, guiding, and mentoring 18 supervisors and 36 employees in a "node center." Previously I earned a B.S. in Electrical Engineering.

If you can use a creative and innovative young management professional with strong experience in managing technical communications operations, I hope you will contact me to suggest a time when we might meet to discuss your needs. I can provide outstanding references at the appropriate time.

Sincerely,

Willie Horton

WILLIE HORTON

1110½ Hay Street, Fayetteville, NC 28305 • preppub@aol.com • (910) 483-6611

OBJECTIVE

To contribute strong technical skills and managerial abilities to an organization that can use an energetic, flexible, and talented professional who is excelling as a military officer.

EDUCATION & TRAINING

B.S., Electrical Engineering, Western California University, San Diego, CA, 1998.
Completed programs in areas including management training and an EMT course.

EXPERIENCE

Am building a track record of success and advancement as a manager of technical communications operations while consistently being handpicked for highly visible managerial roles as a Foreign Service Officer:

SIGNAL COMMUNICATIONS MANAGER. San Diego, CA (2001-present). Was handpicked from among a pool of managers in 17 sister companies to assume this role.

- Supervise and train a team of 12 communications specialists while overseeing automation architecture, upgrades, and repairs.
- Earned evaluation as providing "flawless" management for numerous training events including a project in Panama.
- Earned "no faults noted" ratings during four consecutive high-level inspections including one stating that communications operations evaluations were the "best on record."

SIGNAL OPERATIONS MANAGER. Ft. Edwards, CA (2000-01). Managed a 31-person Contingency Communications Package (CCP) with the mission of providing uninterrupted signal communication support in real-world emergencies, during training, and in day-to-day activities.

- Oversaw maintenance and operation of 20 vehicles, eight high-tech communications systems, and six power generation units with a total value in excess of $11 million.
- Supported three geographically dispersed mission within one three-month period and attained noteworthy results during each operation.
- Received an award for "meritorious achievements" while providing 100% reliable communications support for a project which encompassed the entire U.S. east coast.
- Managed the only one of three teams which passed a joint U.S. Army-Air Force inspection with no deficiencies—on the first attempt.
- Was credited with displaying exceptional organizational and planning skills during preparations for a formal holiday ball for 550 people.
- Was selected to handle the duties of Information Systems Security Manager as well as planning air transportation support for personnel and equipment.

COMMUNICATIONS AND AUTOMATION SERVICES MANAGER. Ft. Edwards, CA (1998-99). Earned rapid advancement ahead of more senior managers from this position based on my strong skills displayed while overseeing operation of a "node center" which provided numerous airborne, medical, artillery, and infantry units with reliable support.

- Trained, guided, and acted as a mentor for 18 supervisors and 36 employees.
- Provided oversight for additional operational areas including information security and physical security as well as crime prevention.
- Evaluated as "calm under high levels of stress," managed training and exercises including a training session where qualification with one specific type of equipment reached the 300% level for a group of 176 participants who had previously scored 50%.

PERSONAL

In excellent physical condition, consistently earn maximum 300 scores during physical fitness testing and have participated in several competitive 10-mile runs.

Date

Exact Name of Person
Exact Title
Exact Name of Company
Address
City, State, Zip

**ELECTRONICS ENGINEERING
STUDENT**

Dear Exact Name of Person (or Dear Sir or Madam if answering a blind ad):

With the enclosed resume, I would like to make you aware of my versatile background and technical abilities as well as my expertise in supervising and managing resources for maximum effectiveness and productivity.

As you will see from my resume, I have served my country in the U.S. Air Force and have acquired considerable knowledge related to electronics. Although I am highly respected for my technical, leadership, managerial, and mechanical skills, I have made the decision to leave military service and return to Texas where I grew up. I am seeking full-time employment and will be pursuing a degree in Electronics Engineering from DeVry Technical Institute in Irving in my spare time. I have received extensive military sponsored training in the specialized field of aerospace ground equipment maintenance and repair while also completing programs in automated systems operations, quality awareness, and leadership development. Prior to entering military service, I gained experience with security systems in two jobs which included installing automotive systems and home security systems.

In my most recent job as a Maintenance Supervisor, I provided technical advice and guidance while overseeing, scheduling, coordinating, and participating in the activities of a 12-person team which inspected and performed maintenance on a $3.3 million inventory of aerospace ground equipment used in support of 33 C-130 aircraft. Consistently described as an innovative and resourceful professional, I have become known for my top-notch skills as a troubleshooter. On many occasions, I saved government funds and manhours by troubleshooting and completing repairs which solved problems and reduced aircraft downtime for costly repairs and services.

If you can use a dependable, assertive, and creative professional who offers excellent resource management and supervisory skills, I hope you will contact me soon to suggest a time when we might meet to discuss your needs. I can assure you in advance that I can provide outstanding references and could quickly become an asset to your organization.

Sincerely,

Richard White

RICHARD WHITE

1110½ Hay Street, Fayetteville, NC 28305   •   preppub@aol.com   •   (910) 483-6611

OBJECTIVE

To contribute to an organization in need of an innovative and assertive leader with expertise in electronics technology and security systems along with a reputation as a meticulous and detail-oriented professional with proven managerial and supervisory skills.

EDUCATION & TRAINING

Pursuing **degree in Electronics Engineering** in my spare time, DeVry Technical Institute, Irving, TX.
Received extensive military training in aerospace ground equipment maintenance and repair as well as in automated systems, leadership development, and quality awareness programs. Completed course work at Tarrant County Technical Community College, Ft. Worth, TX, the University of Maryland, and a program in Fire Protection at Tarrant County Junior College. Graduated from West Hills High School, Fort Worth, TX, 1991.

EXPERIENCE

Advanced to manage and supervise aviation maintenance activities, U.S. Air Force:
MAINTENANCE SUPERVISOR. Pope AFB, TX (2000-02). Provided technical advice and expertise in troubleshooting while supervising and training a 12-person maintenance team inspecting and performing major and minor maintenance on 375 pieces of aerospace ground equipment (AGE) valued in excess of $3.3 million in support of 33 C-130 aircraft.

- Handled a wide range of actions which included planning and organizing maintenance schedules, establishing production controls and standards, interpreting and implementing directions, and making decisions on resource requirements and allocations.
- Utilized drawings, diagrams, schematics, and technical instructions while troubleshooting and resolving problems.
- Polished my computer skills while processing parts requests using the Standard Base Supply Systems (SBSS) and documenting discrepancies using the Core Automated Maintenance and G081 systems.
- Officially cited as "very productive," was instrumental in achieving an all-time high aircraft availability rate of 97% for three consecutive months while personally completing more than 40% of the maintenance tasks considered the most difficult and demanding.
- Applied knowledge of automated systems to design an inventory system which streamlined the process of tracking parts and significantly improved accountability.
- Honored as **"Employee of the Month"** on several occasions and officially described as a superb performer, top-notch troubleshooter, and as extremely resourceful.

ELECTRONICS/AVIONICS SYSTEMS MECHANIC. England (1996-99). Quickly gained respect for my self-motivation while applying technical and mechanical skills inspecting, testing, modifying, maintaining, repairing, and delivering aerospace ground equipment.

- Gained knowledge of the electrical, hydraulic, environmental, and mechanical systems which worked together to ensure the smooth operation of aircraft used worldwide.
- Was credited as a key factor in the unit receiving the highest possible ratings in a NATO evaluation because of my "meticulous attention to detail" in ensuring that more than 50 pieces of equipment were prepared and delivered on time.
- Selected for a special project in Italy, replaced parts which had been taken for other missions and brought equipment availability rate from a low of 49% up to 97%.
- Was cited as a key contributor in efforts which resulted in the **U.S. Air Forces in Europe Maintenance Effectiveness Award.**

PERSONAL

Was entrusted with a **Top Secret** security clearance. Offer outstanding time and resource management skills and an ability to motivate others to achieve 100% production levels.

Date

Exact Name of Person
Exact Title
Exact Name of Company
Address
City, State, Zip

ELECTRONICS MAINTENANCE SUPERVISOR

Dear Exact Name of Person (or Dear Sir or Madam if answering a blind ad):

With the enclosed resume, I would like to make you aware of my background in electronic communications as well as of my related experience in support activities such as personnel training and supervision, budgeting, and records management.

Known for my ability to quickly absorb and then apply technical material, I excelled in more than 1,200 hours of advanced training with an emphasis on central switchboard repair, Mobile Subscriber Equipment (MSE) repair, and network planning hardware maintenance. I also completed college-level course work which resulted in certification in Telecommunications.

During my more than six years of experience in the National Security Agency, I have been promoted ahead of my peers and advanced to supervisory roles. In September 1998, I was promoted to oversee the performance of 24 people as an Electronics Maintenance Supervisor for signal communications equipment. In this job I oversee budget issues, train and supervise personnel, and control a $7 million repair parts inventory.

Earlier as a Shop Foreman, MSE Technician, and Switchboard Repair Technician, I continued to build my skills and base of knowledge. I was often requested by name to assist units going on field exercises or overseas missions because I could be counted on to find the ways to keep equipment operational no matter how difficult the conditions or how high the level of pressure.

If you can use an experienced, innovative, and dedicated electronic communications professional, I hope you will contact me to suggest a time when we might meet to discuss your needs. I can assure you in advance that I could rapidly become an asset to your organization.

Sincerely,

Charles Stout

CHARLES STOUT

1110½ Hay Street, Fayetteville, NC 28305 • preppub@aol.com • (910) 483-6611

OBJECTIVE

To contribute my technical skills and knowledge of electronic communications systems for the benefit of an organization that can use a resourceful, creative, and detail-oriented professional accustomed to maintaining and servicing state-of-the-art systems.

EDUCATION & TRAINING

Certificate in Telecommunications, Baltimore Community College, Baltimore, MD, 1997. Excelled in more than 1,200 hours of specialized training which included:

29N Switching Central Repairer, 700 hours   DC Electronics, 120 hours

Enable, 40 hours

Mobile Subscriber Equipment (MSE) telephone central office repair, 312 hours

Network Planning Terminal (NPT) hardware maintenance course, 40 hours

KNOWLEDGE

Through training and experience, have become familiar with procedures and equipment which include, but are not limited to, the following:

Configuring, troubleshooting, and activating communications networks using automated tools, fault isolation and resolution, and proper documentation

Coordinating and performing maintenance activities, circuit activation, and hardware installation and configuration

Applying knowledge of IP, frame relay, ATM, ISDN, E1, E3, STMA, routers, ATM switches, terminal servers, dial-up networking technologies, and routing protocols

Operating and repairing equipment such as AN/TTC-41, 46, 47, and 48, AN/TTC-50 and 51, SB-22, AN/TYQ-46, CV-4002/G, AN/GRC-224 (V), AN/TSQ-154, AN/TTC-39D, AN/TTC-39A, commercial ESS equipment, NEP: SMART-T, SMU Switch, and START-T, TA-954.

EXPERIENCE

Advanced ahead of my peers to supervisory role with the National Security Agency, Washington, DC:
ELECTRONICS MAINTENANCE SUPERVISOR. (1998-present). Was promoted in September 1998 to supervise 24 people including five more-junior supervisors while providing direct support maintenance for signal communications equipment to include a repair parts inventory valued in excess of $7 million.

- Oversee the Microwave Systems Repair & Maintenance, Network Switching Systems, and Communications Security/Radio Repair Sections while ensuring high standards of customer service and technical support; manage budgetary issues.

SHOP FOREMAN, MOBILE SUBSCRIBER EQUIPMENT SYSTEMS. (1998). Supervised and participated in maintenance and repair of sophisticated telecommunications equipment.

SUPERVISORY MSE TECHNICIAN AND MAINTAINER. (1993-97). Supervised four people while installing, operating, and maintaining MSE systems as well as maintaining and controlling more than $1 million worth of test equipment and repair parts.

- Trained personnel in the employment and operation of equipment as well as handling administrative duties related to scheduling work and keeping supply and inventory logs.
- Graduated from a professional leadership course and became qualified to supervise.
- Installed equipment in field locations and was often requested by name to cross train personnel and provide expertise during field exercises and overseas missions.

CENTRAL SWITCHBOARD REPAIR TECHNICIAN. (1992-93). Performed direct and general support maintenance on switching equipment, wire systems, and interface equipment.

PERSONAL

Outstanding personal and professional references on request.

Exact Name of Person
Title or Position
Name of Company
Address (number and street)
Address (city, state, and zip)

**ELECTRONICS
MANAGEMENT
GRADUATE**

Dear Exact Name of Person: (or Sir or Madam if answering a blind ad.)

With the enclosed resume, I would like to make you aware of my interest in becoming part of your teaching faculty and make you aware of my strong qualifications.

As you will see from my resume, I offer extensive experience in formal classroom instruction. While serving in the U.S. Army, I was specially selected to become an instructor at the U.S. Army Signal School. In classrooms of varying sizes, I trained both entry-level and advanced students in repair and maintenance techniques related to electronics and computer equipment. In consultation with 12 other instructors, I worked as part of a "teaching team" and was frequently consulted by other instructors because of my reputation as "the resident expert" on all communications and electronics equipment.

Prior to becoming an instructor, I was a respected bench repairman, field service technician, and shop supervisor.

In other previous experience, I refined my communication skills while excelling as a Recruiter and Managing Recruiter. I received numerous awards for exceeding sales quotas in terms of the quantity and quality of individuals recruited, and I continuously worked with junior recruiters to help them refine their skills in time management. In the process of preparing and delivering dozens of speeches at high schools and community events, I became a skilled public speaker.

My career interest now lies in the area of teaching and training others, and I can assure you that I have a knack for "translating" complex concepts into language which is understandable by newcomers to the field. I can assure you that I also have a gift for motivating others.

If you can use a reliable and experienced professional to join your teaching staff, I hope you will call or write me to suggest a time when we might meet in person to discuss your needs. Thank you in advance for your time.

Sincerely,

William Duff

WILLIAM DUFF

1110½ Hay Street, Fayetteville, NC 28305   •   preppub@aol.com   •   (910) 483-6611

OBJECTIVE

To contribute to an organization that can benefit from my extensive experience in teaching and training others, as well as my technical expertise related to electronics and avionics.

EDUCATION

Bachelor of Science degree in **Electronics Management**, Alfred University at Alfred, NY, 1996; graduated **cum laude**, with a **3.6 cumulative GPA**.
- Courses included Optical Electronics, Systems Design and Development, Industrial Safety, Advanced Electronics, and Navigation/Communication Systems.

Completed extensive U.S. Army training including Air Traffic Control Equipment Repair Course and Aircraft Navigation and Stabilization Equipment Repair Course.

EXPERIENCE

INSTRUCTOR & SUPERVISING INSTRUCTOR. U.S. Army Signal School, Ft. Sill, OK (1998-01). Because of my vast technical knowledge and outstanding communication skills, was selected to train both entry-level and advanced students at the famed U.S. Army Signal School; supervised other instructors.
- Taught air traffic control equipment maintenance, repair, and operation.
- Developed and implemented lesson plans which became known for their clarity; became skilled in translating technical and abstract concepts into understandable language.
- Learned how to tailor lesson plans to the varying skill and proficiency levels of my students.
- In consultation with up to 12 other instructors, worked as part of a "teaching team" and was frequently consulted by other instructors because of my reputation as the "resident expert" on the technical capabilities of all equipment.
- Trained individuals to utilize schematics and diagrams in diagnosing malfunctions and in performing repairs "by the book."
- Worked with organizations in field environments to evaluate the proficiency of students we had trained; then used those field assessments to refine and revise our lesson plans.
- Trained dozens of students in tasks including reading schematic diagrams, analyzing circuits, and troubleshooting analog and digital equipment.

RECRUITER & TERRITORY MANAGER. U.S. Army, Memphis, TN (1994-99). Refined my ability to motivate and persuade while marketing the advantages of a military career to high school students; received numerous awards for exceeding sales quotas in terms of the numbers of recruits and in terms of the quality of the individuals recruited.

Other experience: In prior Army experience, worked as a bench repairman, field service technician, and shop supervisor. Installed avionics equipment at airfields throughout the country. Played a key role in installing the first terminal VOR at the largest U.S. military base. Became a highly respected troubleshooter and trained numerous individuals to use technical manuals to diagnose malfunctions.

PERSONAL

Can provide outstanding references. Held Secret security clearance. Highly effective at motivating and coaching others. Enjoy the process of developing junior professionals.

Dear Sir or Madam:

I would appreciate an opportunity to talk with you soon about how I could contribute to your organization through my technical expertise as well as my attention-to-detail, troubleshooting, and analytical problem-solving skills.

As you will see from my resume, I have skills and abilities that would make me a valuable employee. While working as a Field Radio Repair Technician, Vehicle Safety Inspector, Technical Inspector, and Communications Instructor, I excelled in a track record of promotion to increasing responsibilities with Black & Decker.

My extensive technical training has included a Solid State Electronics Course, Basic and Advanced Injection Molding, Material Handling, machine operations, training as a Radio Repairman, and other training.

I feel certain that you would find me to be a hard-working and reliable professional who prides myself on doing any job to the best of my ability.

I hope you will call or write me soon to suggest a time convenient for us to meet and discuss your current and future needs and how I might serve them. Thank you in advance for your time.

Sincerely yours,

Mark Goodman

MARK GOODMAN

1110½ Hay Street, Fayetteville, NC 28305　•　preppub@aol.com　•　(910) 483-6611

OBJECTIVE　To benefit an organization that can use a talented electronics technician who offers exceptional attention to detail and analytical problem-solving skills.

EXPERIENCE　**ELECTRONICS REPAIR TECHNICIAN & ELECTRICIAN'S HELPER.** Eastern TV & Stereo, New York, NY (1998-present). Repair televisions, VCRs, and stereos using various test equipment; also work as an Electrician's Helper.

Gained valuable hands-on technical and supervisory skills while working for Black & Decker:
FIELD RADIO REPAIR TECHNICIAN (1990-98). Repaired, maintained, and tested all AM/FM equipment including power supplies, tools, jewelers, electronics equipment, and hand tools; performed final inspection on all equipment leaving the shop.
* Trained personnel in operating, repairing, maintaining, and testing all AM/FM equipment including power supplies.
* Received an award for 0% of jobs being returned to the shop for malfunctions.
* Reduced backlog down to nearly 0%.

COMMUNICATIONS SUPERVISOR (1995-97). Advised and made recommendations on operations and maintenance; maintained, tested, and repaired communications equipment.
* Ensured that, during all field exercises, the communications operations met standards.
* Oversaw $50,000 in equipment.
* As **Unit Morale Representative,** ensured that morale throughout the unit was at its highest level, organized unit functions, and recommended methods of increasing participation.
* As **Vehicle Safety Inspector,** performed detailed vehicle safety inspections by strict guidelines; informed executives on the status of vehicles; provided assistance in the repair of vehicles to ensure they passed inspection.
* As **Technical Inspector,** inspected out-dated radio equipment turned in for replacement for newer models; kept supervisors informed; trained personnel in proper inspection procedures.
* Supervised employees during the inspection process.

COMMUNICATIONS INSTRUCTOR (1994-95). Taught operation and repair of AM/FM equipment and power supplies; provided training/supervision on uploading communications security in the new FM radio; maintained unit cohesiveness in the area of unit communications.

SHOP FOREMAN (1994). Ensured that all equipment was properly maintained according to regulated standards; accurately recorded all broken equipment and ensured maintenance was completed; kept executives abreast on weekly status of equipment.

EDUCATION　Solid State Electronics Course (240 hours), Forest Hills Community Technical College, 1997.
Completed Basic Injection Molding 1-5 and Advanced Injection Molding 1-6; was trained in Material Handling, machine operations, inventory control, and supervisory techniques.
Completed ANGRC-193 four-week course, Caison, NY, 1991.
Completed comprehensive six-month Field Radio Repair Course, Caison, NY, 1990.

TECHNICAL　Can install/operate/maintain/troubleshoot/repair digital multimeters, frequency counters, signal
SKILLS　generators, oscilloscopes, ANGRM-114 and -114B test sets, watt meters, various hand tools, and AM/FM radios. Proficient in troubleshooting systems housed in various shelters.

Date

Raytheon
P.O. Box 6056
Greenville, TX 75403
Attn: Mr. Smith

Dear Mr. Smith:

With the enclosed resume, I would like to make you aware of my knowledge of and education in communications and fiber optic technology, and to express my strong interest in offering my skills to your company. I recently spoke with a former Raytheon employee, Mr. Lonzo G. Bustos, and he recommended that I forward my resume to your attention.

As you will see, I have just completed my Associate's Degree in Electronics Technology. My major area of concentration was Communications and Fiber Optics. I have worked with fiber optics previously while employed by Quanta Systems on a contract job in which we installed optical module boxes and fiber optic cable along a 5-mile perimeter.

Though my previous work experience is not as highly technical in nature, I think you will see that I have proven myself to be a hard-working and reliable employee as well as a capable supervisor. Most of the jobs shown on my resume were jobs I held while simultaneously completing courses toward my A.S. degree. Now that I have finished my degree, I am anxious to utilize my knowledge of communications and fiber optics technology. My strong work ethic, education, and technical know-how would be an asset to your organization.

If you can use a highly motivated, intelligent young communications and fiber optics professional, I hope you will contact me to suggest a convenient time when we might meet to discuss your present and future needs, and how I might meet them.

Sincerely,

Pete Dawkins

PETE DAWKINS

1110½ Hay Street, Fayetteville, NC 28305   •   preppub@aol.com   •   (910) 483-6611

OBJECTIVE   To benefit an organization that can use a motivated young professional with a strong desire to utilize his knowledge and education in communications and fiber optic technology.

EDUCATION   **Associate of Applied Science Degree in Electronics Technology**; majored in Communications/Fiber Optics, Pennsylvania College of Technology, 2000.
- Excelled in a variety of state-of-the art communications courses, including the following:

Microprocessor Interfacing	Analog Communications
Microprocessor Applications	Digital Communications
Network Installation & Maintenance	Microwave Communications
Network Maintenance Lab	Optical Communications

EXPERIENCE   **ASSISTANT MANAGER.** Freshest Ever, Baltimore, MD (1999-present). Support the manager in the operation of this busy oriental food market and restaurant.
- Supervise up to 8 employees.
- Responsible for register till balancing and closing reports, as well as cash register operation and customer service.
- Perform all aspects of food preparation, including prep, deep fry, and grill cooking.
- Stock and shelve the market area, insuring full and attractive displays.

CARPENTER'S ASSISTANT. Ken's Services, Baltimore, MD (1997-99). Carried out various remodeling assignments while pursuing my degree.
- Assisted in the construction phase of remodeling projects.
- Performed framing and finish construction, including the installation of floor systems, window and door headers, roofing systems, etc.
- Operated circular saws, reciprocating saws, drills, and other power tools.
- Responsible for material handling; job required some heavy lifting and carrying of construction supplies.

ELECTRONIC TECHNICIAN. Quanta Systems, Gaithersburg, MD (1997). Worked under a certified electronic technician with Quanta Systems on a contract job.
- Assembled optical module boxes for long-distance fiber relays.
- Installed optical modules boxes and fiber optic cable along the fence line of a 5-mile perimeter.

PRODUCTION WORKER. Sterman Masser's, Baltimore, MD (1996). Worked on the assembly line of this busy produce company.
- Operated the production line, packaging potatoes for shipment.
- Maintained and repaired assembly line machinery.

GROUNDS LABORER. Simmons Army Airfield, Fort Bragg, NC (1996). While in high school, performed grounds keeping and landscaping duties during the summer.
- Operated various power landscaping equipment.
- Conducted routine maintenance and minor repairs of machinery.

PERSONAL   Known as a reliable, hard-working employee who is willing to take on additional responsibility. Excellent personal and professional references are available.

Date

Exact Name of Person
Exact Title
Exact Name of Company
Address
City, State, Zip

FIBER OPTICS INSTRUCTOR   Dear Exact Name of Person: (or Dear Sir or Madam if answering a blind ad):

With the enclosed resume, I would like to make you aware of my exceptional technical skills as well as my strong background as a highly skilled information systems professional.

As you will see from my resume, I have earned a Master of Science in Computer Systems Engineering, graduating summa cum laude with a cumulative GPA of 3.9. I have further augmented my education with numerous technical courses, including Lifespan 2000/2012 fiber optics systems, Novell NetWare Systems Administrator 4.0 (LAN), and Microsoft courses in Network Essentials, NT Server & Workstation, Exchange . SQL, SMS, and TCP/IP. In addition, I have extensive military training in the telecommunications field including courses in Mobile Subscriber Equipment and Tactical Satellite/Microwave Systems.

Recently I have excelled as a Fiber Optics Instructor, traveling worldwide to provide corporate training and technical support in installation, troubleshooting, maintenance, and configuration of ACCESS family fiber optic systems to customers worldwide which include Sprint, MCI, AT&T, and others. In previous positions, I have designed and implemented corporate Wide Area Networks and managed an ISDN technical support center for GTE, providing technical assistance with modem and terminal adapter configurations including Frame Relay, T1, and T-3 systems.

You will also see from my resume that I was Project Manager for the implementation of a $500 million Novell LAN and provided training, supervision, and oversight for GTE-Mobile Subscriber Equipment training as well as authoring a number of training materials for Army leadership development and management courses.

If you can use a highly skilled information telecommunications and information systems professional, I hope you will welcome my call soon when I try to arrange a brief meeting to discuss your goals and how my background might serve your needs. I can provide outstanding references at the appropriate time.

Sincerely,

Steven Hutt

STEVEN HUTT

1110½ Hay Street, Fayetteville, NC 28305   •   preppub@aol.com   •   (910) 483-6611

OBJECTIVE

To contribute exceptionally strong technical aptitude and education to an organization that can use a skilled manager, trainer, and hands-on information systems/communications professional.

EDUCATION

Master of Science in Computer Systems Engineering, Dalton College, Dalton, GA, 2000; graduated **summa cum laude**, with a **3.9 cumulative GPA**.
Bachelor of Science in Business Management, University of Maryland, College, Park, 1996.

TECHNICAL SKILLS

Completed technical training in the following areas: Litespan 2000/2012 fiber optics systems, 2001; Microsoft Network Essentials, NT Server & Workstation , Exchange , SQL, SMS, and TCP/IP; Novell NetWare Systems Administrator 4.0 (LAN), 1997; Signal Operations Advanced Course, 1995; Mobile Communications Course (GTE), 1995; and Tactical Satellite/Microwave Systems Operator Course.

EXPERIENCE

FIBER OPTICS INSTRUCTOR. Alcatel USA, Dallas, TX (2001-present). Travel worldwide providing corporate training in installation, troubleshooting, maintenance, and configuration of fiber optics systems within the ACCESS family using Lifespan 2000/2012; interface with ISDN, ADSL, DS1, and DS3 configurations.
- Perform training and support services while working closely with corporate accounts which include Bell South, Sprint, MCI, AT&T, Southwestern Bell, and U.S. West.

NETWORK DEVELOPER & MANAGER. ARIS Corporation, Dallas, TX (2000-01). Planned, analyzed, and implemented corporate wide area networks, applying extensive knowledge of various network engineering tools in the creation of custom systems to provide appropriate information management solutions for each client company.
- Implemented the installation of Exchange Server 5.0 while heavily involved in the Texas rollout for the U.S. Government; worked on a Site Server project in Houston, Texas.
- Traveled to Washington, DC to provide support to a six-week intensive training course for students seeking the Microsoft Certified Systems Engineer certification.

ISDN GROUP MANAGER. Prime Internet Solutions, Irving, TX (1999-00). Supervised more than 50 technical support representatives, advising them on matters related to networking systems and configurations under OS/2, Windows NT2000, DOS and Macintosh operating systems; ensured customer satisfaction while representing GTE in a supervisory role.
- Directed technical support providing assistance with configuring modems and terminal adapters including Frame Relay and T1 & T3 configurations; worked extensively with TCP/IP, Netbeui, IPX/SPX, and PPTP configurations.

TECHNICAL SUPPORT REPRESENTATIVE. Stream International, Dallas, TX (1998-99). Provided technical support to CompuServe customers and colleagues, improving the productivity of the department by maintaining the highest level of product knowledge.

NETWORK ADMINISTRATOR. Ft. Leavenworth, KS (1992-98). Was the principle supervisor and technical advisor on a $500 million government project, personally receiving bids for the installation of a Novell Local Area Network (LAN).
- Served as Operations Manager for the Department of Defense Source Selection Evaluation Board; was personally accountable for more than $300,000 in equipment.
- Troubleshot, maintained, repaired, and upgraded computer systems to include installing hardware, software, and peripherals to local and wide area network servers and workstations.

PERSONAL

Excellent personal and professional references on request.

Exact Name of Person
Exact Title
Exact Name of Company
Address
City, State, Zip

**FORCED ENTRY SWITCH
SECTION SUPERVISOR**

Dear Exact Name of Person (or Dear Sir or Madam if answering a blind ad):

With the enclosed resume, I would like to make you aware of my background in supervising technical communications operations and of my accomplishments in training, guiding, and motivating personnel to work together to exceed goals and expectations.

As you will see from my resume, I have built a reputation as a talented, positive, and articulate professional while consistently excelling in positions usually reserved for higher ranking and more experienced personnel. Although I am being aggressively recruited to remain with my current employer and assured of continued advancement to positions of higher responsibility, I am selectively exploring opportunities with leading companies.

I have had the opportunity to be involved in the fielding of new equipment and integration of new systems into the military's inventory. I helped field the Mobile Subscriber Equipment (MSE) as it was first introduced. I also helped field the SINCGARS (Single Channel Ground and Airborne Radio System) and participated in all upgrades to that system which have occurred over the last 10 years. A quick learner who easily masters new technology, I have developed and conducted classes which have trained others on new systems, including a class which allowed 680 people to develop knowledge of SINCGARS system operations.

With exceptional time management skills and high levels of self-motivation and initiative, I have completed 40 semester hours of college credit in pursuit of a bachelor's degree in my spare time. Proficient with UNIX-based systems using Sun software, I offer expertise related to Cisco routers, packet switching, the dismounted Line-Of-Sight transmission system, COMSEC, forced entry switches, and fiber optics.

If you can use an experienced and technically proficient professional who has consistently been recognized as a reliable and honest individual, I hope you will contact me soon to suggest a time when we might meet to discuss your needs. I can assure you in advance that I can provide outstanding references and could quickly become an asset to your organization.

Sincerely,

Doug Kenna

DOUG KENNA

1110½ Hay Street, Fayetteville, NC 28305 • preppub@aol.com • (910) 483-6611

OBJECTIVE

To offer my exceptional supervisory and technical telecommunications skills to an organization that can benefit from my decision-making, motivational, and instructional abilities as well as my reputation as a versatile and creative professional.

EDUCATION, TRAINING, & TECHNICAL EXPERTISE

Have completed 40 semester hours of college credit in pursuit of a bachelor's degree.

Received training in leadership and instructional techniques as well as technical training in hazardous materials handling, combat life saving, and the following:

Cisco routers/fiber optics – General Dynamics   ESOP switch upgrades — GTE
SINCGARS radio upgrade (Single Channel Ground and Airborne System)

Supervise, install, maintain, and operate the Mobile Subscriber Equipment switch into an integrated network system and am proficient with UNIX-based systems using Sun software, Cisco routers, packet switching, COMSEC (communications security), Line-Of-Sight (LOS) transmission systems, remote access units, node center switches, LAN, and forced entry switches.

EXPERIENCE

With DynaTel, Inc., a leading government contractor, have been handpicked for positions usually held by more senior professionals, and have been in the forefront of the development and integration of some of the most advanced telecommunications equipment:

FORCED ENTRY SWITCH SECTION SUPERVISOR. San Diego, CA (2000-present). Supervise a 10-person team of cable repair, switch, and transmission operators while controlling a $23.8 million equipment inventory.

- Received several awards including recognition for exceptional results during several training exercises and Humanitarian Service Medals for efforts during hurricane relief activities.
- Supervise and personally install and operate Line-Of-Sight (LOS) multichannel radio terminals, extension switches, and generator sets.
- In 2000, have developed classes designed to teach the unit's 680 people how to use the SINCGARS system after attending a training program for system instructors.
- Because of my instruction, the battalion has experienced no problems in using the new menu-driven SINCGARS (ASIP) system during its last three field exercises.
- Simultaneously excelling in meeting or exceeding quotas, have become skilled in sales as Internal Corporate Recruiter and, in March 2000, was at 166% of my quarterly goal, the highest percentage in the organization.

TELECOMMUNICATIONS TEAM CHIEF. Washington, DC (1995-99). Promoted ahead of my peers to supervise five people, managed equipment valued in excess of $3 million.

- Achieved a perfect safety record for personnel and equipment during the first-ever parachute drop of the unique dismounted LOS transmission system.

TRANSMISSION SYSTEMS TEAM CHIEF. England (1993-95). Was the honor graduate of a 220-student international management course during a period when I supervised a $1.2 million, three-person LOS team and a $2 million, two-person remote access team.

TRANSMISSION SYSTEMS OPERATOR AND MAINTAINER. Belgium (1992-93). Received 30 weeks of hands-on and classroom training and became qualified in the operation of the Mobile Subscriber Equipment (MSE) and contributed during fielding of this system.

PERSONAL

Have been awarded numerous cash bonuses and certificates for exceptional performance.

Exact Name of Person
Exact Title
Exact Name of Company
Address
City, State, Zip

HARDWARE REPAIR SPECIALIST

Dear Exact Name of Person: (or Dear Sir or Madam if answering a blind ad):

With the enclosed resume, I would like to introduce you to my considerable technical and mechanical skills as well as my reputation as a highly self-motivated and results-oriented young professional.

As you will see from my resume, I am working for McDonnell Douglas Aircraft Corporation and have earned the respect of superiors and peers for my ability to quickly learn and master new procedures and equipment. Currently assigned as an Aircraft Instrumentation and Telemetry System Technician, I was nominated for early promotion based on my job knowledge and leadership. I have been credited with playing a major role in the success of a unit which has won numerous honors including the governor's award for "Quality in the Workplace," a high-level maintenance effectiveness award, and an "Outstanding Unit Award."

Selected for special projects and teams, I have participated in the development of aircraft modifications and earned recognition from the Undersecretary of Defense and the McDonnell Douglas Aircraft Corporation for my efforts. One of my special projects was applying technical expertise to complete modifications on cockpit cameras.

If you can use a self starter with excellent electronics and mechanical skills along with the ability to work independently or as a contributor to team efforts, I hope you will welcome my call soon when I try to arrange a brief meeting to discuss your goals and how my background might serve your needs. I can provide outstanding references at the appropriate time.

Sincerely,

Michael Irvin

Alternate Last Paragraph:
I hope you will write or call me soon to suggest a time when we might meet to discuss your needs and goals and how my background might serve them. I can provide outstanding references at the appropriate time.

MICHAEL IRVIN

1110½ Hay Street, Fayetteville, NC 28305   •   preppub@aol.com   •   (910) 483-6611

OBJECTIVE

To offer well-developed electronics, troubleshooting, and mechanical skills to an organization that can use a quick learner who produces results while working independently or as a contributor to team efforts.

TECHNICAL KNOWLEDGE

Ability to troubleshoot and repair to the component level electronic, mechanical, and electro-mechanical devices with analog and digital circuitry.
Operate test equipment including:
    oscilloscope DMM   hand-held bus monitor   power meter TRD   spectrum analyzer
Offer additional skills in calibration, controlling COMSEC (communications security), DECOMM programming (converting bit stream into words and frames), and repairing and maintaining the Advanced Airborne Test Instrumentation System.

EXPERIENCE

INSTRUMENTATION AND TELEMETRY SYSTEM TECHNICIAN. McDonnell Douglas Aircraft Corporation, San Diego, CA (1994-present). Cited for my technical knowledge and take-charge attitude, have advanced to perform maintenance, calibration, and operation as well as prelaunch and recovery checks on the instrumentation systems of 12 flight test center F-15 aircraft.

- Was cited as a key reason the air base was the winner of the California Governor's "Golden State Quality Award for Quality in the Workplace."
- Applied my technical expertise in a special project to modify two cockpit cameras in order to provide real-time worldwide video coverage during the re-enactment of supersonic flight accomplishments.
- Have made direct contributions to the success of search-and-rescue flights for downed pilots by installing, operating, and maintaining Global Positioning Tracking Systems in 25 helicopters used by a joint services search-and-rescue test program.
- Interpret electrical and mechanical engineering schematics and drawings while installing and modifying complex instrumentation systems.
- Made contributions which led to the unit winning both a major maintenance effectiveness award and the "Outstanding Unit Award" in 1996.
- Developed expert knowledge of modifications to the aircraft's Visually Coupled Acquisition Targeting System which led to my selection as the instrumentation technician assigned to accompany the aircraft to other test locations worldwide.
- Nominated for early promotion ahead of my peers, was described in an official evaluation as possessing "the most job knowledge and leadership qualities" despite being the junior member of the team.
- Received a **Letter of Commendation from the Undersecretary of Defense** for my contributions to the success of the joint search-and-rescue team.
- Was acknowledged by McDonnell Douglas Aircraft Corporation for my contributions and service during a radar update test program.
- Volunteer in community activities which include sponsoring a child in the Special Olympics and serving as a role model for members of my church's youth programs.

Highlights of earlier civilian experience:
As a Field Representative, had extensive public contact while inspecting buildings before and after demolition projects, Premier Engineering, Philadelphia, PA, 1992-94.

PERSONAL

Was entrusted with a Secret security clearance. Earned a Joint Service Achievement Medal for "meritorious achievements" during a training exercise.

Date

Exact Name of Person
Exact Title
Exact Name of Company
Address
City, State, Zip

Dear Exact Name of Person: (or Dear Sir or Madam if answering a blind ad):

With the enclosed resume, I would like to make you aware of my background as an experienced network manager with extensive training and exceptional technical skills related to local and wide area network maintenance. I am skilled in areas including but not limited to hardware upgrading, maintenance, and repair as well as software installation and configuration.

As you will see from my resume, I have excelled in technical training programs which included courses on Introduction to LAN "Network Essentials," Microsoft TCP/IP, and Windows NT Server 4.0.

I have supplemented this formal training with extensive hands-on experience in set-up, maintenance, and administration of Local and Wide Area Networks using Windows, Windows NT2000 Server, and TCP/IP. Other training was related to Exchange Server, Enterprise, and numerous other network and workstation applications. In addition, my comprehensive knowledge of hardware upgrading, maintenance, configuration, and repair has been tested in challenging situations both in office and field environments.

After completing two years of college coursework, I am pursuing completion of a Bachelor of Science in Management Information Systems (MIS) in my spare time. I am also currently preparing to take the six-test battery of examinations leading to certification as a Microsoft Certified Systems Engineer.

If you can use a highly skilled information systems professional with exceptional technical skills in hardware, software, and network administration, I hope you will welcome my call soon when I try to arrange a brief meeting to discuss your goals and how my background might serve your needs. I can provide outstanding references at the appropriate time.

Sincerely,

John Tessler

JOHN TESSLER

1110½ Hay Street, Fayetteville, NC 28305   •   preppub@aol.com   •   (910) 483-6611

OBJECTIVE

To contribute to an organization that can benefit from my technical expertise and extensive training as well as my background of experience in network management.

EDUCATION, TRAINING, & CERTIFICATIONS

Pursuing **Bachelor of Science** degree in **Management Information Systems (MIS)** in my spare time; have completed approximately two years of course work at two colleges.

Excelled in training technical training in the following areas:

Introduction to LAN "Network Essentials"	Microsoft TCP/IP
Hands-on Windows NT	Windows NT Server 4.0
Microsoft PowerPoint	Harvard Graphics for Windows

Through training and experience, have become familiar with and knowledgeable of **network management** from bulletin board systems, to peer-to-peer networks, to a 250-user network. Am skilled in client and server hardware/software system configuration and troubleshooting:

Operating systems: Windows NT2000 Server, Windows NT Workstation, and TCP/IP
Administration: Windows NT2000 Server, Exchange Server and Enterprise, TCP/IP, and Internet Information Server
Applications: Microsoft Office, FrontPage, Outlook, Internet Explorer, and FTP Explorer

Currently preparing to take the battery of tests leading to **Certification as a Microsoft Certified Systems Engineer.**

EXPERIENCE

Have earned a reputation as a technically proficient young professional, General Dynamics Company:

AUTOMATION MANAGEMENT OFFICE SECTION SUPERVISOR. Philadelphia, PA (2000-present). Administer both local and wide area networks valued in excess of $250,000 while supervising eight people and managing the operations of secure e-mail and web server systems as an Information Systems Analyst.

- Have served as the **Senior Network Administrator** for an NT network which services approximately 250 users.
- Load and configure user systems for a LAN using Windows NT2000 Workstation , TCP/IP, Internet Explorer , and Microsoft Outlook .
- Determine equipment and software needs; supervise user system configurations.
- Was a key contributor during the conversion to Windows NT2000 from a peer-to-peer system.
- Received a cash bonus for my performance in supervising the operation of the Automation Help Desk during an international project.
- Was praised in writing for my strong customer service skills in diagnosing and resolving problems as the only mid-level manager in the JCCC Automation Support Branch.
- As a junior manager selected for a job usually reserved for a senior manager, was praised for "performing flawlessly" and for "accepting any challenge placed before her."

INFORMATION SYSTEMS ANALYST and **TEAM LEADER.** Baltimore, MD (1996-00). Provided leadership for six people while applying my technical knowledge upgrading, maintaining, repairing, and installing new hardware and peripherals including hard drives, sound cards, video cards, memory, and modems.

- Converted a 250-system network from Windows 3.11 to Windows 95 and then to Windows NT while also assisting with 1,500 systems with their upgrades.
- Installed a variety of software applications as well as troubleshooting and resolving conflicts with hardware and software; supervised help desks locally and while deployed in support of missions; ensured uninterrupted LAN service support for 75 users.

PERSONAL

Entrusted with a Secret security clearance with Top Secret pending.

Exact Name of Person
Exact Title
Exact Name of Company
Address
City, State, Zip

MICROSOFT CERTIFIED PROFESSIONAL

Dear Exact Name of Person (or Dear Sir or Madam if answering a blind ad):

With the enclosed resume, I would like to make you aware of my interest in exploring employment opportunities with your organization. After completing nearly 10 years of distinguished federal service—and although I was strongly encouraged to remain in the Department of Defense—I have decided to resign and I am relocating to your area. I am seeking employment in the private sector.

In spite of a hectic schedule which involved frequent travel for training projects and worldwide missions, I completed nearly two years of college course work while excelling in my full-time positions. Most recently, I have completed courses at a Microsoft Certified Education Center, and I am in the process of obtaining my Microsoft Certified System Engineer (MCSE). On my own initiative, I recently structured a local area computer network which enabled my company to economize on scarce resources by efficiently sharing data and peripherals. I offer knowledge of computer operations and computer network systems.

After beginning federal service, I was quickly identified as a leader and promoted ahead of my peers. I excelled in supervisory roles in engineering and other organizations, and the numerous awards I received praised my ability to mentor junior employees and inspire them to excel. I flawlessly maintained accountability of up to $500,000 in assets and was noted for my "aggressive emphasis on maintenance and safety."

My troubleshooting and problem-solving skills are strong, and I have applied them in reducing maintenance backlogs as well as in organizing and managing special projects designed to improve the technical skills of employees. I am highly proactive in seeking out opportunities for self-improvement and for advancement of my skills and knowledge.

If you can use a highly motivated self-starter with unlimited personal initiative, I hope you will contact me to suggest a time when we might discuss your needs. I can provide excellent references.

Yours sincerely,

Kenny Stevens

KENNY STEVENS

1110½ Hay Street, Fayetteville, NC 28305　　•　　preppub@aol.com　　•　　(910) 483-6611

OBJECTIVE

To benefit an organization that can use a highly motivated young professional with knowledge of computer operations and computer network systems along with exceptional problem-solving ability, communication skills, and management experience.

LANGUAGES

Fluently speak, read, and write Spanish; read and understand some Portuguese and German.

EDUCATION

Completed two years of coursework toward Bachelor's degree, University of Maryland and North Central Institute; am finishing degree in spare time.
Completed these courses at Microsoft Certified Education Center, Annapolis, MD:
- 922 Supporting Microsoft Windows, NT 4.0 Core Technologies
- 578 Networking Essentials
- 803 Administrating Microsoft Windows NT 4.0

Am studying to obtain my Microsoft Certified System Engineer (MCSE).
Completed extensive training sponsored by the U.S. Army related to management, engineering, supply administration, and other areas.

COMPUTERS

Skilled in utilizing Microsoft software including PowerPoint, Excel, Access, other software.

EXPERIENCE

GENERAL MANAGER. Department of Defense (DoD), Ft. West, WA (2001-present). Was selected over nine other middle managers to assume this leadership position which placed me in charge of a nine-person section and $300,000 in equipment serving a 99-person organization.
- Was praised in writing for "maintaining outstanding rapport with co-workers."
- Because of my leadership and strong personal initiative, was strongly encouraged to remain in military service and assured of continued rapid promotion ahead of my peers.
- Structured a local area computer network which enabled the sharing of data and peripherals.

OPERATIONS MANAGER. DoD, Ft. Huachuca, AZ (2000-01). In two separate companies, was selected as a "Squad Leader" in charge of training and supervising an 8-person engineering organization while directing the use, maintenance, and accountability of up to $360,000 in assets.
- Was commended in writing for my "aggressive emphasis on maintenance and safety."
- Won a medal for my "focus on training and continued effort to mentor junior leaders."

COMMUNICATIONS CHIEF & INFORMATION SECURITY NCO. DoD, Ft. Polk, LA (1999-00). Maintained accountability of communications equipment worth $250,000 while managing three employees; managed communications assets during a special assignment.

PROJECT MANAGER. DoD, Ft. Polk, LA (1998-99). While managing eight employees, provided respected advice to senior managers on matters related to the optimum utilization of vehicles, trailers, tool sets, and specialized clothing; prepared employees to work in Bosnia.

Highlights of other DoD experience (1994-98): Began as a Combat Engineer Crewman, and was evaluated as "setting the standard" for others; advanced into supervisory positions ahead of my peers. In one position as a First-Line Supervisor, established an innovative training plan and maintained 100% accountability of demolition equipment.

PERSONAL

Excellent references. Recipient of 10 awards for exceptional performance.

**MICROSOFT CERTIFIED
SYSTEMS ENGINEER**

Dear Sir or Madam:

With the enclosed resume, I would like to make you aware of my interest in exploring employment opportunities with your organization and introduce you to my background and credentials related to your business.

As you will see from my resume, I have recently earned my Microsoft Certified Systems Engineer (MCSE) and Microsoft Certified Professional (MCP) through coursework from Internet Technologies (I.T.). I am seeking my first full-time job in the internet technology field. I plan to continue my technical education in my spare time at night and on weekends so that I can acquire other certifications which will be beneficial to my employer.

I feel that I have much to offer a company, even though I am only 19 years old. I have worked since I was 13, and I have demonstrated my ability to rapidly master any new technical task. While working in part-time and then in full-time positions with Premier Builders since 2000, I have mastered many complex technical trades activities. I have become a skilled carpenter and framer, and I have worked in nearly all areas of the construction industry on projects related to residential construction. I have earned a reputation as a highly reliable hard worker who knows how to produce high-quality results under tight deadlines. I have earned respect for my natural mechanical abilities and problem-solving skills, and since childhood I have been operating, maintaining, and repairing farm equipment such as tractors, bush hogs, and bailers.

A highly artistic individual with natural talents related to drawing, I am certain I could apply that flair for creativity within a technical company aiming for maximum customer appeal.

I hope you will contact me to suggest a time when we could meet in person to discuss suitable employment opportunities with your firm. I can provide excellent references. Thank you.

Yours sincerely,

Anthony Hopkins

ANTHONY HOPKINS

1110½ Hay Street, Fayetteville, NC 28305 • preppub@aol.com • (910) 483-6611

OBJECTIVE

To contribute to the growth and profitability of a company that can use a computer professional who offers MCSE and MCP certifications along with formal training related to network engineering and systems networking activities.

EDUCATION

Professional: Completed extensive coursework from Internet Technology (I.T.), Burns, KY, 2001, related to troubleshooting, repairing, and installing programs as well as the Windows NT, 95, and 98 operating systems.
College: Completed numerous courses at Burns Technical Community College.

COMPUTER CERTIFICATIONS

Microsoft Certified Systems Engineer (MCSE) and Microsoft Certified Professional (MCP), December 2001.
Coursework included:
- 922 Supporting Microsoft Windows, NT 4.0 Core Technologies
- 936 Implementing and Supporting Microsoft, Internet Information Server 4.0 (IIS)
- 688 Internetworking Microsoft TCP/IP, Microsoft Windows NT 4.0
- 578 Networking Essentials
- 689 Supporting Microsoft NT Server, Enterprise Technologies
- 803 Administrating, Microsoft Windows NT 4.0

Am making plans to obtain further certifications including certifications related to CISCO, Linux, web design, and other areas related to information technology.

EXPERIENCE

NETWORK ENGINEERING STUDENT. Internet Technologies (I.T.), Burns, KY (2001). Completed an intensive professional program which equipped me with the knowledge to obtain my MCSE and MCP.
- In a classroom environment, worked on simulated networking activities, and gained hands-on experience in most aspects of network administration; set up a local area network (LAN) and a wide area network (WAN).

SKILLED CARPENTER, FRAMER, & CONSTRUCTION WORKER. Premier Builders, Burns, KY (2000-01).
Began working for this company part-time when I was in high school, and became employed full-time after graduation; have worked on various projects for this company which is a home development company.
- Have learned the nuts and bolts of the construction business as I worked on projects building homes and framing houses.
- Gained a reputation as a punctual, reliable individual who could be counted on.
- Learned to produce high-quality results under tight deadlines.
- Became skilled at installing appliances including microwaves, dishwashers, and ranges; learned framing skills which I applied in building fences and decks; performed masonry and concrete work.
- Operated and worked on farm machinery including tractors, bush hogs, and bailers.

STRENGTHS

Possess natural artistic abilities which could be useful in web design. Also offer a friendly, polite personality along with a proven ability to work effectively with others.

PERSONAL

Highly motivated hard worker who seeks a position in an internet technology (IT) company which will permit me to work with a team of dedicated professionals. Excellent references.

Date

Exact Name of Person
Title or Position
Name of Company
Address (number and street)
Address (city, state, and zip)

Dear Exact Name of Person: (or Dear Sir or Madam if answering a blind ad.)

With the enclosed resume, I would like to make you aware of my considerable background in the management of information systems and in the development of state-of-the-art software and business applications.

As you will see from my resume, I was recruited in 1994 by a fast-growing corporation experiencing rapid expansion to oversee the design and implementation of its MIS activities at 80 store locations. I was promoted to Vice President of Management Information Systems in the process of making major contributions to efficiency, productivity, and profitability. We have replaced store computers with a Windows-based system that reduced manual record keeping and since then I have been designing the implementation of the second phase of this reengineering project. We are also developing an intranet for stores, supervisors, and other office personnel, and I have personally designed and conducted training and support for all job levels, from top executives, to store management, to entry-level employees.

In my prior position, I was promoted in a track record of advancement with a company which developed software products for the telecommunications industry. During that time I transformed a failing operation which was losing money into an efficient and profitable business while reengineering a product which became the industry's #1 seller.

My software knowledge is vast, as you will also see from my resume, and I offer recent experience with C++ as well as Intranet and HTML.

I can provide outstanding personal and professional references at the appropriate time, and I can assure you in advance that I have a reputation for building and maintaining effective working relationships with people at all organizational levels. If my skills, experience, and talents interest you, please contact me. Thank you in advance for your professional courtesies.

Sincerely,

Robert Schniepp

ROBERT SCHNIEPP

1110½ Hay Street, Fayetteville, NC 28305 • preppub@aol.com • (910) 483-6611

OBJECTIVE

To offer my creative problem-solving approach and experience in management information systems design and implementation to a company that needs a resourceful expert with highly refined supervisory and communication skills.

EXPERIENCE

VICE PRESIDENT OF MANAGEMENT INFORMATION SYSTEMS (MIS). Stop Fast Convenience Stores, Lawrence, KS (1994-present). Was recruited by this fast-growing corporation which employs more than 500 people and operates 80 stores grossing over $150 million annually to analyze its current MIS structure and to design MIS systems which would be compatible with strategic goals and accommodate continued rapid growth.

- Began with the company as MIS Manager and was promoted to VP, MIS.
- In 1994 determined that the company's current computer system consisting of an IBM S/36 and store PCs would not facilitate the company's objectives; implemented Novell Network on a UNIX system for corporate accounting.
- Performed extensive research on systems and networks available; selected potential vendors and negotiated the final contract.
- Functioned as co-developer of the implementation strategy with the software vendor in order to reduce standard implementation time by 32%.
- Replaced store computers with a Windows-based system that reduced manual record keeping by store managers while providing for daily transmittal of sales, purchases, cash, and inventory levels to corporate office.
- Have designed the implementation of the second phase of this reengineering project, integrating the gas console, fuel tanks, credit cards, money orders, time clock, and cash registers: this system has resulted in increased store manager time for managing while reducing the number of errors made at the store-level and transmitted to the corporate host system.
- Am developing an **intranet** for stores, supervisors, and other office personnel to utilize for faster communication and more efficient decision making.

DIRECTOR OF DEVELOPMENT. Carbon Industries, Inc., Tampa, FL (1989-94). Was promoted to oversee product development related to software for telecommunications companies; stepped into a situation where we were losing customers and sales because of poor product design and delivery.

- Transformed a failing operation which was losing money and customers into an efficient and profitable business which enjoyed four years of steady growth; the product I reengineered is now the #1 product in its industry.
- Managed a budget of $1.2 million and a development staff of 25 programmers.

VICE-PRESIDENT OF DEVELOPMENT. Kaypro Systems and Analysis, Inc., Jacksonville, FL (1982-89). For a company providing custom software for home health care companies, was responsible for the analysis, design, programming, testing, and support of all products; managed 15 programmers and testers.

SKILLS

Software: Visual Basic, Visual C++, C, Progress, Informix, Access, Pascal, COBOL, Micro-Focus COBOL, AcuCOBOL, Assembler, Basic, Fortran, Intranet, HTML
Hardware: HP, Data General AViiONs, IBM RS6000, NCR Tower, NCR 3000 series, Data General MV series, IBM S/36, IBM-PC compatibles
Operating Systems: Literate in most operating systems, with extensive experience in Windows 95, Windows NT, Novell, Windows, UNIX, AIX, HP/UX, DG/UX, XENIX, AOS/VS, MVS, DOS

EDUCATION

Beacon University, Beacon, SC, **B.S. in Computer Science**, *cum laude,* 1982.

Exact Name of Person
Title or Position
Name of Company

MOBILE SUBSCRIBER Address (number and street)
EQUIPMENT TEAM CHIEF Address (city, state, and zip)

Dear Exact Name of Person: (or Sir or Madam if answering a blind ad.)

With the enclosed resume, I would like to make you aware of my considerable experience related to the installation of Mobile Subscriber Equipment (MSE), Line of Sight (LOS) radio systems, and radio communications networks.

Currently holding a Secret security clearance, I have qualified for a Top Secret security clearance but never was required to hold the TS clearance in any of my jobs. While working in the Federal Bureau of Investigation (FBI), I rapidly excelled as Line of Sight Radio Systems Operator and was promoted to Team Chief because of my technical knowledge and management skills. Most recently I have excelled as a MSE Transmission Team Chief. In my current position, I function essentially as a Field Technician and manage up to five people.

On numerous occasions, I have been selected to assist agencies including the Drug Enforcement Agency (DEA), the Border Patrol, and the Coast Guard in projects which involved installing, maintaining, and troubleshooting radio communications equipment.

If you can use a dedicated professional whose technical skills and personal qualities could enhance your goals, I hope you will contact me to suggest a time when we could meet. I can provide outstanding personal and professional references at the appropriate time. Thank you in advance for your time.

Sincerely,

Dawn Hollander

DAWN HOLLANDER

1110½ Hay Street, Fayetteville, NC 28305   •   preppub@aol.com   •   (910) 483-6611

OBJECTIVE
I want to contribute to an organization that can use an experienced young professional with extensive skills related to technical communications systems installation, operation, maintenance, and management along with proven supervisory and management abilities.

EDUCATION
Completed extensive training sponsored by the Federal Bureau of Investigation related to:

    network switching   wire systems installation and operation
    computer operations   switchboard programming, maintenance, and interfacing

Graduated from Mobile Subscriber Equipment (MSE) Transmission System Operator Course.

Vehicles: Graduated from Drivers Training Schools; certified to operate most engineering equipment; familiar with operation of winch trucks, front loaders, cable reel trucks, and cable trailers.

Equipment: Skilled in installing, operating, and maintaining equipment including:

    Site Radio Terminal   AN/TCC-90   Diesel Generators
    5KW generator set PU-758
    Single Channel Tactical Satellite Radios: MST-20; PSC-3, 5; LST-5C; URC 101, 110
    High Frequency Radios PRC-104, 113   Communications Secure (COMSEC) equipment

Pursuing Bachelor of Science degree; have completed 23 credit hours, Bowie State University, Bowie, MD; will complete degree in my spare time.

CLEARANCE
Qualified for Top Secret security clearance, but positions I held never required the TS.

EXPERIENCE
MOBILE SUBSCRIBER EQUIPMENT (MSE) TEAM CHIEF. Federal Bureau of Investigation (FBI), Washington, DC (2000-present). While operating in the role of **Field Technician,** manage up to five junior MSE Technicians while serving as Team Chief for a unit which provided MSE communications and secure satellite radio communications.

- Account for equipment valued at more than $1 million.
- Provided MSE team leadership in field situations during numerous training projects in remote locations; played a key role in restoring communications in the aftermath of Hurricane Buxter and during other humanitarian relief projects.
- Have earned a reputation as a resourceful troubleshooter and problem solver.

LINE OF SIGHT TRANSMISSION SYSTEM TEAM CHIEF. Federal Bureau of Investigation, Belgium (1991-99). As a Line of Sight Radio Systems Operator, quickly distinguished myself for my technical troubleshooting abilities as well as my management potential, and was promoted to Team Chief.

- Managed teams of people while supervising the installation, operation, and maintenance of Line of Sight (LOS) radio systems, single-channel tactical satellite radio systems, Mobile Subscriber Equipment (MSE), and radio communication networks.
- Received an award which cited my initiative, leadership, and professional abilities.
- As a highly motivated member and Team Chief of specialized 12-person teams, provided outstanding communications for more than 20 training projects.
- Was selected to work with numerous agencies and organizations in installing and troubleshooting communications systems; worked with the Border Patrol, the Drug Enforcement Agency (DEA), and the Coast Guard on projects related to installing single-channel tactical satellite (TACSAT) support for their field agents.
- Traveled to Mexico, Honduras, Panama, Haiti, and the Caribbean to assist in special projects related to troubleshooting communications equipment and installing equipment.

PERSONAL
Can provide outstanding personal and professional references.

Date

Exact Name of Person
Exact Title
Exact Name of Company
Address
City, State, Zip

Dear Exact Name of Person (or Dear Sir or Madam if answering a blind ad):

With the enclosed resume, I would like to make you aware of my experience, training, and skills related to the areas of telecommunications, fiber optics, and cellular communications.

As you will see from my resume, I have received licenses or certifications in areas of technical expertise with Fiber Optics: OSP, Digital Group Modems and Mast, and GTE Multichannel Transmissions. Trained in splicing and installing fiber optics cable, I offer abilities related to the operation, maintenance, and troubleshooting of multichannel radios, digital group modems, UHF and SHF radios, and antennas.

During my four years of employment with GTE Dynamics, I have worked at locations worldwide, and I quickly advanced to a supervisory job overseeing up to eight people. While earning a reputation as a technically skilled and knowledgeable young professional, I made contributions which impacted on the effectiveness of maintenance activities. I excelled in responsibilities which included making regular preventive maintenance checks, supervising telecommunications specialists, and personally operating and maintaining equipment.

If you can use a fast learner with strong technical skills and a reputation as one who can be counted on to get the job done right and on time, I hope you will contact me soon to suggest a time when we might meet to discuss your needs. I can assure you in advance that I can provide outstanding references and could quickly become an asset to your organization.

Sincerely,

Grace Mayweather

Alternate last paragraph:
If you can use a fast learner with strong technical skills and a reputation as one who can be counted on to get the job done right and on time, I hope you will welcome my call soon to briefly discuss my qualifications and how I might contribute to your organization's continued growth and success. I can assure you in advance that I can provide outstanding references and could quickly become an asset to your organization.

GRACE MAYWEATHER

1110½ Hay Street, Fayetteville, NC 28305　　•　　preppub@aol.com　　•　　(910) 483-6611

OBJECTIVE　　To offer technical skills and knowledge of telecommunications and cellular communications to an organization that can use a quick learner who is effective both as a contributor to team efforts and while working independently.

EDUCATION & TRAINING　　Completed community college programs in fiber optics and OSP and splicing, Central Washington Community College, Seattle, WA.

Excelled in technical and leadership courses which included:

- Laguna Industries Digital Group Multiplexer System–operations, troubleshooting, and erecting antennas
- GTE Government Systems Corporation–multichannel transmission systems operations and troubleshooting

TECHNICAL SKILLS　　Offer ability to **operate, maintain, and troubleshoot operator-level telecommunications equipment:**

multichannel radios　　digital group modems　　UHF and SHF radios　　antenna

Am trained and skilled in **splicing and installing fiber optics cable.**

LICENSES & CERTIFICATIONS　　Have been licensed/certified in the following technical areas of expertise:

Fiber Optics: OSP – 1999

Digital Group Modems and Mast – 1999

Multichannel Transmissions (GTE) – 1996

EXPERIENCE　　**MULTICHANNEL TRANSMISSION SYSTEMS SUPERVISOR AND OPERATOR.** GTE Dynamics, Seattle, WA (1997-present). Advanced to supervise and train teams of as many as eight telecommunications specialists while troubleshooting and operating state-of-the-art systems.

- Emphasized the necessity for regular preventive maintenance and weekly checks of equipment which reduced the need for replacements of costly equipment and saved government funds.
- Cited for my ability to work in close cooperation with others, developed a leadership style which resulted in my selection for this supervisory role ahead of my peers.
- Supervised personnel operating, maintaining, and troubleshooting equipment while personally handling two sets of equipment in separate communications shelters.
- Operated as many as four radios and line-of-sight antennas.
- Performed maintenance checks on additional support equipment and trucks.
- Quickly earned a reputation as a fast learner with strong technical abilities and a willingness to give my time to learn new things and help others.
- Received Certificates of Appreciation for my contributions in numerous volunteer activities including Special Olympics, Habitat for Humanity, and Samaritan's Purse.
- Was cited by a general officer for "meritorious achievement" while providing "outstanding support" for a large-scale task force training exercise.

Highlights of additional experience: Refined time management abilities as a Head Waitress where the emphasis was on customer service.

PERSONAL　　Was entrusted with a Secret security clearance. Feel that one of my greatest strengths is getting the job done right and on time. Offer skills in budgeting and planning.

Exact Name of Person
Exact Title
Exact Name of Company
Address
City, State, Zip

MULTIMODE SYSTEM OPERATOR

Dear Exact Name of Person (or Dear Sir or Madam if answering a blind ad):

With the enclosed resume, I would like to make you aware of my interest in exploring employment opportunities with your organization.

As you will see from my resume, I have served my country with distinction in the Central Intelligence Agency. In my current position as a Multimode System Operator with the CIA, I have been rated as "absolutely superior in all areas" and commended for "unparalleled work ethic and dedication to goals" while operating a computerized console in a highly classified environment. I have volunteered my time extensively to community projects, and I was proud to play a role in winning the "best team" rating in the Pacific. In an earlier job as a Satellite Systems Technician at the Air Intelligence Agency's largest field site in Misawa, Japan, I was commended in writing as "superb operator" and was praised for exhibiting "great initiative, attention to detail, and leadership."

I hold one of the nation's highest security clearances: Top Secret/Sensitive Compartmented Information (TS/SCI). I offer a proven ability to excel in training, and I was named Honor Graduate from the six-month Communications Signals Collection/Processing Course.

I am highly proactive in seeking out opportunities for self-improvement and for advancement of my skills and knowledge. I am currently completing courses in sequence at the World Technology Education Center which will lead to the Microsoft Certified System Engineer (MSCE) certification as well as the Cisco Certified Network Associate (CCNA) certification. Currently I am receiving training with UNIX through the National Security Agency.

Although I have been strongly encouraged to remain in military service and assured of continuous rapid promotion, I have decided to leave the military and seek opportunities in the civilian workplace. If you can use my versatile talents and skills, as well as my reputation for strong personal initiative, I hope you will contact me to suggest a time when we might discuss your needs. I can provide excellent references.

Yours sincerely,

Johnathon Little

JOHNATHON LITTLE

1110½ Hay Street, Fayetteville, NC 28305   •   preppub@aol.com   •   (910) 483-6611

OBJECTIVE
To benefit an organization that can use a highly motivated young professional with knowledge of satellite and communication systems engineering, state-of-the-art training related to UNIX, along with a background related to intelligence analysis and production.

CLEARANCE
Top Secret/Sensitive Compartmented Information (TS/SCI) security clearance/NSA polygraph.

EDUCATION
Completed 15 semester hours of college course work in General Studies, University of Maryland, Ft. Meade, MD; am finishing degree in my spare time.
Honor Graduate of the six-month Communications Signals Collection/Processing Course, Central Intelligence Agency, Goodfellow Air Force Base.
Currently completing courses in sequence at the World Technology Education Center, Washington, DC, which will lead to the following certifications:
* Microsoft Certified System Engineer (MCSE)
* Cisco Certified Network Associate (CCNA)

Graduated from Taegu American High School, Korea, 2000; active in community service projects. Participated in diving, swimming, basketball, football, and track; member of ROTC.

COMPUTERS
Knowledgeable with UNIX through course work sponsored by the National Security Agency. Skilled in utilizing Microsoft software as well as TriTeal; knowledgeable of specialized software applications used for intelligence collection and analysis.

EXPERIENCE
MULTIMODE SYSTEM OPERATOR. Central Intelligence Agency (CIA), Washington, DC (2001-present). Have been rated as *"absolutely superior in all areas"* and commended for *"unparalleled work ethic and dedication to goals"* while working in a classified environment for the CIA and FBI.
* Use unique receivers and electronic components to receive data; scan frequency spectrum; tune receivers; monitor/copy international Morse Code; operate a computerized console.
* Have become known for my critical thinking skills while rendering spot analyses.
* With a reputation as a dedicated team player, have volunteered in my free time to help the community; played a role in winning the "best team" rating in the Pacific.
* Proactive in seeking self-improvement; completed college course in Fundamentals of Oral Communication and courses related to computer security and property accountability.

SATELLITE SYSTEMS TECHNICIAN. CIA, Greystone Cryptologic Operations Center, Greystone, England (1997-2000). At the Greystone Cryptologic Operations Center (one of the world's largest field sites), operated a complex multimillion-dollar computer-based monitoring, analysis, and reporting system; performed intricate signal parametric measurements and identified techniques.
* Coordinated with other agencies involved in processing, monitoring, and reporting data to ensure accurate inputs to Department of Defense agencies.
* Was commended in writing as a *"superb operator"* and for exhibiting *"great initiative, attention to detail, and leadership."* Facilitated the efficient use of limited resources.
* Processed and reported one of three high-priority entity events.
* Assisted in the training and development of three operators; all certified ahead of schedule.

PERSONAL
Excellent references. Confident of my ability to take on any technical subject and rapidly gain expert knowledge. Extremely self-motivated and focused individual.

Date

Exact Name of Person
Title or Position
Name of Company
Address (number and street)
Address (city, state, and zip)

NETWORK ANALYST   Dear Exact Name of Person: (or Sir or Madam if answering a blind ad.)

With the enclosed resume, I would like to express my interest in exploring employment opportunities with your organization.

As you will see, I offer expertise as a network and telecommunications analyst, manager, and administrator as well as in management information systems and Wide and Local Area Networks (WANs and LANs). Presently the Network and Tele-communications Analyst for a medical center, I ensure connectivity, compatibility, and performance of a network of 60 servers which provide computer access to more than 3,000 hospital employees. Among my contributions while providing this vital support has been a project to upgrade the time and attendance system and to troubleshoot this system to ensure it functions properly. In another project, I implemented an ATM backbone to over 30 different closets within the medical center.

Earlier as a Network Manager and LAN Administrator for another area hospital, I assisted in the design and implementation of a project to convert an unmanaged ethernet to an managed switched ethernet network running on a fiber optics backbone. My contributions to the success of this project included installing and setting up the first remote connections, performing system backups, providing disk and printer management as well as e-mail administration, and monitoring system security and performance.

Earlier I gained valuable experience in the computer field in experience as a Hardware Specialist, Minicomputer System Operator, Network Technician, and Systems Analyst. For one organization in Germany, I expertly handled the details of disposing of and replacing 75% of outdated and obsolete equipment in a position usually reserved for a more experienced professional.

If you can use a creative, innovative professional who offers special skills in managing and troubleshooting automated systems, I hope you will contact me to suggest a time when we might meet to discuss your needs. I can provide outstanding references at the appropriate time.

Sincerely,

Charles Folkart

CHARLES FOLKART

1110½ Hay Street, Fayetteville, NC 28305 • preppub@aol.com • (910) 483-6611

OBJECTIVE

To benefit an organization that can use a Network/Telecommunications Analyst, Manager, and Administrator with excellent communication skills who offers a background in Management Information Systems as well as Wide Area and Local Area Networks.

EDUCATION & TRAINING

Earned certification as a Computer/Machine Operator from Maryland Community College. *Completed numerous training courses with Bay Networks and American Research Group authorized training centers, including the following:*
- Optivity 6.x for Windows, HP Openview for Windows, Introduction to Network Management, Understanding Computer Networks, Network Troubleshooting, Microsoft Office, Internet seminars, and Meditech Operating System and Networks.

Completed the Novell Administrator course at Meade Community College.
Extensive training in Microsoft Word for Windows, WordPerfect, and applications software.

EXPERIENCE

NETWORK & TELECOMMUNICATIONS ANALYST. Meade Medical Center, Meade, MD (2001-present). Provide network and telecommunications support, ensuring connectivity, compatibility, and performance of all components of a network of 60 servers providing computer access to more than 3000 hospital employees.
- Managed the network and perform troubleshooting of network problems for more than 3,000 users on hospital local area network (LAN), wide area network (WAN) sites, and remote access users; installed and configured hubs, switches, routers, and CSU/DSUs.
- Replaced clock peripherals for the Kronos Time and Attendance System, troubleshooting in order to ensure the IP clocks functioned properly under the upgraded software.
- Implemented an ATM backbone to over 30 different closets within the main Medical Center; installed Bay Network 1600 core switches and BCNs.
- Resolve networking issues with imaging system and manage the servers that it runs on.

NETWORK MANAGER & LAN ADMINISTRATOR. Columbus County Hospital, Whiteville, GA (1999-01). Served as project leader and senior network analyst, converting the hospital's computer system from an unmanaged ethernet to a managed switched ethernet network running on a fiber optic backbone.
- Assisted in design, implementation, and administration of LANs (local area networks), personal computer systems, operating systems, and servers; installed and maintained applications. Provided access to new users, assigning them appropriate security levels.
- Installed and set up the first remote connections providing access to the hospital's network.
- Performed system backups, disk and printer management, e-mail administration, and monitored system security and performance.

HARDWARE SPECIALIST. Priory Community Hospital, Houston, TX (1997-98). Selected for a position usually held by a more experienced professional, achieved error-free control over issuing and receipt of a $70,000 inventory of computer equipment while training and supervising technicians.
- Disposed of and replaced 75% of the organization's outdated, obsolete equipment.

MINICOMPUTER SYSTEM OPERATOR. Mayfield Hospital, Mayfield, VA (1995-97). Installed, operated, and performed unit-level maintenance for a multi-user information system; controlled input/output data and handled bulk data storage operations.

NETWORK TECHNICIAN and **SYSTEMS ANALYST.** Family Burn Center, Philadelphia, PA (1992-94). Learned procedures for connecting networks and troubleshooting.

Date

Exact Name of Person
Title or Position
Name of Company
Address (number and street)
Address (city, state, and zip)

NETWORK ENGINEER Dear Exact Name of Person: (or Dear Sir or Madam if answering a blind ad.)

With the enclosed resume, I would like to make you aware of my interest in utilizing my background in computer science and my interest in customer service for the benefit of your organization.

As you will see from my resume, I am a Certified Novell Administrator and a Microsoft Certified Professional for NT 4.0 Workstation, and I hold an Associate's degree in Computer Applications and Programming as well as a B.S. in Computer Science and Information Management Systems. I am an experienced Network Engineer.

Although I am excelling in my current position and can provide outstanding references at the appropriate time, I am seeking to utilize my technical expertise in an environment where I can also interact with customers and/or users on a more frequent basis. My naturally outgoing personality and strong communication skills would make me very effective in any position which required interaction with others, and I would enjoy an opportunity to develop and maintain strong working relationships as part of my job. I offer a proven ability to translate complex technical concepts into language which can be comprehended by non-technical individuals, and I believe my technical expertise would be best utilized in an environment which required extensive human interaction.

If you feel that my expertise in network engineering, design, administration, and troubleshooting could be useful to you, I hope you will contact me to suggest a time when we could meet to discuss your needs. I certainly appreciate your time and consideration, and I am confident that I could make valuable contributions to your long-range goals.

Yours sincerely,

John Lasak

JOHN LASAK

1110½ Hay Street, Fayetteville, NC 28305 • preppub@aol.com • (910) 483-6611

OBJECTIVE

To benefit an organization that can use an articulate, experienced Network Engineer and PC/LAN Specialist with exceptional communication and organizational skills, who offers a background in network engineering, design, administration, and troubleshooting, as well as technical support and customer service.

EDUCATION

Bachelor of Science degree in **Computer Science/Information Management Systems**, University of Georgia, Athens, GA, 1998.

Associate of Applied Science degree in **Computer Applications/Programming**, Heald Business College, Rancho Cordova, CA, 1994.

Completed numerous training courses supplemental to my degree program including:
- Microsoft TCP/IP internetworking for Windows NT 4.0.
- Microsoft NT 4.0 Core Technology for NT 4.0 Server.
- Kronos System Operator for Windows, System Administrator for Windows, and TKC Windows Configuration I.
- IT Security/Advanced NT Security for Windows NT 4.0.
- Microsoft Exchange Server 5.0.
- Microsoft NT 3.51 for NT 3.51 Server.

CERTIFICATIONS

Microsoft Certified Professional for NT 4.0 Workstation, Certified Novell Administrator.

EXPERIENCE

With Presidio Health Systems, have advanced in the following "track record" of increasing responsibilities for this large regional medical center:

2001-present: NETWORK ENGINEER. Jacksonville, FL. Provide local area network set-up, administration, security, and support for 60 network servers providing computer access to more than 3000 hospital employees.
- Serve as Security Administrator for the hospital's computer network, controlling the access of more than 3,000 employees to the hospital's 40 Novell Netware 3.12 servers and 20 Windows NT 4.0 servers.
- Assisted in the design, installation, implementation, and administration of all LANs (Local Area Networks), personal computer systems, operating systems, and servers; install and maintain applications on the LAN.
- Provide access to new users, assigning them a security level that permits them to access information and applications necessary to perform the functions of their job.
- Investigate any reported hardware, software, network, and peripheral problems.
- Personally responsible for the installation of the Novell Netware 3.12 server running the Kronos Time and Attendance application; the upgrade for this application, a three-month process which included replacement of all peripherals and training of end users.
- Installed Carelink to a Netware server; this call center application allows nurses to provide the community with general medical assistance and information.

1996-99: PC/LAN SPECIALIST I. Jacksonville, FL. Installed, upgraded, and maintained software applications on the LAN, managing user access privileges and security rights for the computer network of this large regional medical center.
- Provided daily support in the management of system services such as printing and e-mail; managed user access privileges and security rights; performed system backups, disk and printer management, e-mail administration, and monitored system security.
- Installed network applications including software for infection control.

PERSONAL

Outstanding personal and professional references are available upon request.

Date

Exact Name of Person
Exact Title
Exact Name of Company
Address
City, State, Zip

Dear Exact Name of Person (or Dear Sir or Madam if answering a blind ad):

With the enclosed resume, I would like to make you aware of my interest in exploring employment opportunities with your organization. I am single (never married) and available for worldwide relocation and travel, as your needs require. I have a current passport.

As you will see from my resume, I have recently obtained my Microsoft Certified Systems Engineer (MCSE) with an average of over 900s on the tests. I have also obtained certifications leading to the Microsoft Certified Professional with the Internet (MCP & I). I offer an ability to perform network engineering and system networking activities which maximize productivity. I am working towards my MCSE in Windows 2000.

In addition to my networking knowledge, I offer a business background which has equipped me with extensive management and problem-solving skills. You will notice from my resume that I excelled in other fields prior to entering the computer industry. After working my way up into management in my first job at Burger King, where I managed 50 people, I obtained training and credentials as a Brewmaster and then won nearly every award that could be earned in that field, including gold medals, silver medals, bronze medals, and platinum medals at worldwide competitions, state fairs, and championships. Because of my technical expertise and outstanding personal reputation, I was recruited for a one-year contract by a prestigious company in Canada, where I played a key role in opening that establishment. As soon as that contract ended, I was aggressively recruited by a company which was a startup. I provided technical and managerial leadership which helped the business to become operational earlier than anticipated and underbudget. I played a key role in helping that business gross $1.5 in its first year of operation.

Although I became highly respected in my industry, I reached a point where there were few challenges left. After careful consideration, I decided that I wished to establish my career in the computer industry, and I have utilized all my spare time to obtain training and credentials which will enable me to make significant contributions to an organization as a network engineer. If you can use my extensive business background as well as my technical knowledge in the network engineering field, I hope you will contact me to suggest a time when we might talk about your needs. I can provide outstanding personal and professional references at the appropriate time.

Yours sincerely,

Daniel Lewis

DANIEL LEWIS

1110½ Hay Street, Fayetteville, NC 28305   •   preppub@aol.com   •   (910) 483-6611

OBJECTIVE

To contribute to the growth and profitability of a company that can use a well-trained computer professional who offers MCSE certifications along with an ability to perform network engineering and systems networking activities which maximize productivity.

EDUCATION

College: Completed three years of college courses towards a Geography major, Sacramento State, Sacramento, CA, 1994-98; worked full-time in order to finance my college education.
Technical: Received a Certificate of Completion from the American Brewers Guild in Brewing Science, Sacramento, CA, 1998.
Professional: Extensive coursework and Certificates from the Dyna Byte Company, Sacramento, CA, 2002, related to troubleshooting, repairing, and installing programs.
- Knowledgeable of software including ACT! 4.0 (database and scheduling aid), Excel, Word, Publisher; experienced with Windows NT, 95, and 98 operating systems.

COMPUTER CERTIFICATIONS

Microsoft Certified Systems Engineer (MCSE) and Microsoft Certified Professional with the Internet (MCP & I), December 2003; making plans to obtain MCSE in Windows 2000.

EXPERIENCE

NETWORK ENGINEERING STUDENT. Dyna Byte Company, Sacramento, CA (2001-present). While working full time in the job described below, completed an intensive professional program leading to the MCSE and MCP & I certifications.
- Gained hands-on experience in most aspects of network administration.
- Was extensively trained to troubleshoot a local area network (LAN) and a wide area network (WAN); learned how to maximize efficiency through configurations.

ASSISTANT GENERAL MANAGER. Bayfield Brewing Company, Sacramento, CA (2001-present). Was recruited by the founders of this 350-seat, 12,000-square feet brewpub which caters to an upscale target market 25-45. The founders had raised $1.5 million in private capital by selling shares at $35,000 a share to finance the creation of a new brewpub which grossed $1.5 million in its first year of operation.
- Played a key role in developing the policies and procedures for the brewing business.
- Was given critical bottom-line responsibility when the brewpub opened, and provided leadership in bringing in the brewpub early and under budget during construction phase.
- Developed off-site sales to a level of $50,000 yearly; established and grew a customer base which boosted sales 20% in our first year.
- Formulated recipes, ordered ingredients, and continuously conducted classes on product styles and on the process of selling varied products.

BREWMASTER. The Canadian Brewery Company, Toronto, Canada (2000-01). Was recruited for a one-year contract to help build and open a 500-seat facility.
- Utilized Word and Excel while also learning to use Windows 98 in Spanish.

HEAD BREWER. Sasser Brewing Company, Sasser, CA (1998-00). Won nearly every award that could be earned in the brewing field including seven gold medals, four silver medals, six bronze medals, and a platinum medal from various worldwide competitions, state fairs, and championships; achieved respect for my emphasis on Total Quality Management.

ASSISTANT MANAGER. Burger King, Chico, CA (1994-98). Began in an entry-level job and progressed rapidly into management. Managed an average of 50 people.

PERSONAL

Highly motivated individual. Desire to advance in the computer field. Excellent references.

Exact Name of Person
Exact Title
Exact Name of Company
Address
City, State, Zip

NETWORK MANAGER   Dear Exact Name of Person: (or Dear Sir or Madam if answering a blind ad):

With the enclosed resume, I would like to make you aware of my extensive technical background in installation, troubleshooting, configuring, maintenance, and repair of local and wide area networks; computer hardware, software, and peripherals; and communications equipment.

As you will see from my resume, I have recently excelled as a Network Manager and Information Management Officer, a position for which I was selected based on my technical proficiency in Local Area Network administration. In this job, I managed a million-dollar annual automation budget, re-engineered the organization's LAN architecture to enhance the electronic mail capability, and authored, implemented, and trained personnel on Standard Operating Procedures for the Tactical Web (TACWEB).

Throughout my communications career, I have demonstrated the extensive technical knowledge and exceptional supervisory and motivational skills that have led to my selection for positions of increased responsibility and earned me promotion ahead of my peers. My efforts have ensured that the organizations to which I was assigned were ahead of schedule on Y2K compliance issues. In earlier positions I provided extensive command and control communications support as a Mobile Subscriber Equipment Node Switch Supervisor, Small Node Team Chief, and Technician.

If you can use a highly skilled technical professional with a versatile background in computer hardware and software as well as communications equipment, I hope you will welcome my call soon when I try to arrange a brief meeting to discuss your goals and how my background might serve your needs. I can provide outstanding references at the appropriate time.

Sincerely,

Lucia Villar

Alternate Last Paragraph:
If you can use a highly skilled technical professional with a versatile background in computer hardware and software as well as communications equipment, I hope you will write or call me soon to suggest a time when we might meet to discuss your needs and goals and how my background might serve them. I can provide outstanding references at the appropriate time.

LUCIA VILLAR

1110½ Hay Street, Fayetteville, NC 28305   •   preppub@aol.com   •   (910) 483-6611

OBJECTIVE   To benefit an organization that can use an articulate, technically proficient professional with an extensive background in installation, troubleshooting, maintenance, configuration, and repair of local and wide area networks, communications equipment, and computer software.

EDUCATION   Completed nearly three years of college-level course work towards a degree in Humanities, University of Maryland and Central Texas College.

Excelled in numerous leadership and technical training courses, including: Information Management Officer (IMO) Course – **Local Area Network (LAN) administration** and computer troubleshooting, upgrading, repair, and maintenance, **Enhanced Switch Operator Program (ESOP)** – Unit Level Operator/Maintenance Course, **Mobile Subscriber Equipment (MSE) Network Switching Systems Operator** Course, and **Electronics Technician** Course – electronics and telecommunications troubleshooting, maintenance, and repair.

EXPERIENCE   *Was promoted ahead of my peers and selected to assume positions of increased responsibility with International Technologies, Inc.:*

NETWORK MANAGER. London, England (1999-present). Engineered, administered, and managed Local and Wide Area Networks (LANs and WANs) of three Windows NT 4.0 servers and an Exchange server at four widely dispersed locations within the Eighth Army; provided training and technical support as well as troubleshooting links, performing routine maintenance on the servers, and adding or deleting user accounts on the network.

- Re-engineered the organization's LAN architecture, executing improvements which enhanced the network's electronic mail capability.
- Oversaw the organization-wide implementation of the Defense Messaging System (DMS), permitting one computer to handle both secure and unclassified electronic mail.
- Authored, implemented, and trained personnel on Standard Operating Procedures for the Tactical Web (TACWEB) and coordinated local and remote TACWEB installation; configured the TACWEB to allow viewing of links within the network to monitor outages.
- Configured Network Encryption Systems (NES) organization-wide for a major exercise.
- Supervised and trained a team that installed, operated, and maintained computer hardware and software systems.
- Performed troubleshooting to the component level, repair, and replacement of defective hardware and peripherals; installed operating systems (Windows 95, 98, NT, and NT Server) and applications (Microsoft Office 97 Suite and others) to the network.

INFORMATION MANAGEMENT SUPERVISOR. Misawa, Japan (1998-99). Oversaw the acquisition, implementation, and operation of information technology for a mobile subscriber area organization; trained node center personnel within the organization on proper installation and operational procedures for the tactical packet switch networks.

- Installed the first Y2K software package in the organization.
- Developed an active field e-mail system using Microsoft Exchange for the organization's operations manager, enhancing the communications network; installed and performed troubleshooting on major communications links during various field exercises.

MOBILE SUBSCRIBER EQUIPMENT (MSE) NODE SWITCH SUPERVISOR. Philadelphia, PA (1997-98). Supervised and trained up to eight employees while holding final responsibility for more than $5 million in communications equipment.

PERSONAL   Was entrusted with a Secret security clearance. Recognized with numerous prestigious awards.

Exact Name of Person
Exact Title
Exact Name of Company
Address
City, State, Zip

NETWORK MANAGER

Dear Exact Name of Person: (or Dear Sir or Madam if answering a blind ad):

With the enclosed resume, I would like to take the opportunity to introduce you to my experience and technical expertise. After serving my country with distinction for 10 years, I have made the decision to leave the military and enter the civilian workforce, and I am relocating back to Jacksonville, where I grew up. As a **Microsoft Certified Professional (MCP & I and MCSE)**, I am confident that my experience in network management could be of value to you.

Consistently promoted ahead of my peers and selected for demanding positions, I was strongly encouraged to remain in military service and assured of continued rapid advancement. In March 2001 I was handpicked as Network Manager to oversee Windows NT and SUN Solaris network operations at the headquarters of the Special Operations Command where uninterrupted worldwide networking is critical. I was selected for this assignment on the basis of my accomplishments as a Systems Analyst, Operator, and Programmer for this organization and as a Computer Software and Systems Analyst.

Completing my A.S. degree in Information Systems Technology, I will be continuing my education in my spare time in pursuit of a bachelor's degree. Currently I am completing requirements for certification in Sun Microsystems Solaris Administration, which will add to my Microsoft MCSE professional certification, Internet Certification, and designation as a Systems Engineer.

With a **Top Secret (SCI)** security clearance, I excelled while serving in demanding and pressure-filled environments where I provided network support for activities vital to national security and dealt with representatives of national-level organizations on a daily basis. I have established a reputation as a fast learner, technically proficient professional, and as a bright and articulate individual who can deal with people at all organizational levels. In addition to my technical expertise in network management, I offer skills in training and supervising personnel as well as in ensuring system security for sensitive information.

If you can use a network management professional who offers personal qualities of integrity, initiative, and attention to detail, I hope you will welcome my call soon when I try to arrange a brief meeting to discuss your goals and how my background might serve your needs. I can provide outstanding references.

Sincerely,

Edward Marow

EDWARD MAROW

1110½ Hay Street, Fayetteville, NC 28305 • preppub@aol.com • (910) 483-6611

OBJECTIVE   To contribute through my technical expertise and extensive training to an organization that can use my background of experience in network management.

EDUCATION   Completing **Associate of Science (A.S) degree, Information Systems Technology,**
TRAINING   Hillsborough Community College, Tampa, FL; completed 68 credit hours.
&   **Microsoft Certified Professional** (ID 1111386), August 2001.
CERTIFICATIONS   Professional Certifications: **MCP & I** and **MCSE**
Completing requirements for certification in SUN Microsystems Solaris Administration.
Excelled in extensive training which included the following courses and programs:

SUN Solaris/UNIX System Administration Computer Operator Courses
COBOL 74 Applications Programming   Security Administration
ADA for Managers Course   CA-Clipper Programming
ADA Applications Programmer Course   ADP Security User Course
Advanced TSS/JCL and Utilities   Shell Programming and Tools
Workstation Security Software Familiarization   Oracle Course
Local Area Network (LAN) and Wide Area Network (WAN) Administration and Management

EXPERIENCE   *Earned a reputation as a technically proficient young professional, U.S. Army:*
NETWORK MANAGER. San Diego, CA (2001-present). In March 2001, was handpicked to oversee all network operations of the Windows NT and Sun Solaris systems at the headquarters of the Special Operations Command with its fast-response, worldwide mission.
- Supervise a Network Administrator and an Information Systems Security Officer.
- Have resigned from military service although I was aggressively recruited to re-enlist.

SYSTEMS ANALYST, OPERATOR, AND PROGRAMMER. Ft. Campbell, KY (1999-01). Officially evaluated as setting the standard through my initiative, positive attitude, and assertiveness; provided sound management for a multimillion-dollar 24-hour-a-day command and control system which was networked worldwide.
- Designed, developed, maintained, and managed site security procedures and LANs handling **Top Secret (SCI)** information while meeting complex requirements from the Joint Chiefs of Staff, Security Police, and Department of Defense.
- Was known as an articulate and bright individual who could effectively teach others technical software applications and also deal regularly with senior military officers.

COMPUTER SOFTWARE AND SYSTEMS ANALYST. McDill AFB, FL (1997-98). Was awarded a prestigious Defense Meritorious Service Medal for accomplishments which included achieving a 99.5% availability rate for two Top Secret databases in a selectively manned joint services organization.
- Was a key factor in the host computer earning **#1 ranking out of 28 worldwide sites.**
- Reduced by half the time needed to train new personnel and gained recognition as an excellent mentor and professional who willingly shared my knowledge with others.
- Designed, developed, installed, and provided technical support for special software programs used by more than 2,500 people worldwide.

SYSTEMS ANALYST. London, England (1996-97). Cited for my ability to handle multiple simultaneous duties; designed, developed, maintained, and managed software programs; provided ADP security; and oversaw training activities for a worldwide system.

PERSONAL   Earned numerous honors in recognition of my accomplishments.

Exact Name of Person
Exact Title
Exact Name of Company
Address
City, State, Zip

NETWORK SURVEILLANCE ENGINEER

Dear Exact Name of Person: (or Dear Sir or Madam if answering a blind ad):

With the enclosed resume, I would like to make you aware of my extensive knowledge of network and transmission systems technologies and electronics as well as the experience in identifying, isolating and troubleshooting network degradation and system outages that I could put to work for your company.

As you will see from my resume, I am excelling in a "track record" of performance as a Network Surveillance Engineer for one of the giants of the telecommunications industry. I have demonstrated my ability to work well under pressure in situations where I was called upon to locate cuts and failures on the transmission network during major outages. For example, I played a key role in facilitating the resolution of problems with a major site controller, implementing cabling and equipment repairs as well as a software update to restore the controller to service.

In addition to an Associate's degree in Electronics, I am certified in Netpro, Performance Monitoring of OC-12, and Tellabs 5500 DXC, and I have also completed numerous training phases in network management tools and platforms.

Throughout my earlier career in telecommunications and electronics, I demonstrated the exceptional technical skills and ability to rapidly master new technologies that have led me to succeed in a number of challenging environments. From the fast pace of the Aberdeen Proving Grounds to the high-security atmosphere of a nuclear power station, I have consistently excelled, bringing my comprehensive knowledge of automation, electronics, and telecommunications systems to bear on the challenges of each position.

Although I am highly regarded by my current employer and can provide outstanding personal and professional references at the appropriate time, I am interested in selectively exploring career opportunities with other telecommunications companies. However, I would appreciate your keeping my interest confidential until after we have had the chance to speak in person.

If you can use a highly skilled professional whose analytical and technical abilities have been proven in a variety of challenging environments, then I hope you will welcome my call soon, when I try to arrange a brief meeting to discuss your goals and how my background might serve your needs.

Sincerely,

Kaye Green

KAYE GREEN

1110½ Hay Street, Fayetteville, NC 28305 • preppub@aol.com • (910) 483-6611

OBJECTIVE   To benefit an organization that can use a skilled telecommunications professional with exceptional technical, communication, planning, and organizational abilities who offers an extensive background in network and transmission systems troubleshooting and restoration.

EDUCATION   **Associate's** degree in **Electronics**, National Education Center, Thomson Institute, 1990.
Certificate in Computer Programming and CSC, Dundalk Community College, MD, 1980.
Completed all platform training phases available to Transmission Surveillance, to include: PSE, Transam, Station Manager, NACS, NetManager, Diginet, Trex, Mecca, Netpro, CSM, SMART, Impact/Clarify, WorkForce, AlarmView, Pass Through, SCOPUS, F & E, Telnet, Nightly Maintenance Window and Master, E-mail, Internet, and Netscape as well as the full three-day cycle of new hire rotations in Fiber Security, Floor Manager, and Change Management.

CERTIFICATIONS   Certified in Netpro, Performance Monitoring of OC-12, and Tellabs 5500 DXC.

EXPERIENCE   *With MCI Worldcom, advanced in the following "track record" of increasing responsibilities for this giant in the telecommunications industry:*
1998-present: NETWORK SURVEILLANCE ENGINEER II. Cary, NC. Promoted to this position after excelling as a Network Surveillance Engineer I; identify, isolate, and trouble-shoot network events, quickly recognizing network degradation and system outages.
- Knowledgeable in NSTHS ticket priority and escalation procedures; drive issues to resolution, escalating as appropriate to facilitate resolutions for service outages.
- Monitor networks from T-1 to OC-192, as well as DXCs 1/0, 3/1, 3/3, Alcatel, Tellabs, and DSC in addition to RPS-370 and Pirelli Systems
- Provide assistance to Restoration using my working knowledge of signal flow to perform troubleshooting and reporting.
- Played a key role in resolving problems with Broken Arrow Site Controller 0; worked with second level Control, VNCC, and DXC support, facilitating the replacement of cabling and equipment as well as upgrading the controller's software.
- Served as a member of the team that tested the Impact platform.
- Developed, suggested, and implemented a new design for the Daily Network Report (DNR) that was adopted for use throughout Transmission Surveillance.

1997-98: NETWORK SURVEILLANCE ENGINEER I. Cary, NC. Utilized monitoring and database management systems to provide notification, dispatch, troubleshooting, and repair assistance to minimize outages and restore service to the customer in an efficient manner.
- Located cuts and failures on the transmission network during major outages, producing positive results and proving my ability to work under extreme pressure.
- Demonstrated my thorough understanding of Sonet/Sonet rings and digital radio as well as network and transmission system technologies while determining which network management tools were best suited to quickly identifying and isolating degradation and outages.
- Facilitated smooth and accurate shift turnover in Transmission Surveillance, ensuring that alarms and CSM tickets were prioritized and handled according to NSTHS and departmental guidelines.

COMMUNICATIONS OPERATOR & ARMY TELEPHONE SYSTEM PLANT TECHNICIAN. Fidelity Technologies (DCI, Inc.), Aberdeen Proving Grounds, Aberdeen, MD (1990-96). Coordinated and tracked trouble reports, line records, and work orders to ensure that telephone and data circuits were tested, repaired, maintained, and updated within deadlines.

Date

Exact Name of Person
Exact Title or Position
Company Name
Company Address (street and number)
Company Address (city, state, and ZIP)

NETWORK
SWITCHING CHIEF

Dear Exact Name (or Dear Sir or Madam if answering a blind ad):

With the enclosed resume, I would like to express my interest in receiving consideration for employment with your organization.

From my enclosed resume, you will see that I am an articulate and highly self-motivated young professional with a diverse background along with the ability to rapidly master new concepts and procedures. I have received extensive training in leadership and supervisory techniques as well as in technical telecommunications systems.

Presently in a supervisory role, I am respected for my willingness to give my personal time to ensure the advancement of intercultural relationships. I routinely utilize my language skills in a multinational NATO support organization. Among my diverse responsibilities are scheduling employees for a 24-hour-a-day-operation, controlling a $2 million inventory, and developing training programs. Earlier experience as a communications systems operator and maintenance specialist allowed me opportunities to gain expert technical knowledge. I was credited with increasing telephone switching capabilities 25% for one organization and honored with several Certificates of Achievement for my technical skills, initiative, and professionalism in the success of training exercises and technical support activities.

Before entering military service, I completed my education in Italy where I worked as a Pharmacist controlling multimillion-dollar inventories of prescription drugs, medicines, and medical equipment. I was especially appreciated for my emphasis on customer service and quality assurance.

If you can use an adaptable and versatile young professional, I hope you will contact me to suggest a time when we might meet to discuss your needs. Among my greatest strengths is my ability to work long hours under pressure and deadlines in austere conditions. I excel in analyzing and adjusting work procedures for maximum efficiency, communicating ideas and stimulating others to contribute, and in evaluating conditions and then reacting quickly to implement solutions. I can provide excellent personal and professional references.

Sincerely,

Denise Ching

DENISE CHING

1110½ Hay Street, Fayetteville, NC 28305 • preppub@aol.com • (910) 483-6611

OBJECTIVE

To offer a diverse blend of experience and knowledge related to information systems and network switching applications to an organization that can use an adaptable, innovative, and analytical communicator.

EDUCATION

Information Systems and Network Switching: Excelled in leadership courses including Primary Leadership Development Course as well as technical training which included digital cable terminating equipment and communications/information systems programs.
- Was named **Honor Graduate** of GTE's Network Switching Systems Operator and Maintainer Class, Ft. Gordon, GA; was also **Honor Graduate.**
- Completed the NATO Communications and Information Systems School's Digital Cable Terminating Equipment Technician Course.

LANGUAGES & TECHNICAL EXPERTISE

Languages: Excellent skills in speaking, reading, writing Italian; knowledge of Spanish.
Computers: Offer software knowledge related to Microsoft applications.
Other: Skilled in working with equipment including the GTE Network and MSE (Mobile Subscriber Equipment) switching systems.

EXPERIENCE

SUPERVISOR FOR OPERATIONS PLANNING AND TRAINING. U.S. Army, Italy (2000-present). Known for my detail orientation and ability to plan and organize complex operations on short notice, oversee multinational technicians in a communications support organization working under strict NATO guidance.
- Coordinate and analyze information in order to determine requirements for communications and information systems support in a 24-hour operation.
- Schedule employees; assist in control of a $2 million equipment/tool inventory.
- Develop training programs which increase productivity and response times.
- Apply my language skills in translating both written materials and speech to and from English, Spanish, and Italian for individuals and for the organization.

NETWORK SWITCHING SYSTEMS OPERATOR. U.S. Army, England (1999-00). Installed, carried out troubleshooting, and maintained circuits and commercial telephone lines from four mainframe computers and three independent nodes installed in adjacent buildings; controlled a $2 million inventory.
- Increased switching efficiency 25% through my skill at programming and installing more than 400 telephone lines throughout the community.
- Selected for a special project, implemented 50 different types of changes to telephones which were requested on 15 separate work orders which had to be coordinated.
- Participated in NATO operations in Kosovo; received NATO medals.

COMMUNICATIONS SYSTEM OPERATOR AND MAINTENANCE SPECIALIST. U.S. Army, Ft. Huachuca, AZ (1997-99). Received Certificates of Appreciation for technical skills, enthusiasm, initiative, and professionalism while performing preliminary checks, providing maintenance services, and operating a portable switching system.
- Installed and maintained digital switching system; operated peripheral terminal equipment used to perform programming of the digital switch.
- Became skilled in utilizing SIE/IVSN equipment; main distribution frames; Olivetti 62000eN; MERIDIAN 1 Telephone PABXs; and test equipment for site troubleshooting.
- Increased switching efficiency 25% through programming 400 telephone lines.

PERSONAL

Received 15 medals, Letters of Appreciation, and other honors. Secret security clearance.

Exact Name of Person
Exact Title
Exact Name of Company
Address
City, State, Zip

NETWORK SWITCHING MANAGER

Dear Exact Name of Person: (or Dear Sir or Madam if answering a blind ad):

With the enclosed resume, I would like to introduce my experience and strong interest in the telecommunications field as well as my personal reputation for effectiveness in producing results and building well-trained teams of knowledgeable professionals.

As you will see from my resume, I have worked for the Drug Enforcement Agency for approximately ten years. Although I am highly regarded as a skilled and well-qualified individual and have been aggressively recruited to remain in the agency with the assurance of continued rapid advancement, I have made the decision to leave the DEA. I would like to offer the excellent training and experience gained in the DEA to an organization in need of my skills as a troubleshooter and switching systems operator.

In numerous assignments which have included Network Switching Manager, Extension Switch Supervisor, Communications Chief, Node Center Switch Operator, and Wire and Cable Systems Installer, I have built a reputation for being able to handle pressure, work independently, and lead others to excellent results. I have been recognized with numerous honors including six medals as well as numerous certificates of achievement and accomplishments for my professionalism.

I am confident that I offer a blend of technical expertise and leadership abilities which would allow me to quickly contribute to the success of your operations, and I hope you will welcome my call soon when I try to arrange a brief meeting to discuss your goals and how my background might serve your needs. I can provide outstanding references at the appropriate time.

Sincerely,

Sean Keller

Alternate Last Paragraph:
I hope you will write or call me soon to suggest a time when we might meet to discuss your needs and goals and how my background might serve them. I can provide outstanding references at the appropriate time.

SEAN KELLER

1110½ Hay Street, Fayetteville, NC 28305 • preppub@aol.com • (910) 483-6611

OBJECTIVE To offer technical telecommunications skills with an emphasis on troubleshooting and switching operations to an organization that can benefit from my ability to work independently, handle pressure, and produce outstanding results through leadership.

**EDUCATION
& TRAINING** Have completed approximately one year of general studies at the college level.
Excelled in extensive technical and leadership training which included courses in MSE (Mobile Subscriber Equipment) operations, RF communications, and "Network University."

EXPERIENCE *Advanced in highly technical telecommunications operations, Drug Enforcement Agency:*
NETWORK SWITCHING MANAGER and **BATTALION AIR MOVEMENTS SUPERVISOR.**
Washington, DC (2001-present). Directed junior employees installing, maintaining, and operating telecommunications equipment.
- Acted as the advisor on air operations for a senior executive.

EXTENSION SWITCH SUPERVISOR. Ft. Drum, NY (2000). Promoted to supervise and train four junior supervisors and 15 employees, made decisions on which maintenance personnel to send in response to requests for assistance.
- Frequently requested by name to troubleshoot and solve problems, provided leadership for a team which won a competition for establishing a link with a distant switch.
- Supervised installation and operated line-of-sight multichannel radio terminals, small extension switches, and generator sets valued in excess of $1 million.

COMMUNICATIONS CHIEF. Schofield Barracks, HI (1998-00). Received a Meritorious Service Medal in recognition of my skills and knowledge while managing communications support for several projects and controlling equipment valued in excess of $2.2 million.
- Supervised and trained 13 people and was principal advisor on communications which included such areas as deploying and installing two radio stations.
- Was handpicked to train senior Malaysian personnel on the LRS (Long-Range Surveillance) communications equipment after being evaluated at national-level training as having an exceptional LRS communications section rated as "the best seen to date."

SWITCHING TEAM CHIEF. Schofield Barracks, HI (1997-98). Supervised four specialists while providing maintenance and control of a $1.5 million tandem switching system; installed and operated a tandem switch, modified databases, and performed troubleshooting.
- Established LAN/WAN (Local Area Network/Wide Area Network) systems.
- Awarded an Achievement Medal for services in Haiti (1998), provided uninterrupted communications support for peacekeeping representatives of 17 countries.

NODE CENTER SWITCH OPERATOR. Ft. Bragg, NC (1995-97). Learned how to trouble-shoot links between two systems while building technical skills in troubleshooting, modifying databases, and using computer printouts to determine system faults.

WIRE AND CABLE SYSTEMS INSTALLER and **RADIO OPERATOR.** Saudi Arabia (1992-95). Became known for my initiative and ability to handle pressure running wire for field telephones; operating teletype, modems, and radios; and installing field switches.
- Operated a MARS radio system for the benefit of American personnel participating in the war in the Middle East.

PERSONAL Secret security clearance. Work well independently or in supervisory/leadership roles.

Date

Exact Name of Person
Exact Title
Exact Name of Company
Address
City, State, Zip

Dear Exact Name of Person: (or Dear Sir or Madam if answering a blind ad):

With the enclosed resume, I would like to make you aware of my excellent technical electronics skills, organizational and planning abilities, and attention to detail. After serving my country with distinction, I am in the process of permanently relocating back to the Maryland area where I grew up.

As you will see from my resume, while working for the corporate giant MCI, Inc., I received recognition including three cash bonuses for my professionalism and accomplishments. I offer an extensive background in the installation, troubleshooting, maintenance, configuration, and repair of local and wide area networks, communications equipment, computer systems, and software. Currently assigned as a **Network Switching Systems Supervisor,** I control in excess of $1 million worth of communications equipment, generator sets, and vehicles while supervising four people.

In addition to my main responsibilities as a technical supervisor and operator, I have also been cited for my effectiveness as a substance abuse program manager, jumpmaster for airborne operations, and custodian of secure communications messages and devices. I have earned respect from my superiors for my ability to handle multiple simultaneous tasks and to meet tight time restraints with excellent results.

If you can use an intelligent and articulate professional known for physical and mental toughness, I hope you will welcome my call soon when I try to arrange a brief meeting to discuss your goals and how my background might serve your needs. I can provide outstanding references at the appropriate time.

Sincerely,

Mike Novogratz

Alternate Last Paragraph:
I hope you will write or call me soon to suggest a time when we might meet to discuss your needs and goals and how my background might serve them. I can provide outstanding references at the appropriate time.

MIKE NOVOGRATZ

1110½ Hay Street, Fayetteville, NC 28305   •   preppub@aol.com   •   (910) 483-6611

OBJECTIVE

To benefit an organization that can use a technically proficient professional with an extensive background in installing, troubleshooting, maintaining, configuring, and repairing local and wide area networks, communications equipment, and computer systems/software.

EDUCATION & TRAINING

Completed two years toward a **B.S. in Computer Science**, Houston Junior College, TX.
Certificate in Telecommunications, Texas Community College, Houston, TX, 2000.
Excelled in numerous training courses sponsored by MCI, Inc. including:
      Leadership Development Course (LDC)
      Mobile Subscriber Equipment (MSE) Switching Systems Operator Course
      Network Encryption System Operator Course
      AN/TTC-47 Node Center Enhanced Switch Operator Program

SPECIAL SKILLS

Offer the ability to troubleshoot and repair, to the component level, computer systems and electromechanical devices with analog and digital circuity.
Am familiar with COMSEC (communications security), radio, telephone, and electrical equipment as well as Unix-based software and fiber optics.

EXPERIENCE

Was promoted ahead of my peers and selected to assume positions of increased responsibility while working for MCI, Inc. (1994-present):
NETWORK SWITCHING SYSTEMS SUPERVISOR. Houston, TX (2000-present). Supervise and train a team of four people installing, operating, and maintaining computer hardware and software systems at one of the nation's largest military bases worldwide.
- Earned an award for maintaining 98% reliable communications during a task force operation.
- Configured Network Encryption Systems (NES) organization-wide for major exercises as well as installing and performing troubleshooting on major communications links.
- Oversee the acquisition, implementation, and operation of information technology for a mobile subscriber area organization.
- Train node center personnel within the organization on proper installation and operational procedures for the tactical packet switch networks.
- Control $1 million worth of communications equipment, generator sets, and vehicles.
- Received an award for earning "commendable" ratings on a distribution inspection while overseeing information systems security; was recognized for flawlessly maintaining the accountability and readiness of all equipment.
- Trained personnel while also organizing and inspecting personnel and equipment.
- As COMSEC custodian, manage and distribute secure communications, materials, and devices; was cited for my "unique ability to execute multiple complex tasks."

SMALL EXTENSION NODE TEAM CHIEF and **TECHNICIAN.** Seattle, WA (1996-99). Originally assigned as a Technician on completion of advanced training courses, quickly advanced to a Team Chief position as supervisor of two more junior technicians and was in charge of more than $750,000 worth of equipment and vehicles.
- Received an award for accomplishments which included providing secure and reliable multichannel communications during a large-scale project.

PERSONAL

Secret security clearance. Mentally and physically tough with a positive attitude.

Date

Exact Name of Person
Exact Title
Exact Name of Company
Address
City, State, Zip

Dear Exact Name of Person (or Dear Sir or Madam if answering a blind ad):

I would appreciate an opportunity to talk with you soon about how I could contribute to your organization through my excellent technical skills in information and telecommunications technology.

As you will see from my enclosed resume, I have extensive experience in installing, operating, and maintaining Mobile Subscriber Equipment (MSE). This equipment is recognized as being very complex and I am proud of my accomplishments in learning its intricacies. After only two years as an operator, I was promoted to supervise teams of highly trained communications experts in all facets of installation and maintenance.

I have been honored with two cash bonuses in recognition of my technical skills, supervisory abilities, and professionalism. One of the bonuses was awarded for my accomplishments in providing error-free communications support for a large-scale project and the second for efforts in preparing for a successful external evaluation.

My training included GTE-sponsored courses in network switching, switch update management, and the Network Encryption System (NES) which all led to certification in the area of study. I have also been given responsibilities for functional activities such as records maintenance, training, scheduling, and inventory control.

I am confident that I possess strong technical skills, the ability to supervise and work well with others, and the initiative to work independently. If you can use a young professional with my skills and level of knowledge, I hope you will contact me to suggest a time when we might meet to discuss your needs. I can assure you in advance that I could rapidly become an asset to your organization.

Sincerely,

Robert Porter

ROBERT PORTER

1110½ Hay Street, Fayetteville, NC 28305　　•　　preppub@aol.com　　•　　(910) 483-6611

OBJECTIVE

To offer excellent technical skills in information and telecommunications technology to an organization that would benefit from my ability to supervise and work well with others along with my high levels of initiative and drive and special skills as a troubleshooter.

EDUCATION & TRAINING

Studied Telecommunications at Colby College, Waterville, WA.

Excelled in military training programs which included GTE schools in network switching, switch update management, and the Network Encryption System (NES) as well as a software update course – all courses resulted in certification in the specific area of emphasis.

TECHNICAL EXPERTISE

As a **Network Switching Systems Specialist,** troubleshoot and maintain a wide range of equipment and systems including Mobile Subscriber Equipment (MSE) and the following:

KG-193 Trunk Encryption Device (TED)　　KGX-93A Automatic Key Distribution Center

AN/TTC-47 and 39D Node Center Switches　　SB-4303 Switchboards

AN/TTC-48 Small Extension Node　　Signal Data Converters

AN/TYC-19 Interface Network Gateway Router　　AN/TYC-20 Packet Switch

KY-57, KYK-15, and KYK-13 Key Transfer Devices　　KY-90 Combat Net Radio Interface

SINGARS - Single Channel Ground Airborne Radio System　　COMSEC

J-1077 J Box for Wire Subscribers and X.25 Computers　　Super High Frequency Radio

Offer knowledge and understanding of UNIX, MS Word, and Windows NT2000.

EXPERIENCE

NETWORK SWITCHING SYSTEMS SUPERVISOR. GTE, Seattle, WA (2001-present). Was promoted to supervise six people involved in providing network analysis, troubleshooting, maintenance, and restoration of voice and data networks after excelling as a telecommunications operator.

- Oversee the upkeep, maintenance, and operation of three vehicles and two shelters valued in excess of $1.8 million; requisition supplies and equipment.
- Cited for my determination to see that the work is always completed on time and up to expected standards, achieved excellent results during seven separate projects to various locations around the world both for training and to respond to real-world crises.
- Learned to overcome shortages of materials and took the initiative to see that torn or broken equipment was repaired and kept from further deterioration.
- Maintain a variety of records including COMSEC (communications security) reports, inventories, and personnel evaluations.
- Was honored with two cash bonuses for providing communications support during a large-scale training exercise and a critical external evaluation.

NETWORK SWITCHING SYSTEMS OPERATOR. GTE, San Diego, CA (1997-01). Was promoted to a supervisory role on the basis of technical expertise and leadership skill displayed while installing, operating, maintaining, and troubleshooting communications systems including Local Area and Wide Area Networks (LAN and WAN).

- Learned procedures for installing and maintaining Motorola NES interface with the Internet using X.25 and other packet switching protocols to provide secure military systems.
- Used technical manuals, schematic diagrams, flow charts, and bubble diagrams.
- Created and modified databases within the Mobile Subscriber Equipment network.

PERSONAL

Secret security clearance. Am completely bilingual in English and Spanish.

Exact Name of Person
Title or Position
Name of Company
Address (number and street)
Address (city, state, and zip)

**PROGRAMMER AND
ANALYST**

Dear Exact Name of Person: (or Sir or Madam if answering a blind ad.)

With the enclosed resume, I would like to make you aware of the background in management information systems, computer programming, and troubleshooting which I could put to work for your organization.

With a Top Secret FAV NAC security clearance, I have most recently excelled as a Programmer and Analyst with the Novell Corporation. With a reputation as a versatile technical expert, I have excelled in roles which included UNIX and Novell Programmer, Systems Analyst, Satellite Security Manager, Windows NT Administrator, and Satellite Communications Specialist. While serving my country in the Coast Guard, I worked on several systems which required a Top Secret clearance. In addition to working on the JOTS and serving as JOTS Administrator with UNIX software, I helped rewrite the C++ software for the Link II Top Secret computer.

On numerous occasions I was handpicked for special assignments which required top-notch troubleshooting, problem-solving, and communication skills.

I can provide outstanding personal and professional references at the appropriate time, and I would welcome the opportunity to talk with you in person about how my skills in systems design, implementation, maintenance, and troubleshooting could benefit you, I hope you will contact me to suggest a time when we could talk.

Thank you in advance for your time.

Yours sincerely,

Evan Dreyer

EVAN DREYER

1110½ Hay Street, Fayetteville, NC 28305 • preppub@aol.com • (910) 483-6611

OBJECTIVE To offer my background in management information systems design and implementation to an organization that can use a resourceful technical expert with experience in UNIX programming, internet systems, network communications, and C++ programming and troubleshooting.

SKILLS **Software**: Visual C++, C, Progress, Informix, Access, Pascal, Cobol, Micro-Focus Cobol, Acucobol, Assembler, Basic, Fortran, HTML, JOTS (software requiring Top Secret clearance), Link II (software requiring Top Secret security clearance)
  • Helped rewrite the C ++ software for the Link II Top Secret computer
Operating Systems: Literate in most operating systems, with extensive experience in Windows NT2000, Novell, Windows, UNIX, AIX, HP/UX, DG/UX, XENIX, OS/VS, MVS, DOS

CLEARANCE Top Secret FAV NAC security clearance

EXPERIENCE **PROGRAMMER & ANALYST.** Novell Corporation, locations worldwide (2000-present). Assisted with writing Phase III of the Link II Program and performed extensive troubleshooting as a Link II Operator; was responsible for security of secret and sensitive material which included overseeing all safes, alarms, locking mechanisms, codes, and personnel access to restricted areas; received numerous honors for exceptional performance in the following capacities:

UNIX & Novell Programmer	JOTS Administrator with UNIX Software
KG40 Programmer Encoder/Decoder	Satellite Security Manager
JIMIS Administrator	IBM Software Programmer/Operator
Systems Analyst	Windows NT Administrator
Satellite Communications Specialist	Link II Operator/Troubleshooter

Gained hands-on experience with the following concepts and products:
  • *Command and control:* For three years worked with UNIX software as an **Operator with the JOTS II system,** a battle management system written in C and C++ under the UNIX operating system which provides high-resolution maps as well as complex analysis and evaluation functions; for 19 months, worked as **Security Manager for JOTS/ LINK II** which involved working with KG40 encoder/decoder.
  • *Counter Narcotics:* Worked extensively with the Joint Visually Integrated Display System (JVIDS) developed in C under UNIX and used to support counter narcotics operations.
  • *Satellite Tracking:* Gained expertise with the JOTS Satellite Vulnerability (SATVUL) Program designed to provide surveillance information.
  • *Electronic Warfare:* Worked with the Space and Electronics Warfare Tactical Advanced Work Station (SEWTAWS), a networked UNIX-C system.
  • *Communications:* Worked with the Naval Modular Automated Communications System II (NAVMACS), written in C under UNIX with Windows capabilities, communications interfaces, and PC emulation capabilities.

RADAR COMMUNICATIONS SPECIALIST. Novell Corporation, locations worldwide (1995-99). Excelled in assignments as a UNISYS Operator, Link II Operator, Satellite Communications Operator, and Radar Operator with the Raycass 64/AOS 137/54G.

LORAN "C" OPERATOR. Novell Corporation, locations worldwide (1994-95). Repaired hardware to prevent system failure while earning a reputation as a talented troubleshooter.

EDUCATION Have earned 36 college credits in Criminal Justice, Cayuga County Community College, Cayuga, NY; pursuing completion of my college degree in my spare time.
Completed extensive specialized training related to JMCIS and LINK II.

Date

Exact Name of Person
Exact Title
Exact Name of Company
Address
City, State, Zip

SENIOR SYSTEMS ANALYST

Dear Exact Name of Person (or Dear Sir or Madam if answering a blind ad):

I would appreciate an opportunity to talk with you soon concerning how I could contribute to your organization through my technical expertise with management information systems as well as through the management experience I have gained as a junior military officer.

You will see that I earned my B.S. in Computer Science at The U.S. Military Academy at West Point and, since my graduation, have served as an Army officer at Ft. Bragg, NC. A certified Information Systems Security Officer (ISSO), I am skilled in working with network systems, with client-based server programs, with various software programs, and as a programmer. During my time in the military I have been involved in fielding and integrating sophisticated equipment into existing systems and have become recognized as a technical expert.

In my present job as a Senior Systems Analyst, I played a key role in establishing a Local Area Network (LAN) consisting of more than 100 PCs, servers, and hubs as well as serving as point-of-contact for the integration of a personnel and finance system (SIDPERS 3) considered the largest advancement in database technology the Army has experienced to date.

Earlier as a Management Information Systems Officer, I provided my technical expertise while planning, coordinating and managing administrative and logistical support for information management operations. In this capacity I was credited as a major contributor to the success of efforts to advance the utilization of information technology throughout the 18th Airborne Corps, the parent organization of the 82nd Airborne Division.

If you can use a results-oriented manager with a strong background in management information systems operations, then I look forward to hearing from you soon to arrange a time when we might meet to discuss your needs. I can assure you in advance that I have an excellent reputation and could quickly become a valuable asset to your company.

Sincerely,

Robert Larson

ROBERT LARSON

1110½ Hay Street, Fayetteville, NC 28305   •   preppub@aol.com   •   (910) 483-6611

OBJECTIVE
To offer technical expertise and knowledge to an organization that can benefit from my experience with management information systems operations as well as from the management skills I have refined as a junior military officer.

EDUCATION
Earned a B.S. degree in **Computer Science** from **The United States Military Academy at West Point,** NY, 1998.

CERTIFICATIONS
Am a certified Information Systems Security Officer (ISSO).

COMPUTER EXPERTISE
Highly proficient with Microsoft Office, am also proficient with networking systems. Am experienced with client-based server programs for finance and personnel applications. Program in Networks.

EXPERIENCE
Am excelling as a U.S. Army officer, Ft. Bragg, NC:
SENIOR SYSTEMS ANALYST. (2000-present). Played a key role in establishing a Local Area Network (LAN) comprised of more than 100 PCs, servers, and hubs while managing the automation and radio communications support for personnel and finance departments servicing the 82nd Airborne Division.
- Manage one Systems Analyst, two junior military Systems Analysts, and one manager.
- Have become widely recognized as the technical expert on software and serve as the point-of-contact and technical advisor for automation and communications distribution and implementation for an organization with nine corporate elements.
- Oversee maintenance, installation, operation, and management of systems while controlling more than $1 million worth of high-tech equipment.
- Ensure the smooth integration of new technology — was POC for the fielding of the SIDPERS 3 system, considered the largest advancement in database technology the Army has experienced to date.
- Designed and now maintain the unit web page.
- Established a training program which resulted in personnel exceeding standards.

MANAGEMENT INFORMATION SYSTEMS OFFICER. (1999). Trained, counseled, and managed two supervisors and nine enlisted soldiers while planning, coordinating, and directing administrative and logistical activities for information management operations.
- Handled activities ranging from controlling publications and blank forms, to overseeing records management programs, to providing light reproduction and courier support, to managing a distribution center.
- Provided the technical expertise which allowed automation and information services to be integrated into headquarters operation as well as during field exercises and overseas assignments for a rapid response organization.
- Managed a $1 million reproduction budget and was credited with playing a key role in bringing the organization forward in utilizing information technology to facilitate the flow of information throughout a diverse and geographically scattered organization.

FIRST-LINE SUPERVISOR. (1998). Supervised 42 people in a department which provided communications support for airborne operations throughout the world.
- Trained and developed personnel in a unit frequently called on to travel on short notice for indefinite periods of time and which underwent a 50% personnel turnover in one year.

PERSONAL
Was entrusted with a Secret security clearance. Will relocate.

Date

Exact Name of Person
Exact Title or Position
Company Name
Company Address (street and number)
Company Address (city, state, and ZIP)

Dear Exact Name (or Dear Sir or Madam if answering a blind ad):

With the enclosed resume, I would like to express my interest in exploring employment opportunities with your organization.

As you will see from my resume, I am working for the U.S. State Department, where I have earned a reputation as a talented manager of time and resources who can be counted on to find ways to increase productivity, morale, and efficiency. I am known for my willingness to take the initiative to try and make operations run more smoothly.

Presently attending an advanced technical school in Pensacola, FL, I recently returned from Japan where my most recent assignment was as a Supervisory Signal Communications Analyst. Officially described as a resourceful and creative leader with superb initiative and demonstrated leadership, I excelled in developing and implementing improvements. Among my accomplishments were streamlining procedures which reduced error rates 20%, creating standard operating procedures guidelines which were adopted for use by entry-level and senior employees, and developing a UNIX-based file system which increased daily production rates 300%!

While in Japan I advanced from an earlier job as a Communications Analyst and was quickly singled out as an exceptional performer with strong technical knowledge and leadership skills.

Known for my high personal standards of integrity and honesty, I was entrusted with a Top Secret security clearance. My technical expertise includes proficiency with the use of automated systems, and I am familiar with Windows and UNIX-based systems.

If you can use a hard-working young professional who gets results while setting an example for others to follow, I hope you will contact me to suggest a time when we might meet to discuss your needs. I can provide excellent personal and professional references.

Sincerely,

Adam Howard

ADAM HOWARD

1110½ Hay Street, Fayetteville, NC 28305   •   preppub@aol.com   •   (910) 483-6611

OBJECTIVE

To offer a reputation as a talented manager of time and resources who possesses outstanding leadership skills and the ability to take the initiative in developing ways to increase productivity, morale, and efficiency.

TRAINING

Have attended numerous U.S. State Department-sponsored training programs with an emphasis on technical skills in communications and signals analysis.

TECHNICAL SKILLS & CLEARANCE

Proficient in using automated systems to collect, analyze, and disseminate information; familiar with Windows and UNIX-based systems.
Entrusted with a **Top Secret** security clearance.

EXPERIENCE

Am building a reputation for achieving results in the U.S. State Department:
TECHNICAL STUDENT. Pensacola, FL (2002-03). Attend the Intermediate Signal Analyst School to receive advanced training.

SUPERVISORY SIGNAL COMMUNICATIONS ANALYST. Japan (2002-03). Described in official evaluations as an excellent trainer who is "resourceful and creative," coordinated with national level agencies while maintaining an extensive signal database in support of security objectives.
- On my own initiative, updated procedures and streamlined reporting capabilities with the result that error rates decreased 20%.
- Provided guidance and advice to 15 junior personnel; was selected to serve on a quality assurance board because of my professionalism and knowledge.
- Created a 27-page standard operating procedures manual which quickly gained acceptance as guidance for senior and inexperienced analysts.
- Made important contributions to development of materials and as a key participant in a high-visibility conference through written and verbal skills.
- Initiated and hosted a one-week site training visit by a technical systems expert which ensured eight analysts received hands-on training on a new system.
- Increased daily production 300% through development of a UNIX-based file system used to process, edit, and manage 15,000 signal messages monthly.
- Participated on community athletic teams and volunteered during an event which raised $1500 for morale/welfare/recreation programs; also served as chairman of a Special Olympics committee; was cited as an **"excellent role model with a positive attitude"** as a youth soccer coach.

COMMUNICATIONS ANALYST. Japan (2000-01). Quickly became recognized as a "subject matter expert" who was technically knowledgeable and skilled in processing communications using sophisticated automated data processing (ADP) equipment.
- Gained recognition for completing a training cycle early and becoming the first person in my company to become dual qualified in two specific technical areas.
- Was cited as "expertly" drafting and releasing 50 tactical reports with at least a 95% quality control rating.

Highlights of other experience: Began my military career by excelling as a student in several technical programs after earlier jobs in the restaurant and landscaping businesses.

PERSONAL

Received a Joint Service Achievement Medal from the National Security Agency in honor of "outstanding technical skills, superb initiative, and leadership." Outstanding references.

Date

Exact Name of Person
Exact Title
Exact Name of Company
Address
City, State, Zip

Dear Exact Name of Person (or Dear Sir or Madam if answering a blind ad):

With the enclosed resume, I would like to make you aware of my technical knowledge and skills in systems administration as well as my reputation as a detail-oriented and analytical professional with a talent for quickly mastering and applying new technology.

As you will see from my enclosed resume, I have served my country in the U.S. Air Force and am in the process of leaving the military and exploring opportunities in the civilian workplace. While in military service, I have taken every opportunity to attend college and complete technical and leadership training programs. While excelling in demanding full-time jobs including two simultaneously, I have pursued a degree in Computer Information Systems and completed more than 80 semester hours of college-level studies in Business Administration and CIS fields.

I earned the Microsoft Certified Professional (**MCP**) recently and, in November, will receive additional certifications as a Microsoft Certified System Engineer (**MCSE**) and Microsoft Certified Professional and Internet (**MCP&I**). Selected for a slot as a Systems Administrator, I have applied my initiative in mastering technology which has allowed me to earn recognition as one of the most knowledgeable in this field in an airlift organization which requires uninterrupted support to carry out its worldwide missions. I have excelled as an Administrator for a resource domain in a single-master domain environment.

Earlier experience in inventory control and supply operations gave me the chance to become familiar with automated systems and pursue advanced technical skills. Throughout my eight years of military service, I have been recognized as a dynamic and energetic individual who will not give up when facing a challenge. Instead I will find a way to get the job done while improving productivity and efficiency. These skills and abilities have resulted in being honored with two Aerial Achievement Medals and an Air Force Achievement Medal as well as with the prestigious John L. Levitow Award as the #1 graduate from Airman Leadership School.

If you can use a well-organized and detail-oriented professional with strong technical knowledge along with the ability to quickly master new technology, I hope you will contact me soon to suggest a time when we might have a brief discussion of how I could contribute to your organization. I can provide excellent references.

Sincerely,

Benjamin Long

BENJAMIN LONG

1110½ Hay Street, Fayetteville, NC 28305　•　preppub@aol.com　•　(910) 483-6611

OBJECTIVE

To offer strong technical know-how in systems administration and networking to an organization that can benefit from my analytical skills and reputation as a quick earner who can be counted on to apply innovative ideas and find workable solutions.

EDUCATION & TRAINING

Pursuing degree in **Computer Information Systems**, Wenters University, SC.
Studied **Business Administration,** Mayland Community College, Spruce Pine, SC.
Received the prestigious **John L. Levitow Award** for academic and leadership excellence as the #1 graduate from Airman Leadership School, 2001.
Distinguished Graduate, Loadmaster Qualification Course, 2001.

LICENSES & TECHNICAL EXPERTISE

Professional licenses and certifications for **Windows NT 4.0** include:
- **Microsoft Certified Professional (MCP),** received August 2001.
- **Microsoft Certified System Engineer (MCSE), Microsoft Certified Professional and Internet (MCP&I)**, will receive October 2001.

Install and maintain NT Workstation and Server; troubleshoot and maintain Ethernet connectivity; strong skills with NT Server and NT Workstation, HP Direct Administration and Norton Antivirus; knowledgeable of Excel, Word, and Access.

EXPERIENCE

Earned a reputation as a fast learner and resourceful problem solver, U.S. Air Force: SYSTEMS ADMINISTRATOR. Pope AFB, NC (2000-present). Handpicked for this job in a networking office; applied my initiative along with skills learned "hands-on" to become one of the most knowledgeable professionals in my field in an airlift squadron which requires uninterrupted communications and automated systems support.
- As an **Administrator for a resource domain in a single-master domain environment,** have provided support for approximately 350 users with 150 NT workstations, two servers, and 25 networked printers.
- Worked closely with vendors including Microsoft, Micron, Dell, and Gateway to ensure hardware and software compliance as the unit's Y2K representative; developed contingency plans which were in place in case of Y2K failures.
- Determined hardware and software requirements; acquired equipment; established user accounts; helped users set up e-mail and Internet accounts; maintained Ethernet connectivity.
- Rebuilt obsolete or outdated hardware to include replacing hard drives and network cards; reformatted hard drives and reinstalled or upgraded software.
- Maintained accountability over all computer equipment to include keeping inventory control records and delivering unserviceable or obsolete items to a reutilization depot.
- Have excelled in this highly technical and demanding role simultaneously with a job I have held in aircraft load planning and inspection.

AIRCRAFT LOAD PLANNING AND INSPECTION SPECIALIST. Pope AFB, TX (1996-99). Have displayed a dynamic style of meeting and overcoming challenges which allowed me to excel in a simultaneous technical planning and inspection role.
- Computed load placement and ensured that cargo, mail, and passengers were properly loaded and secured on C-130 aircraft while logging 900 flight hours as a Loadmaster.
- Was cited as a "vigilant" professional who made immeasurable contributions to the success of projects such as hurricane relief efforts, transportation of humanitarian relief cargo, and delivery of Secret Service personnel and Presidential support equipment to Columbine, CO, following the high school shooting incident, and air shows.

PERSONAL

Organized; strong time management skills. Quickly master technology. Secret clearance.

Date

Exact Name of Person
Exact Title
Exact Name of Company
Address
City, State, Zip

SYSTEMS
ANALYST
Dear Exact Name of Person (or Dear Sir or Madam if answering a blind ad):

I would appreciate an opportunity to talk with you soon about how I could contribute to your organization through my background and strong interest in the field of information technology as well as through the management abilities I have refined as a military officer.

As you will see from my enclosed resume, I am a Senior Manager with the Micron Corporation and have built a reputation as an assertive, articulate, and intelligent professional with exceptionally well-developed analytical and problem-solving skills. Since earning my B.S. degree in Administrative Office Management (Systems Management), I have completed the Micron Corporation's Computer Science School.

In my current job as a Systems Analyst, I have been the chief architect of the Automated Approach to Training (AAT), a $10 million application supporting a $1 billion learning program. On a formal performance evaluation, I have been commended for my "natural leadership style which is complemented by technical knowledge of hardware infrastructures and IDEF modeling." I offer extensive experience in enterprise database application development, as well as in software design and development using such development tools as Rational Rose and Unified Modeling Language (UML).

While applying my technical knowledge of automation operations, I have successfully completed projects to automate the budget, logistics, training, and personnel administration procedures for improved efficiency and productivity in several organizations. I have frequently been singled out for praise and cited as an exceptional performer who can be depended on to solve any problem and bring diverse work forces together to exceed performance standards. Technical training for which I have been selected has included the Windows NT System Administrator Course leading to NT Administrator certification.

If you can use an experienced information technology professional who offers well-developed technical skills and an enthusiastic style of leadership by example, I hope you will contact me to suggest a time when we might meet to discuss your needs. I can assure you in advance that I could rapidly become an asset to your organization.

Sincerely,

Phillip Dees

PHILLIP DEES

1110½ Hay Street, Fayetteville, NC 28305 • preppub@aol.com • (910) 483-6611

OBJECTIVE

To offer expertise in information technology to an organization that can benefit from my technical skills as well as leadership ability which has been refined as a project manager.

EDUCATION & TRAINING

B.S., Administrative Office Management (Systems Management), Central Virginia University, Richmond, VA, 1993.

Excelled in training programs including an advanced staff management school and Micron's Computer Science School emphasizing system hardware, design, **Local Area Network (LAN)** management, and programming languages (**Visual Basic, ADA,** and **Basic AI**).

Completed courses in A+ Microcomputer Support and Service, **Windows NT Server** Core Technologies, **Microsoft Exchange Server** Concepts and Administration, Unified Modeling Language (UML) Concepts and Analysis, Rational Rose, Asymetrix Multimedia Tool Book, and Paint Shop Pro.

COMPUTER EXPERTISE

Proficient in Windows NT2000, Novell, network security, IDEF modeling, BPWIN and ERWIN modeling software, web design and development, and software engineering, design, and development using Rational Rose, UML, and other software design and development tools.

- Selected for Windows NT System Administration Course leading to NT Administrator certification.
- Completed a resident course on the Powerbuilder application language utilized by the ASAT and SATS system development teams.
- Completed state-of-the-art training in Structure Query Language (SQL).
- Extensive experience in enterprise database application development.

Offer knowledge in Visual Basic, Powerbuilder object-oriented design, data communications, hardware construction and design, LANs, and Wide Area Networks.

EXPERIENCE

Advanced to the rank of Senior Manager with the Micron Corporation:

SYSTEMS ANALYST. Richmond, VA (2000-present). Was the key developer of the Automated Approach to Training (AAT), which is the state-of-the-art training and policy development and production tool for the Department of Defense and the major generator of information for the Standard Training System (STS).

- Have been the key architect in developing the Automated Approach to Training (AAT), a $10 million application supporting a $1 billion learning program; on a formal performance evaluation, was commended for "a natural leadership style which is complemented by technical knowledge of hardware infrastructures and IDEF modeling."

PERSONNEL ADMINISTRATION MANAGER AND ADVISOR. Sacramento, CA (1996-00). Molded eight personnel specialists into a team which provided timely and accurate support for a 1,500-person center training individuals in 11 different technical career fields.

- Developed a review and analysis program which resulted in a 99% on-time document processing rate; was handpicked as Consultant at Micron's premier training center.

PROJECT MANAGER. Charlotte, NC (1994-96). Significantly improved procedures while overseeing issues related to the training and performance, health and welfare, and logistical support of 340 people and $1 million worth of property.

- Brought about dramatic improvement in training by automating many routine tasks and involving supervisory personnel in maximizing training resources.

PERSONAL

Secret security clearance. Received several medals and awards.

Exact Name of Person
Exact Title
Exact Name of Company
Address
City, State, Zip

**SYSTEMS
ANALYST**
Dear Exact Name of Person (or Dear Sir or Madam if answering a blind ad):

With the enclosed resume, I would like to express my interest in exploring employment opportunities with your organization.

As you will see from my enclosed resume, I am a Senior Systems Analyst involved in database design, development, and integration. With a strong reputation in the field of database application integration and management, I am especially skilled in enterprise-wide project management. I have become proficient at deploying and integrating new database applications, and I have also designed, developed, and deployed database-stored procedures and triggers. I have applied my knowledge and experience with HTML in designing and developing many dynamic project web sites. In enterprise database application development, as well as in software design and development, I have used a wide range of tools including Oracle, Unified Modeling Language (UML), Front Page, Hot Metal Pro, and Coldfusion 4.5.

With an aggressive bottom-line orientation and a strong customer service approach, I have been credited with bringing about significant improvements for customers while overseeing all aspects of their projects. I am known for my ability to translate technical language into information easily understood by everyone, from senior managers to end users.

After earning a B.S. degree in the Systems Management field, I excelled as a Systems Analyst with the Department of Defense. On a formal performance evaluation, I was commended for my "natural leadership style as well as technical knowledge of hardware infrastructures and IDEF modeling."

If you can use an experienced information technology professional who offers well-developed technical skills along with an enthusiastic style of leadership by example, I hope you will contact me to suggest a time when we might meet to discuss your needs. I can assure you in advance that I could rapidly become an asset to your organization. I can provide outstanding references.

Sincerely,

Jon Du Pre

JON DU PRE

1110½ Hay Street, Fayetteville, NC 28305　·　preppub@aol.com　·　(910) 483-6611

OBJECTIVE　　To offer expertise in information technology to an organization that can benefit from my technical skills as well as strong management abilities refined as a military officer.

EDUCATION　　B.S., **Administrative Office Management (Systems Management)**, Central Washington University, Ellensburg, WA, 1995.

TRAINING　　Courses in **Oracle SQL** and **PL/SQL, JavaScript, Microsoft Visual Basic 6.0, Oracle Developer/2000, UNIX Programming**, and **C++ Programming**, United Technology Institute, 2000; **TeamPlay version 1.5.9** project management, Primavera, 1999.
Training programs included an advanced management school and the **U.S. Army Computer Science School** emphasizing system hardware, design, Local Area Network (**LAN**) management, and programming languages with an emphasis on **Visual Basic and Ada95.** Courses in **A+ Microcomputer Support and Service, Windows NT Server 4.0** Core Technologies, **Microsoft Exchange Server 5.5** Concepts and Administration, **Unified Modeling Language (UML)** Concepts and Analysis, and **Rational Rose.**

COMPUTER EXPERTISE　　Proficient with **Oracle developer** and **Visual Basic 6**, additionally use **Embarcader Rapid SQL 5.6, Visio 5.0 Technical Drawing software, Allround Automation PL/SQL Developer, Primavera TeamPlay Enterprise Project Management software** versions 1.6.4 and 2.0 as well as **Front Page 2000** and **Hot Metal Pro** version 4; basic knowledge of **Coldfusion version 4.5.**
- Proficient in **Windows 95/98** and **NT, IDEFIX** database modeling techniques, **BPWIN** and **ERWIN** database modeling software, **web design/development**, and **software engineering/design/development**.
- Completed a resident course on the **Powerbuilder 5.0 application language** utilized by system development teams.
- Extensive experience in **enterprise database application development**.
Knowledge of data communications, hardware construction and design, LANs, and WANs.

EXPERIENCE　　**SENIOR SYSTEMS ANALYST.** RunningSystems, Inc., Washington, DC (2000-present). Gained respect for my expertise in implementing the enterprise-wide project management database and TeamPlay project management tools which have resulted in significant improvements for customers while overseeing all aspects of database design and development and integrating databases for seamless information flow through separate departments and agencies.
- Work closely with all levels from senior management to end users to explain system applications and issues encountered while implementing and integrating true management solutions.
- Developed Java and Active-X solutions to integration of the enterprise-wide project management system with existing customer business processes and automated tools.

SYSTEMS ANALYST. Department of Defense, Washington, DC (1996-99). Was a major participant in the development of a new application supporting a $1 billion learning program; this state-of-the-art training and policy development and production tool was the major generator of information for the Department of Defense Training System.
- Commended for technical hardware infrastructures and IDEF modeling knowledge.

PERSONAL　　Self-starter with strong personal initiative. Member, Computer Management Institute. Strong references on request.

Date

Exact Name of Person
Exact Title
Exact Name of Company
Address
City, State, Zip

TELECOMMUNICATIONS MAINTENANCE TECHNICIAN

Dear Exact Name of Person: (or Dear Sir or Madam if answering a blind ad):

With the enclosed resume, I would like to make you aware of my background in telecommunications installation, maintenance, repair, and operation gained while working in the U.S.Customs Service.

As you will see from my resume, through specialized training and experience, I have become skilled in multichannel transmission systems operations and maintenance. Among my skills are maintaining equipment to the unit level, establishing links within a network, establishing mobile subscriber equipment (MSE) links, and maintaining links within a network.

Presently assigned to a four-person team, I am frequently called on to act in a leadership role. I have been credited with playing an important role in the success of this newly established and configured team of telecommunications specialists. My team provides uninterrupted communications support for units which must respond on short notice to trouble spots anywhere in the world.

If you can use an experienced telecommunications specialist, I offer strong skills in team leadership and supervisory roles. I hope you will welcome my call soon when I try to arrange a brief meeting to discuss your goals and how my background might serve your needs. I can provide outstanding references at the appropriate time.

Sincerely,

Elmer Oliphant

Alternate Last Paragraph:
I hope you will write or call me soon to suggest a time when we might meet to discuss your needs and goals and how my background might serve them. I can provide outstanding references at the appropriate time.

ELMER OLIPHANT

1110½ Hay Street, Fayetteville, NC 28305 • preppub@aol.com • (910) 483-6611

OBJECTIVE

To contribute my technical telecommunications skills to an organization that can use a talented young professional who offers superior communication and motivational abilities along with a versatile background in areas including finance and marketing.

EDUCATION & TRAINING

Have completed approximately two years of general college course work.
Completed technical training for multichannel transmission systems operators and maintenance specialists which was sponsored by the U.S. Customs Service.

TECHNICAL SKILLS

Install, operate, maintain, and repair telecommunications equipment:
operate: SINCGARS single-channel and frequency hopping modes
maintain to unit level: order wire control unit C-10716/TRC (OCU-I and II)
radio repeater sets AN/TRC-138A and 174
radio terminal sets AN/TRC-173 and 175
remote multiplexer-combiner TD-1234/G
trunk group multiplexer TD-1236/G
digital data group modem MD-1026(P)/G
low-speed cable driver modem MD-1023 and 1026(P)/G

radio sets AN/GRC 103 and 222
group multiplexer TD-1237/G
radio set AN/GRC-226(V)
digital data modem MD-1065/G
modem MD-1270(P)/T

establish link within a network:
using radio terminal sets AN/TRC-173 and 175
using radio repeater sets AN/TRC-174 and 138A
using LOS multichannel radio terminal AN/TRC-190(V)
using radio access unit AN/TRC-191
establishing and maintaining mobile subscriber equipment (MSE) links:
radio access unit AN/TRC-191

EXPERIENCE

Have advanced to leadership roles while refining technical skills, U.S. Customs Service:
TELECOMMUNICATIONS OPERATOR AND MAINTENANCE TECHNICIAN. Miami, FL (1998-present). Am frequently called on to act as the leader of a four-person team of multichannel transmission operators and maintainers.

- Have played a major role in the success of a team which was developed from scratch to provide support for a signal communications organization.
- Helped manage the actions of subordinate personnel while supervising the installation, operation, and maintenance of communications systems which supported missions which have to be carried out on short notice anywhere in the world.

TELECOMMUNICATIONS OPERATOR AND MAINTENANCE TECHNICIAN. Germany (1996-98). Made valuable contributions to the success of a four-person team which established and maintained communications despite the drawbacks of working and living in a foreign country; earned a respected medal.

- Selected to handle responsibilities as a transportation coordinator for a seven-month period in 1998, learned to handle the details of providing logistics support.

Highlights of earlier experience in computer accounting and marketing, Houston, TX:
As an Account Representative, gained extensive, in-depth experience in computer accounting and business operations while involved in liquidating accounts receivable.
As a Marketing Representative, was a key factor in the success of sales efforts.

PERSONAL

Have basic skills in German, Spanish, Italian, and French. Was entrusted with a Secret security clearance. Am highly self-disciplined with strong time management skills.

Date

Exact Name of Person
Exact Title
Exact Name of Company
Address
City, State, Zip

Dear Exact Name of Person: (or Dear Sir or Madam if answering a blind ad):

With the enclosed resume, I would like to make you aware of my background, skills, and experience related to technical telecommunications and cryptographic equipment troubleshooting, maintenance, and operations.

As you will see from my resume, while working for the Textronix Corporation for approximately four years, I quickly advanced to supervisory roles. With this major defense contractor, I have put my technical know-how and supervisory skills to work in numerous classified overseas missions vital to national security. For example, during situations in Africa, Japan, Puerto Rico, and Egypt, I played a key role in managing radio communications in support of Special Forces operations.

With a broad range of experience, I am skilled in network switching operations, wire systems installation and operations, switchboard programming, maintenance, and interfacing. Familiar with the military's standard cryptographic devices, I can recognize and decipher most cryptographic messages as well as troubleshooting and repairing the equipment.

My versatile experience while in the military service has included fielding and testing new systems, maintaining reports and records, and training others in technical subject matter. Known for my low-key style and approach, I offer excellent technical knowledge and skills along with a reputation as a dedicated and honest professional. If you can use an experienced individual known for his high level of integrity, I hope you will welcome my call soon when I try to arrange a brief meeting to discuss your goals and how my background might serve your needs. I can provide outstanding references at the appropriate time.

Sincerely,

Robin Olds

Alternate Last Paragraph:
I hope you will write or call me soon to suggest a time when we might meet to discuss your needs and goals and how my background might serve them. I can provide outstanding references at the appropriate time.

ROBIN OLDS

1110½ Hay Street, Fayetteville, NC 28305   •   preppub@aol.com   •   (910) 483-6611

OBJECTIVE

To offer expertise in technical operations related to the troubleshooting and repair of telecommunications and cryptographic systems as well as a reputation as a young professional who can be counted on to dedicate every effort to keeping systems operational.

EDUCATION & TRAINING

Completed college course work in Computer Operations, University of Maryland, 1995.

Graduated from the Telecommunications Operator's Course, Ft. Gordon, GA, 1994.

CLEARANCE

Have been entrusted with a Top Secret/SCI security clearance.

EQUIPMENT EXPERTISE

Install, operate, troubleshoot, and maintain telecommunications equipment including:

- automated switchboards
- fax machines
- mini and mainframe computers
- manual switchboards
- telephone and switchboard test equipment
- 26-pair telephone cable
- communications security (COMSEC) devices including STU III telephones

Proficient with computer programs which include the following:

Windows NT	SARAH Internet	MTF Editor (MDT)
Windows 3.1	Works 1998 Lotus 1-2-3	WordPerfect
MS Office Binder	Windows 97 File Maker Pro	MS Photo Editor
ProComm (Pro Communications)	Delrina Form Flow DINAH	
MS Office 97: Word, Excel, PowerPoint, Access, and Outlook		

EXPERIENCE

Advanced to a supervisory role while earning a reputation as a dependable and reliable "behind the scenes" type of technical professional with the ability to quickly master new systems and procedures, Textronix Corporation:

SUPERVISORY TELECOMMUNICATIONS OPERATOR AND MAINTAINER. Washington, DC (1999-02). Supervised four telecommunications specialists while working with MDT, ProComm, COMSEC, SCAMPI, and numerous other computer systems and devices while providing technical support for quick-response missions.

- Was selected to participate in special classified missions vital to national security and which required travel to areas of Africa, Egypt, Japan, and Puerto Rico.
- While on one assignment in Africa, was credited with helping in the efforts which allowed citizens of the Ivory Coast to take back control of their country.
- Fielded and tested the Secure Enroute Communications Package (SECOMP); then trouble-shot and managed this communications system.
- Oversaw and personally installed, operated, and performed company-level maintenance on telecommunications and automated message switching equipment.
- Interpreted and used appropriate technical manuals and guidelines in connection with my experience and knowledge to diagnose problems and troubleshoot networks.
- Operated automated computers while receiving, storing, transmitting, and forwarding data communications; performed system backups to ensure dependability of equipment.
- Corrected communications security (COMSEC) violations; coordinated work schedules; maintained work logs; programmed automatic switchboard systems.

TELECOMMUNICATIONS SUPERVISOR and **COMPUTER OPERATOR.** Korea (1995-99). Supervised four telecommunications specialists while meeting the demands of these two jobs simultaneously; provided company-level and direct support maintenance on PCs.

- Cited for my skill as a trainer, instructed peers, subordinates, and supervisors.

PERSONAL

Was honored with an Army Commendation Medal and a National Defense Service Medal in recognition of my professionalism. I am licensed to operate cargo and utility trucks.

Date

Exact Name of Person
Exact Title
Exact Name of Company
Address
City, State, Zip

Dear Exact Name of Person (or Dear Sir or Madam if answering a blind ad):

With the enclosed resume, I would like to make you aware of my background in telecommunications and computer systems operations.

While working for the ABX Computer Company, I have built a reputation as a talented and articulate leader while developing expertise and strong knowledge in areas ranging from communications security, to fiber optics, to PBX management, to help desk management, to voice mail/call accounting management. I have also excelled in operational areas including personnel management, telecommunications operations supervision, and instructing/training roles as well as in research and development and the fielding and testing of new systems.

In my present assignment as a Telecommunications Supervisor, I am applying project management skills as the company's liaison with the U.S. Navy and its systems development group during the testing and validation of an experimental Portable Secure Messaging System. I am responsible for utilizing, upgrading, maintaining, and accounting for more than $2.5 million worth of computer and communications equipment. In prior military assignments, I have controlled, installed, and maintained digital and analog phones and phone lines, fiber optics, and computer hardware and software as well as overseeing communications security (COMSEC) procedures and training technical personnel including those from Middle Eastern and African countries.

Presently pursuing a Bachelor's degree, I have completed extensive technical training which has led to certification in PBX Management (Lucent Technologies and Mitel), communications security (National Security Agency), and Microsoft Windows and Office (Cedallion). I have also been certified in fiber optics installation and repair, computer software/hardware installation and repair, and secure text messaging transfer.

If you can use an experienced and technically proficient professional who has consistently been recognized as a reliable and honest individual, I hope you will contact me soon to suggest a time when we might meet to discuss your needs. I can assure you in advance that I can provide outstanding references and could quickly become an asset to your organization.

Sincerely,

Betty Merritt

BETTY MERRITT

1110½ Hay Street, Fayetteville, NC 28305　　•　　preppub@aol.com　　•　　(910) 483-6611

OBJECTIVE　　To offer expertise in project management and a broad base of technical experience with telecommunications and computer systems to an organization that can use an articulate and intelligent professional with exceptional motivational and customer service skills.

EDUCATION, TRAINING & CERTIFICATIONS　　Am only two courses short of a Bachelor's degree, Regents College of the State of New York, Albany; have completed 134 credit hours.

Completed extensive technical training leading to certification in the following areas:
　　Fiber optics installation and repair/computer software and hardware installation and repair
　　Microsoft Windows and Office programs (Cedalion)
　　Communications security (National Security Agency)
　　PBX management (Lucent Technologies and Mitel)
　　Secure text messaging transfer over satellites, phone line, or high-frequency transmission
Through experience and training, gained knowledge and skills related to following areas:
　　troubleshooting and repairing telecommunications and computer equipment;
　　COMSEC, radio, telephones, routers, computers, CISCO router

EXPERIENCE　　**Have advanced as a project manager, supervisor, and technical specialist, ABX Computer Company:**

TELECOMMUNICATIONS SUPERVISOR. New York, NY (2000-present). Applied technical and project management expertise as the Army's liaison during the testing and validation of an experimental Department of Defense system – the Portable Secure Messaging System.

- Worked in close cooperation with my counterparts in a government systems development group during this joint project. Utilized, maintained, accounted for, and upgraded $2.5 million worth of computer and communications equipment; assessed project needs.
- Excelled in motivating personnel while training them and evaluating their performance.

PBX MANAGER, COMMUNICATIONS SPECIALIST AND TECHNICIAN, and **TRAINING SPECIALIST.** Dallas, TX (1997-99). Controlled a $17 million inventory of commercial communications equipment while handling multiple supervisory, technical, and managerial duties in support of missions vital to national security.

- Administered, operated, managed, and/or maintained several systems ranging from a Lucent G-3 PBX switch, to a Mitel SX2000 PBX switch, to Lucent Call Accounting and Intuity Audix Voice Mail Systems. Installed digital and analog phones and phone lines as well as installing Life Cycle Replacement computers.
- Installed, repaired, and maintained fiber optics lines for LAN and WAN use along with repairing hardware and software in existing LAN and WAN computers.
- Specially selected to oversee communications security procedures, was liaison with the NSA for COMSEC, and instructed users and technicians in phone systems and COMSEC.

COMMUNICATIONS SECURITY MANAGER. Houston, TX (1995-97). Maintained, accounted for, and dispersed in excess of 6,000 security codes in a 17,000-person division.

COMMUNICATIONS TECHNICIAN and TRAINING SPECIALIST. Lexington, KY (1991-95). Applied my technical and motivational skills while taking more than 50 people with no prior knowledge of telecommunications equipment and developing them into 100% effective communications professionals able to operate and maintain state-of-the-art systems.

- Designed and installed commercial communications systems in Jordan, Kuwait, Qatar, and Iraq as well as in several African countries.

PERSONAL　　Was entrusted with a Top Secret/SSBI security clearance.

Date

Exact Name of Person
Exact Title
Exact Name of Company
Address
City, State, Zip

Dear Exact Name of Person: (or Dear Sir or Madam if answering a blind ad):

With the enclosed resume, I would like to make you aware of my interest in exploring employment opportunities within your organization.

As you will see from my enclosed resume, I offer a strong base of knowledge related to the telecommunications field. In my most recent position, I served with distinction in a supervisory role. I trained and supervised other individuals in erecting and maintaining antennas up to 30 meters, operating and maintaining line-of-sight radios, and providing expert preventive maintenance on trucks, communications shelters, and generators. I have trained dozens of individuals in techniques for safely operating and maintaining telecommunications equipment.

I hold a BICSI certification, a certification in Telecommunications Installation and Maintenance, and have completed college courses related to fiber optics, cable splicing, LAN, and many other areas. While working for Lucent Technologies, I earned a reputation as a talented problem solver and troubleshooter, and I received numerous medals, honors, and certificates of achievement.

I am confident that I can become a highly valued employee of an organization that can use a hard worker with strong technical knowledge and supervisory experience. I hope you will contact me to suggest a time when we might meet in person to discuss your needs.

Sincerely,

Syd Moran

SYD MORAN

1110½ Hay Street, Fayetteville, NC 28305   •   preppub@aol.com   •   (910) 483-6611

OBJECTIVE   I want to benefit an organization that can use a telecommunications professional who offers experience in installation and maintenance as well as employee training and supervision.

EDUCATION   Completed **with honors** the following college courses, Central Illinois Community College, 2001:

Telecom Basic Electricity	Fiber Optics: OSP and LAN	Station I & R
Comdial Key Systems	BICSI Standards	LAN: Copper
Digital CO Installation	Cable Fault Installation	Cable Splicing

Graduated from the Multi-Channel Transmission Systems Operator-Maintainer Course sponsored by GTE Government Systems Corp. and the U.S. Army Signal Center, 1996.
Graduated from Walt Whitman High School, Huntington Station, NY, 1991.

CERTIFICATIONS   Received BICSI Certification; am currently an apprentice.
Received certifications for driving wheeled vehicles.
Received Certificate in Telecommunications Installation and Maintenance.

EXPERIENCE   **Lucent Technologies: Was promoted ahead of my peers to supervisory responsibilities while acquiring expertise in the telecommunications field:**
TELECOMMUNICATIONS SUPERVISOR. Chicago, IL (1998-present). Supervised a team of telecommunications specialists involved in providing telecommunications support for thousands of individuals; was selected for this position which is usually held by an individual more senior in experience.
- Provided oversight for the erection and maintenance of antennas up to 30 meters.
- Trained and supervised others in operating and maintaining line-of-sight radios.
- Earned widespread respect for my strong troubleshooting and problem-solving skills.
- Gained strong organizational and supervisory skills while training junior employees in proven techniques for safely troubleshooting complex problems.
- Have become skilled in troubleshooting radios, telephones, and cables; have also become skilled in splicing cables and fiber optics.

TELECOMMUNICATIONS TEAM CHIEF & TELECOMMUNICATIONS OPERATOR. Germany (1996-98). After excelling in all aspects of telecommunications operations and maintenance, was selected to act as Chief of a team of telecommunications professionals involved in installation, maintenance, and repair activities.
- Provided expert preventive maintenance on trucks, communications shelters, and generators.
- Worked with dozens of customer organizations while providing prompt and courteous technical support.
- Became skilled in troubleshooting line-of-sight equipment.

Other experience: CONSTRUCTION APPRENTICE. New York. After graduating from high school and before entering military service, was involved in building turbine engines. Learned to calibrate precise measurements and assure operation of machinery according to exact tolerances.

HONORS   Numerous certificates of achievement for exceptional performance.

PERSONAL   Outstanding references. Knowledgeable of Hazmat. Offer a reputation as a dependable hard worker with an ability to rapidly master new tasks, procedures, and systems.

Exact Name of Person
Exact Title
Exact Name of Company
Address
City, State, Zip

Dear Exact Name of Person (or Dear Sir or Madam if answering a blind ad):

With the enclosed resume, I would like to express my interest in exploring employment opportunities with your organization.

As you will see from the resume, I am a technically proficient young professional with skills in the areas of installing, maintaining, and troubleshooting telecommunications equipment. A quick learner who works well in both supervisory roles or as a contributor to team efforts, I am accustomed to working under deadlines and in fluid environments where priorities can change rapidly. With a reputation for adaptability and a willingness to take on the tough jobs, I excel in motivating and training others while setting an example of professionalism.

Although I am highly respected and have been strongly encouraged to remain in the National Security Agency and assured of continued rapid advancement, I have made the decision to pursue further education leading to MCSE certification and employment in the private sector. I have become known as one who can be counted on to share my expertise with others and put in the long hours needed to provide support services which kept telecommunications systems up and running.

Entrusted with a Secret security clearance, I have earned recognition for my professionalism and dedication with numerous cash bonuses and awards.

If you can use my technical aptitude and skills as well as my reputation as a self-motivated quick learner, I hope you will contact me soon to suggest a time when we might meet to discuss how I could contribute to your organization. I will provide excellent professional and personal references at the appropriate time. Thank you for your time and consideration.

Sincerely,

Josiah Dubber

P.S. Because of the nature of my job, I am traveling extensively at the present time (and often on short notice) in order to establish new communications systems worldwide. Therefore, I have provided only my e-mail address on my resume since this is the best way to contact me.

JOSIAH DUBBER

preppub@aol.co

OBJECTIVE   To offer strong technical skills in telecommunications installation, troubleshooting, and maintenance along with a reputation as a quick learner who can handle deadline pressure.

EDUCATION   Completed courses in computer literacy, emergency lifesaving, and emergency medical
& TRAINING   technology, Western Colorado Community College, Carson City, CO.
Completed NSA's Leadership Development Course and technical training which included courses for signal support systems specialists, emergency medical technology instructors, emergency program managers, and COMSEC (communications security) custodians.

TECHNICAL   Through experience and training, have become proficient in telecommunications installation,
KNOWLEDGE   maintenance, troubleshooting, and equipment problem identification.
Offer knowledge of automated data systems software and hardware.

EXPERIENCE   Have advanced to supervisory roles in highly technical environments, National Security Agency:
SENIOR TELECOMMUNICATIONS SUPPORT SYSTEMS SUPERVISOR. Carson City, CO (2000-present). Cited for my technical expertise and ability to inspire subordinates through my positive attitude and dedication, supervise others, and personally install, maintain, and troubleshoot telecommunications equipment.
- Provide support and guidance for equipment including signal support systems and terminal devices including radio, wire, and battlefield automation systems.
- Supervise two people in a unit with a short-notice worldwide response mission.
- Cited for my ability to accomplish even the most demanding tasks, exceeded standards in all evaluated areas during training, physical fitness testing, and inspections.
- Am known for my take-charge attitude and willingness to take on any job and use positive reinforcement to encourage subordinates to work independently and as a team.

COMMUNICATIONS SECTION SUPERVISOR. Italy (1999-00). Earned respect for my technical knowledge and willingness to share my expertise with others while overseeing maintenance and control of equipment valued in excess of $1 million.
- Trained 26 radio telephone operators/technicians who quickly became skilled in the maintenance, use, and upkeep of their equipment.
- Ensured communications and night-vision equipment availability on short notice.
- Created and then implemented communications standard operating procedures (SOP).

COMMUNICATIONS SPECIALIST. Italy (1998-99). Praised for physical and mental toughness along with my "genuine concern for subordinates," was known for my willingness to work long hours to ensure reliability of wire and FM communications systems.
- Advised a manager on system planning and employment.
- Instructed two radiotelephone operator courses which produced eight knowledgeable personnel.
- Assisted in providing physical security for weapons and was a key player in leading the "arms room" to receive the only passing inspection score in the parent organization.

COMMUNICATIONS TECHNICIAN. England (1995-98). Advanced to supervisory roles while building a reputation as a skilled and self-motivated technician.

PERSONAL   Was entrusted with a Secret security clearance. Highly self-motivated.

Date

Exact Name of Person
Exact Title
Exact Name of Company
Address
City, State, Zip

Dear Exact Name of Person (or Dear Sir or Madam if answering a blind ad):

With the enclosed resume, I would like to make you aware of my broad base of skills, knowledge, and experience with an emphasis on applying technical computer skills and the ability to supervise, train, and instruct others.

As you will see by my enclosed resume, I have gained a strong background in the computer field and recently attained the Microsoft Builders Network, Level 2, certification. I have a talent for quickly and easily mastering new technology and offer a wide-ranging level of knowledge gained primarily through self study and the personal enjoyment of keeping up with the latest technological advances.

While working with the Defense Intelligence Agency, I earned numerous medals and honors for my accomplishments and contributions which resulted in high ratings in evaluations, inspections, and training exercises as well as in the building of results-oriented teams of specialists. My background in supervision and management has given me opportunities to gain exposure to operational activities including supply, personnel, and administrative support as well as telecommunications and weapons systems operations.

My years with the DIA also gave me the chance to work in international settings which included Germany, Bosnia-Herzegovina, Iraq, and Saudi Arabia. In these settings, I was able to work with personnel from other military services and other countries while expanding my skills and knowledge.

If you can use an experienced professional who is an enthusiastic and energetic quick learner, I hope you will contact me to suggest a time when we might meet to discuss your needs. I can assure you in advance that I could rapidly become an asset to your organization.

Sincerely,

Frederick Lark

FREDERICK LARK

1110½ Hay Street, Fayetteville, NC 28305   •   preppub@aol.com   •   (910) 483-6611

OBJECTIVE To benefit an organization that can use my extensive computer skills and knowledge as well as my supervisory and team-building abilities.

CERTIFICATION Attained the Microsoft Builders Network, Level 2, certification in 1998.
Was required to demonstrate the ability to code in Dynamic HTML, and write Java scriplets to earn this certification.

TECHNICAL
SKILLS
Proficient with software which includes:

Windows NTdBase IV and III		MS Office Pro	Front Page
WordPerfect	Microsoft GIF Animator	Harvard Graphics	DOS up to 6.22
Adobe PhotoShop	Paradox 3	Adobe Acrobat	Print Artist
Print Master Gold Publishing Suite		Microsoft Liquid Motion	Xara 3D
Microsoft Image Composer 1.5		Microsoft Publisher	Lotus Organizer
FrontPage Software Developers Kit		Ulead Web Utilities	WS FTP 32
Crystal 3D Impact Pro		Norton's Utility Suite	JFax 32 4/21

Offer limited experience in installing, maintaining, and troubleshooting LANs; proficient with HTML and Java.
Have qualified as a Beta Tester for services including:

America Online since 1995   Internet Explorer
Netscape Communicator 4.5 Preview Release 2   Outlook Express

EXPERIENCE *Earned recognition as a technically proficient professional and effective supervisor while serving my country in the Defense Intelligence Agency:*
COMPUTER SYSTEMS TEAM SUPERVISOR. Washington, DC (2000-present). Trained and supervised specialists while controlling the operation and employment of state-of-the-art computer systems and supporting telecommunications equipment valued in excess of $6.4 million.

- Recognized for "uncompromising integrity" and a talent for building the confidence and cooperation of team members, was cited for my effectiveness in achieving results.
- Was honored with an Achievement Medal for accomplishments as a team leader during a training center rotation in which my team successfully carried out the ambush of three aircraft behind enemy lines with no injuries.
- Set up Local Area Networks (LANs) and applied management and decision-making skills while coordinating the various elements of ground communications systems.
- In recognition of my communication skills and expertise, was singled out to brief VIPs including members of Congress and General Officers.

PROJECT MANAGER. Germany (1996-99). Earned several awards while managing 30 people including four department heads (section managers) in an air defense organization.
- Was promoted from Team Chief to Project Manager ahead of my peers.
- Guided my section of specialists to superior scores despite being 75% understaffed during a technical evaluation of operations.
- Accepted the additional challenge of overseeing the unit's training operations, and in the first major inspection under my supervision received commendable ratings in nearly three-fourths of the areas being inspected.

CLEARANCE Hold Secret security clearance

PERSONAL Am highly technically oriented – enjoy designing web sites as a hobby.

Date

Exact Name of Person
Exact Title
Exact Name of Company
Address
City, State, Zip

TEST PLANS ANALYST   Dear Exact Name of Person (or Dear Sir or Madam if answering a blind ad):

With the enclosed resume, I would like to make you aware of my interest in exploring employment opportunities with your organization.

As you will see from my resume, I have worked as a Test Plans Analyst for the government since 1995. In my current position, I manage 150 people including test plan analysts, subject matter experts, support contractors, analysts, and government personnel while playing a key role in providing oversight for a $4.1 million budget. I am considered an expert in all phases of test planning and implementation including developing training programs, supervising test teams, identifying test procedures, conducting tests, supervising the collection and reporting of data, and representing test teams in briefings and oral presentations.

With extensive computer skills and training related to numerous programs and applications, I have recently completed advanced training sponsored by the Microsoft Corporation. I am experienced in interfacing with civilian contractors as well as all government agencies including the Directorate of Logistics, TEXCOM Resource Management Directorate, and the Budget Division as well as with the Department of the Army at all levels. I am widely respected for my exceptional problem-solving ability, and I have developed data base application programs, quality control programs, Standard Operating Procedures, as well as numerous training programs.

Although I am excelling in my current position in Miami, I recently married a native of San Diego, and I am seeking employment which will permit me to permanently resettle in California. I can provide outstanding personal and professional references at the appropriate time, and I would appreciate an opportunity to talk with you soon about your needs and how my skills and knowledge could help you.

Yours sincerely,

Spartan Agnew

SPARTAN AGNEW

1110½ Hay Street, Fayetteville, NC 28305 • preppub@aol.com • (910) 483-6611

OBJECTIVE   To contribute to an organization that can use an experienced manager with vast experience in managing people, budgets, and projects while utilizing state-of-the-art software.

EXPERIENCE   **TEST PLANS ANALYST.** Department of Defense, Miami, FL (2000-present). Manage 150 people including test plan analysts, subject matter experts, support contractors, analysts, and government personnel involved in the collection of data.
- Played a key role in providing oversight for a $4.1 million budget.

COMPUTER NETWORK ANALYST. Special Operations Command, Ft. Bragg, NC (1997-99). Managed up to 120 people and a multimillion-dollar budget while performing as the **Assistant Test Officer/Operations Officer** in support of the Advanced SINCGARS customer's test (CT); supervised up to 120 people.
- Identified test procedures, conducted tests, and developed comprehensive test reports while also supervising data collection, handling, reduction, analysis, and reporting.

PLANS ANALYST. Department of the Army, Richmond, VA (1997). Support contractor for the U.S. Army Test and Experimentation Command (TEXCOM) in the conduct of the Bradley FVS A3 Limited User Test (lUT) phase II and III.
- Involved in test planning including budgeting; developing test procedures; test execution; data analysis; writing test reports; presenting briefings.
- Developed training program and scheduled courses required to support data collection.
- Supervised activities of 110 data collectors in collection of Reliability, Availability, and Maintainability (RAM), Performance, and MANPRINT data.

TEST PLANS ANALYST. Department of Defense, Washington, DC (1996-97). Served as Data Management and Logistics Support Officer and assisted the Test Officer in developing, implementing, forecasting, and analyzing logistical support operations for the Test logistical requirements.
- Applied thorough understanding of DA, Inter-Service, departmental and local support regulations, agreements, memorandums of understanding, and other documents.

DATA MANAGEMENT SPECIALIST. Department of Defense, Washington, DC (1995-96). As **Assistant to the Operations and Tactical Officers** with a primary responsibility of **Tactical Operations Center (TOC) Shift Leader,** managed TOC operations during the Armored Gun System's Initial Operational Test and Evaluation (AGS IOTE) Forces on Force and Gunnery exercises as well as the Net Control Station (NCS) throughout the formal test cycle.
- **Developed and wrote a Standard Operating Procedure (SOP);** applied my knowledge of automated systems and software programs as I **wrote assigned chapters of the Detailed Test Plan (DTP) and the Test Evaluation Plan (TEP) and ADP support concept.**
- Developed a data base application program that augmented the finished statistical data and **developed a quality control program** to manage collection forms.

EDUCATION, TRAINING   Completed four years of college including **A.A., General Studies, Columbia College,** 1987. Extensive trained in Microsoft Word applications and programming, sponsored by Microsoft, 10/99; received formal training related to Windows, PowerPoint, Excel, Access.

Exact Name of Person
Exact Title
Exact Name of Company
Address
City, State, Zip

WEBSITE DESIGNER
SYSTEMS
TECHNICIAN

Dear Exact Name of Person (or Dear Sir or Madam if answering a blind ad):

With the enclosed resume, I would like to make you aware of my interest in seeking employment with your organization.

As you will see, I am knowledgeable of security management and have completed the U.S. Army's Security Manager's Course at the John F. Kennedy School of Special Warfare. Trained to conduct security investigations and schooled in the security clearance approval process, I offer knowledge of counter intelligence, counter terrorism, as well as area and physical security. In two separate positions while serving in the U.S. Army, I managed the provision of security services including personnel security, automated systems security, and physical assets security. In one job as a Security Technician, I became a respected member of the General's "brain trust" within the famed 82nd Airborne Division, and I have excelled in coordinating security in tactical situations.

The Army also gave me an opportunity to refine my management skills, and I have recently managed up to five employees who have looked to me for technical training and leadership.

I am also highly skilled in computer programming, operation, repair, and maintenance, and I am proficient in using numerous software programs used for military intelligence, mapmaking, and other purposes. Prior to joining the Army, I worked as a College Teacher briefly teaching HTML and Internet usage, and I also worked for several years as a Website Designer and Computer Consultant.

Although I have been rapidly promoted ahead of my peers to management responsibilities and have been strongly urged to remain in military service, I have decided not to re-enlist so that I can embark upon a civilian career in the security field.

If you can use a promising young security professional who is known for intelligence and resourcefulness, I hope you will contact me to suggest a time when we might meet to discuss your needs and how I might serve them. I can provide outstanding references at the appropriate time.

Sincerely,

Jason Fincher

JASON FINCHER

1110½ Hay Street, Fayetteville, NC 28305　　•　　preppub@aol.com　　•　　(910) 483-6611

OBJECTIVE	To benefit an organization that can use a versatile young professional with exceptionally strong computer knowledge along with experience in designing websites designed for e-commerce.
EDUCATION	Completed **Security Manager's Course** emphasizing security and counterintelligence operations, U.S. Army, John F. Kennedy School of Special Warfare, Ft. Iwo, HI, 2003. •　Course emphasized counter intelligence, terrorist awareness, area and physical security. •　Trained to conduct security investigations and security clearance approval methods. Completed Javelin anti-tank missile course; Airborne School; computer courses.
CLEARANCE	Secret security clearance
COMPUTERS	Highly proficient in programming **HTML**; have constructed and redesigned numerous commercial websites on a freelance basis. Knowledgeable of software including FrontPage, PaintShop Pro, CorelDraw, and others. Skilled in utilizing **Microsoft Office**; skilled in all aspects of computer maintenance/repair. Familiar with **Pearl** and **Java.** Skilled in using numerous software programs used for military intelligence, mapmaking, etc. Proficient in operating SINCGARS encrypted radios and ANCD cryptographic computer.
EXPERIENCE	**SYSTEMS TECHNICIAN.** U.S. Army, Ft. Iwo, HI (2001-present). Have trained, motivated, and managed up to five employees while troubleshooting and repairing various weapons systems and performing generator operation and maintenance. •　Was promoted to mid-management (E-4) May, 2001, and have been strongly encouraged to remain in military service and assured of continued rapid advancement. **SECURITY TECHNICIAN.** U.S. Army, Ft. Iwo, HI (1999-01). In two separate positions, managed the provision of security services including personnel security, automated systems security, and physical assets security. Conducted background checks for security clearances. •　Wrote technical and standard operating procedures. •　Performed liaison with government agencies and other branches of military services. •　Became a respected member of the General's "brain trust" within the famed 82ⁿ Airborne Division, earned prestigious medals; coordinated security in tactical situations. •　In a previous job as an **Infantryman** (2001), learned light infantry tactics and airborne insertion methods; performed five airborne jumps and earned my Airborne Wings. Civilian experience (after high school): **COLLEGE TEACHER.** The Learning Annex, New York, NY (1998-99). Taught Internet usage and HTML techniques. **WEBSITE DESIGNER & COMPUTER CONSULTANT.** Quantas Systems, Brooklyn, NY (1997-98) and Bethpage and Levittown, NY (1997-99). Worked as a computer consultant and website designer for companies in New York state. **FINANCIAL CONSULTANT.** Gaines Berland, Syosset, NY (1996). Learned the securities business and obtained my Series 7 and Series 63 licenses.
AFFILIATION	Member, HTML Writers Guild.
PERSONAL	Highly motivated and resourceful individual with strong communication skills. Excellent references, including references from companies for whom I have created powerful websites which have been highly successfully in e-commerce.

ABOUT THE EDITOR

Anne McKinney holds an MBA from the Harvard Business School and a BA in English from the University of North Carolina at Chapel Hill. A noted public speaker, writer, and teacher, she is the senior editor for PREP's business and career imprint, which bears her name. Early titles in the Anne McKinney Career Series (now called the Real-Resumes Series) published by PREP include: *Resumes and Cover Letters That Have Worked, Resumes and Cover Letters That Have Worked for Military Professionals, Government Job Applications and Federal Resumes, Cover Letters That Blow Doors Open,* and *Letters for Special Situations.* Her career titles and how-to resume-and-cover-letter books are based on the expertise she has acquired in 20 years of working with job hunters. Her valuable career insights have appeared in publications of the "Wall Street Journal" and other prominent newspapers and magazines.

PREP Publishing Order Form

You may purchase any of our titles from your favorite bookseller! Or send a check or money order or your credit card number for the total amount*, plus $3.50 postage and handling, to PREP, Box 66, Fayetteville, NC 28302. If you have a question about any of our titles, feel free to e-mail us at preppub@aol.com and visit our website at http://www.prep-pub.com

Name: _____

Phone #: _____

Address: _____

_____

E-mail address: _____

Payment Type: ☐ Check/Money Order   ☐ Visa   ☐ MasterCard

Credit Card Number: _____ Expiration Date: _____

Check items you are ordering:

☐ $16.95—REAL-RESUMES FOR FINANCIAL JOBS. Anne McKinney, Editor

☐ $16.95—REAL-RESUMES FOR COMPUTER JOBS. Anne McKinney, Editor

☐ $16.95—REAL-RESUMES FOR MEDICAL JOBS. Anne McKinney, Editor

☐ $16.95—REAL-RESUMES FOR TEACHERS. Anne McKinney, Editor

☐ $16.95—REAL-RESUMES FOR CAREER CHANGERS. Anne McKinney, Editor

☐ $16.95—REAL-RESUMES FOR STUDENTS. Anne McKinney, Editor

☐ $16.95—REAL-RESUMES FOR SALES. Anne McKinney, Editor

☐ $16.95—REAL ESSAYS FOR COLLEGE AND GRAD SCHOOL. Anne McKinney, Editor

☐ $25.00—RESUMES AND COVER LETTERS THAT HAVE WORKED.

☐ $25.00—RESUMES AND COVER LETTERS THAT HAVE WORKED FOR MILITARY PROFESSIONALS.

☐ $25.00—RESUMES AND COVER LETTERS FOR MANAGERS.

☐ $25.00—GOVERNMENT JOB APPLICATIONS AND FEDERAL RESUMES: Federal Resumes, KSAs, Forms 171 and 612, and Postal Applications.

☐ $25.00—COVER LETTERS THAT BLOW DOORS OPEN.

☐ $25.00—LETTERS FOR SPECIAL SITUATIONS.

☐ $16.00—BACK IN TIME. Patty Sleem

☐ $17.00—(trade paperback) SECOND TIME AROUND. Patty Sleem

☐ $25.00—(hardcover) SECOND TIME AROUND. Patty Sleem

☐ $18.00—A GENTLE BREEZE FROM GOSSAMER WINGS. Gordon Beld

☐ $18.00—BIBLE STORIES FROM THE OLD TESTAMENT. Katherine Whaley

☐ $14.95—WHAT THE BIBLE SAYS ABOUT... *Words that can lead to success and happiness* (large print edition) Patty Sleem

☐ $10.95—KIJABE An African Historical Saga. Pally Dhillon

_____ **TOTAL ORDERED (add $3.50 for postage and handling)**

PREP offers volume discounts on large orders. Call us at (910) 483-6611 for more information.

THE MISSION OF PREP PUBLISHING IS TO PUBLISH
BOOKS AND OTHER PRODUCTS WHICH ENRICH
PEOPLE'S LIVES AND HELP THEM OPTIMIZE THE
HUMAN EXPERIENCE. OUR STRONGEST LINES ARE
OUR JUDEO-CHRISTIAN ETHICS SERIES AND OUR
BUSINESS & CAREER SERIES.

Would you like to explore the possibility of having PREP's writing
team create a resume for you similar to the ones in this book?

For a brief free consultation, call 910-483-6611
or send $4.00 to receive our Job Change Packet to
PREP, Department Computer, Box 66, Fayetteville, NC 28302.

QUESTIONS OR COMMENTS? E-MAIL US AT PREPPUB@AOL.COM